Navigating Stylistic Boundaries in the Music History Classroom

At a time of transformation in the music history classroom and amid increasing calls to teach a global music history, *Navigating Stylistic Boundaries in the Music History Classroom* adds nuance to the teaching of varied musical traditions by examining the places where they intersect and the issues of musical exchange and appropriation that these intersections raise. Troubling traditional boundaries of genre and style, this collection of essays helps instructors to denaturalize the framework of Western art music and invite students to engage with other traditions—vernacular, popular, and non-Western—on their own terms.

The book draws together contributions by a wide range of active scholars and educators to investigate the teaching of music history around cases of stylistic borders, exploring the places where different practices of music and values intersect. Each chapter in this collection considers a specific case in which an artist or community engages in what might be termed musical crossover, exchange, or appropriation and delves deeper into these concepts to explore questions of how musical meaning changes in moving across worlds of practice. Addressing works that are already widely taught but presenting new ways to understand and interpret them, this volume enables instructors to enrich the perspectives on music history that they present and to take on the challenge of teaching a more global music history without flattening the differences between traditions.

Esther M. Morgan-Ellis is Associate Professor of Music History at the University of North Georgia.

Modern Musicology and the College Classroom

Series Editor: James A. Davis, *SUNY Fredonia*

Modern Musicology and the College Classroom is a series of professional titles for current and future college instructors of musicology in its broadest definition—encompassing music history, ethnomusicology, music theory, and music courses for all majors. Volumes feature a basic introduction to a significant field of current scholarship, a discussion of how the topic impacts pedagogical methodology and materials, and pragmatic suggestions for incorporating these ideas directly into the classroom.

Listening Across Borders
Musicology in the Global Classroom
Edited by James A. Davis and Christopher Lynch

Teaching Electronic Music
Cultural, Creative, and Analytical Perspectives
Edited by Blake Stevens

Race and Gender in the Western Music History Survey
A Teacher's Guide
Horace J. Maxile, Jr. and Kristen M. Turner

Music, Gender, and Sexuality Studies
A Teacher's Guide
Jacqueline Warwick

Disability and Accessibility in the Music Classroom
A Teacher's Guide
Alexandria Carrico and Katherine Grennell

Teaching Music History with Cases
A Teacher's Guide
Sara Haefeli

Navigating Stylistic Boundaries in the Music History Classroom
Crossover, Exchange, Appropriation
Esther M. Morgan-Ellis

For more information about this series, please visit: www.routledge.com/Modern-Musicology-and-the-College-Classroom/book-series/MMCC

Navigating Stylistic Boundaries in the Music History Classroom
Crossover, Exchange, Appropriation

Edited by Esther M. Morgan-Ellis

NEW YORK AND LONDON

Designed cover image: © Jan Sochor / Getty Images

First published 2024
by Routledge
605 Third Avenue, New York, NY 10158

and by Routledge
4 Park Square, Milton Park, Abingdon, Oxon, OX14 4RN

Routledge is an imprint of the Taylor & Francis Group, an informa business

© 2024 selection and editorial matter, Esther Morgan-Ellis; individual chapters, the contributors

The right of Esther Morgan-Ellis to be identified as the author of the editorial material, and of the authors for their individual chapters, has been asserted in accordance with sections 77 and 78 of the Copyright, Designs and Patents Act 1988.

All rights reserved. No part of this book may be reprinted or reproduced or utilised in any form or by any electronic, mechanical, or other means, now known or hereafter invented, including photocopying and recording, or in any information storage or retrieval system, without permission in writing from the publishers.

Trademark notice: Product or corporate names may be trademarks or registered trademarks, and are used only for identification and explanation without intent to infringe.

ISBN: 978-1-032-54251-5 (hbk)
ISBN: 978-1-032-54252-2 (pbk)
ISBN: 978-1-003-41595-4 (ebk)

DOI: 10.4324/9781003415954

Typeset in Sabon
by Deanta Global Publishing Services, Chennai, India

Contents

Contributors   vii

Introduction: Teaching Liminal Musicking   1
ESTHER M. MORGAN-ELLIS

PART I
Denaturalizing Western Art Music   13

1. European Art Music is an Ethnic Music: Fraying the Edges in a Music History Classroom   15
D. LINDA PEARSE AND SANDRIA P. BOULIANE

2. From Beijing to Paris: Teaching Music of the Global Eighteenth Century   40
QINGFAN JIANG

3. "Song of the Spirit Dance" and Native American Songs: Teaching about Appropriation in Late Nineteenth- and Early Twentieth-Century Symphonic Compositions   62
ERINN E. KNYT

4. Examining Vernacular Borrowings to Denaturalize Western Art Music: The Case of "Hoe-Down"   85
ESTHER M. MORGAN-ELLIS

PART II
Teaching Blended Musics　　　　　　　　　　　　　　　　　　103

5　Music of the Hyphen: Diaspora Music as Process and Product　　105
　　VARSHINI NARAYANAN

6　African-Focused Approaches to Teaching African Popular
　　Music in Western Classrooms　　　　　　　　　　　　　　　124
　　ALABA ILESANMI

7　Por ti seré: Jarocho Fusion and Revivalism in "La Bamba"　　140
　　GREGORY REISH

PART III
Training Global Musicians　　　　　　　　　　　　　　　　　155

8　From Brazilian Worship Houses to a U.S. College:
　　Recontextualizations of Afro-Brazilian Religious Music and
　　Movement　　　　　　　　　　　　　　　　　　　　　　　157
　　MARC M. GIDAL

9　Crossing Over Popular and Classical Traditions through
　　Musical Theater　　　　　　　　　　　　　　　　　　　　179
　　ALEX BÁDUE

10　The Anti-Colonial Conservatory: The Case of the University
　　"Folk Band"　　　　　　　　　　　　　　　　　　　　　　197
　　CHRISTOPHER J. SMITH

　　Index　　　　　　　　　　　　　　　　　　　　　　　　　*221*

Contributors

Alex Bádue is Assistant Professor of Music at Hamilton College. He is the author of *Why Aren't They Talking? The Sung-Through Musical from the 1980s to the 2010s* (2022). He conducts research and has published on the compositional process, musical structure, reception, and social impact of musicals by Jason Robert Brown, William Finn, Michael John LaChiusa, Jonathan Larson, and Jeanine Tesori, as well as Disney's Broadway musicals. He also researches the interactions between Latin American and U.S. American popular music industries in the 1940s and 1950s.

Sandria P. Bouliane is Associate Professor of Musicology at Université Laval, Québec. She conducts research on cultural borrowings and transfers between Canadian and American linguistic and musical communities. Her approaches draw on popular music studies, interdisciplinary research, and critical historiography focusing on cultural life. As principal investigator of the projects La vie musicale au Québec and the Laboratoire d'archives vivantes et de recherche sur la vie musicale she aims to facilitate the integration of a diverse set of musical practices and encounters moving across languages, ethnicities, genders, and socio-economic borders.

Marc M. Gidal, Ph.D., is Associate Professor of Music (Musicology) at Ramapo College of New Jersey, a public liberal arts college. He is the author of *Spirit Song: Afro-Brazilian Religious Music and Boundaries* (Oxford, 2016) and research articles in the journals *Ethnomusicology*, *Ethnomusicology Forum*, *Latin American Music Review*, *American Music*, *Americas: A Hemispheric Music Journal*, and *Civilisations*. He is writing a book about Brazilian jazz in New York City.

Alaba Ilesanmi is a Mellon/ACLS Dissertation Innovation Fellow and McKnight Doctoral Fellow at Florida State University, where he directs the pan-African ensemble, *Afro-Nyota*. His research interest is broadly in Global Black cultures and music, exploring themes of identity, cultural politics, and globalization. He holds advanced music theory and performance certificates from the Associated Board of the Royal Schools of Music (ABRSM) and Trinity College, London; a bachelor's degree in music education from the University of Texas at Tyler; a EC-12 music teaching certification; and a master in musicology from Florida State University.

Qingfan Jiang is Assistant Professor of Musicology at the Peabody Institute of Johns Hopkins University. Her research focuses on the musical exchange between China and Europe in the seventeenth and eighteenth centuries. Her article "In Search of the 'Oriental Origin': Rameau, Rousseau, and Chinese Music in Eighteenth-Century France" was published in *Eighteenth Century Music* (2022). Before joining Peabody, Jiang held a postdoctoral fellowship at the Institute of Sacred Music at Yale University. She earned her Ph.D. in Historical Musicology from Columbia University in 2021.

Erinn E. Knyt is Professor of Music History at the University of Massachusetts, Amherst. Knyt specializes in nineteenth- and twentieth-century music and has published extensively about Ferruccio Busoni. Both of her books, *Ferruccio Busoni and His Legacy* (2017) and *Ferruccio Busoni as Architect of Sound* (2023) were awarded American Musicological Society Book Subventions. Her forthcoming book, *Johann Sebastian Bach's "Goldberg Variations" Reimagined,* is under contract with Oxford University Press. Knyt was also awarded the 2018 American Musicological Society Teaching Award, and she has published in the *Journal of Music History Pedagogy.*

Esther M. Morgan-Ellis is Associate Professor of Music History at the University of North Georgia, where she also directs the orchestra and coaches the old-time string band. She researches participatory music-making practices of the past and present. Her work on the U.S. community singing movement can be found in her monograph, *Everybody Sing! Community Singing in the American Picture Palace* (2018), and in a wide range of musicological journals. She is also co-editor of *The Oxford Handbook of Community Singing* (2024). As a scholar of teaching and learning, she served as editor and lead author of the open-access music appreciation textbook *Resonances: Engaging Music in Its Cultural Context* (2020) and has contributed a variety of writings to the *Journal of Music History Pedagogy.*

Varshini Narayanan is a PhD candidate in Music and Theater and Performance Studies at the University of Chicago. Their research focuses on the music-making practices of the South Asian diaspora, with a particular emphasis on Indo-jazz fusion and cross-cultural performance. Varshini is a lifelong practitioner of Carnatic music and performs widely on the Carnatic flute. They hold a B.A. in Anthropology from Princeton University.

D. Linda Pearse is Associate Professor of Music at Mount Allison University and Canada Research Chair in Music, Contact, and Conflict. Pearse draws on her extensive experience as a performer and instructor of early European art music and its histories to combine artistic and musicological methodologies informed by studies in musicology (McGill) and performance (Schola Cantorum Basiliensis, Indiana University Bloomington). Her work on intercultural collaboration brings together historians, artists, and cultural knowledge keepers to test theoretical insights within collaborative environments. These projects produce both performative and written outputs, bringing diverse perspectives to bear on the entanglements of early European music with others.

Gregory Reish is Professor of Music History at Middle Tennessee State University and Director of the Center for Popular Music, one of the nation's premier American music research archives. He is active as an integrative scholar-performer-producer of old-time country, bluegrass, Tejano and other musics. He has performed at venues and festivals in the U.S., Mexico, Japan, and China, and produced and engineered numerous albums of traditional music. His publications cover topics as varied as the music of Italian modernist composer Giacinto Scelsi, the original fiddle music of bluegrass innovator John Hartford, and the political orientation of early country music. Reish was a Fulbright grant winner to Italy for his dissertation research in the 1990s, and in 2023 he served as Fulbright-García Robles U.S. Studies Chair at the University of Veracruz, Mexico.

Christopher J. Smith is Professor, Chair of Musicology, and Director of the Vernacular Music Center at Texas Tech University. His monographs are *The Creolization of American Culture: William Sidney Mount and the Roots of Blackface Minstrelsy* (2013) and *Dancing Revolution: Bodies, Space, and Sound in American Cultural History* (2019). His next books are *Sounding History*, with Thomas Irvine, a global history of the soundscapes of imperial encounter; *Situational Genius: The Practice of the American Bandleaders*; and *The Teacher's Guide to Arts Practice Research in the Undergraduate Classroom*. He is the producer, co-host, and showrunner for the podcasts *Sounding History* and *Voices from the Vernacular Music Center*.

Introduction
Teaching Liminal Musicking

Esther M. Morgan-Ellis

This volume is predicated on the usefulness of teaching "difference" in order to help students better understand the cultural specificity of their own practices, values, and experiences. Each of the authors probes a site of cultural intersection at which one approach to musicking comes into contact or conflict with another. The nature of these intersections is diverse, as are their locations within works, genres, and institutions. In each case, however, the author privileges perspectives that have not always found a home in Westernized music education, thereby challenging received wisdom about what music means, how it should be categorized, and—crucially—how it should be taught in college and graduate settings.[1]

The central concept of "crossover, exchange, appropriation" was adopted to index three significant modes of intercultural contact. In the first, an artist grounded in one cultural context applies their practices and values to another. In the second, artists grounded in disparate cultural contexts collaborate as equals. In the third, an artist takes, as they see fit, from the music of another culture, molding the appropriated material to their own context without concern for its original significance or usage. It is by no means an aim of this volume to define or police musical appropriation; indeed, few of the authors engage with the concept or even use the term. As these chapters make clear, analytic engagement with appropriative techniques is more productive than cursory condemnation. Additionally, many of the intersections that authors explore do not fit easily into any of these three categories. Indeed, several authors argue completely new models for understanding cross-cultural synthesis and invention. All the same, I have retained the titular triad as evocative of the typical relationships that underpin liminal musicking and as a reminder of the power imbalances that characterize intercultural encounters.

Modern institutions concerned with the teaching, performance, and marketing of music tend to silo traditions and styles off from one another. In university music departments, we typically teach about art, vernacular, and popular musics in different courses. Festivals celebrate narrowly defined musical categories, record labels confine their efforts to niche genres, and musicians associate themselves with distinct communities. This volume confirms that musical difference is real and significant, yet it argues that the study of liminal musicking promises rich pedagogical rewards. By leading our students to probe the cracks between distinct (or seemingly distinct) musical practices, we encourage them to question so-called "universal" knowledge and recognize their own subjective identities as cultural actors.

This volume, while not principally concerned with the movement to "decolonize" higher education, certainly contributes to those efforts. Discussions of decolonization consider how to counter the legacy of Eurocentrism—and its attendant privileging, not only of European epistemologies and repertoires but of whiteness and masculinity—that provides the foundation for formal music study in modern institutions of higher education.[2] While expressing skepticism that total decolonization is possible, scholars repeatedly argue that it is still necessary to pursue decolonial pedagogical strategies.[3] Michael Figueroa, using language that calls to mind the aims of this collection, describes these as "techniques intended to break the shackles of colonial, imperial, and/or Eurocentric thinking about what music is, who makes it and listens to it, and how it functions in human societies."[4] Chapter authors offer a variety of tools that the classroom teacher can use to dismantle received structures and build new knowledge.

Organization and Contents

This volume is divided into three sections. Within each section, the chapters are connected in both thematic and practical terms. The authors pursue closely related questions and can be brought into conversation with one another. They are also writing for instructors working in related pedagogical environments. The first section primarily addresses instructors teaching Western art music courses. The second section considers the teaching of styles and practices that fall outside of the Western art music framework. And the final section considers the grounding of practical musicianship training in historical and cultural contexts.

Part I: Denaturalizing Western Art Music

For better or worse, most music departments require students to complete survey courses in the history of Western art music, or what is typically termed "classical music."[5] These courses most often bear the straightforward title "music history," with the attendant connotations of comprehensiveness and universality. In practice, however, students encounter a narrow historical narrative that considers canonic works of the Euro-American tradition only within their immediate cultural contexts. These courses are offered within departments that similarly claim to teach "music," but that in fact impart the values and practices of Western art music developed within a closely bounded geographic area and temporal span. It is therefore necessary to resist the "naturalization" of Western art music as universally relevant and meaningful.

The chapters in this section offer strategies for making the practices and values of Western art music opaque and, therefore, visible to students. Although the first chapter, "European Art Music is an Ethnic Music: Fraying the Edges in a Music History Classroom," was not commissioned as an introduction to the section, it could hardly fill the role more perfectly. D. Linda Pearse and Sandria P. Bouliane have partnered over the course of several years to redesign their approach to teaching music history, employing techniques that "decenter Europe and show that European art music never existed in isolation." In the first part of their chapter, which merits close consideration, they carefully outline the theoretical frameworks and pedagogical approaches that underpin their work. Then, in a pair of case studies, each supplemented by five detailed pedagogical plans, they demonstrate their method in action.

In the first case study, Pearse and P. Bouliane present an approach to teaching troubadour song that broadens the geographical scope to include the Muslim Iberian Peninsula, with an emphasis on the activities of the Qiyan (enslaved Iberian singing girls and women). In doing so, they accept Edgard Morin's writings about complex thinking as an invitation to "stop looking for infallible proof of an Arab, goliard, liturgical, or folkloric influence (or the absence of one), and instead, to focus on the contacts, encounters, and crossovers that flourished in each place and time." In the second case study, they use a motet by Giovanni Gabrieli as the starting point to explore conflict and cultural exchange between Europeans and Ottomans in the seventeenth century. Their pedagogical plan begins by examining the motet through a variety of lenses, and then proceeds to consider Janissary music, transcriptions of Ottoman music-making by the Polish-born 'Alī Ufukī, and issues of historically informed performance practice. In both cases, Pearse and Bouliane provide enough historical and pedagogical detail for an instructor to implement their lessons with minimal preparation.

Qingfan Jiang is in perfect sympathy with Pearse and P. Bouliane, and her chapter, "From Beijing to Paris: Teaching Music of the Global Eighteenth Century," further explores approaches to teaching global music history. Jiang reports on a course she taught at Yale University, contextualizing her work in the need for cross-cultural perspectives in the music history classroom. Her approach, which brings students into contact with a variety of primary sources, presents the music of China and France as being of equal importance. In addition to introducing musical examples from both societies, she considers Chinese perspectives on French music and French perspectives on Chinese music, as well as compositions resulting from intercultural contact.

Jiang shares two complete lessons, providing the reader with all of the necessary material to replicate her work. This includes historical details, translated passages from primary sources, and discussion questions. In the first lesson, Jiang leads students to consider Emperor Kangxi (1654–1722) and his son Emperor Yongzheng (1678–1735) as interpreters of Western scientific thought, which included the discipline of music. She examines how the two rulers accepted European knowledge as a gift given to China out of respect, undertaking its study as an opportunity to "both restore China's ancient knowledge and to rectify the errors in Western knowledge." In the second lesson, she draws three musical examples into conversation: a Kun opera, a French opera by Jean-Philippe Rameau, and a piece of Catholic liturgical music used in Beijing that integrated Kun and European styles. She considers Chinese responses to French music alongside Rameau's accounts of Chinese music theory, which betray his mistaken assumptions about non-Western cultures. Her final example is a setting of the Lord's Prayer transcribed by the French missionary Jean-Joseph-Marie Amiot using an experimental combination of staff and gongche notation. Although Amiot was largely frustrated in his attempts to bring Chinese and French musical practices into mutual agreement, Jiang reports that students are often enthralled by the balanced and respectful blend of styles represented in this piece of music.

While the first two chapters outline approaches to teaching a global music history, the work of Erinn E. Knyt remains rooted in Western art music pedagogy. This makes her techniques more practical for many instructors to implement. Knyt takes the canonized repertoire and stories of the music history sequence as a starting place, and then demonstrates how that material can become a gateway for the introduction of marginalized musics and musicians. While her chapter, "'Song of the Spirit Dance' and Native American Songs: Teaching about Appropriation in Late Nineteenth- and Early Twentieth-Century Symphonic Compositions," is specific to the Indianist movement of the late nineteenth and early twentieth centuries, the technique she employs can be applied to any canonic repertoire that draws on vernacular tradition or claims to represent ethnic identity.

Knyt suggests a method for engaging students more deeply with topics they usually encounter in the study of Antonín Dvořák's Symphony No. 9 "From the New World." She broadens the curriculum to include two other Indianist composers, Edward MacDowell and Ferruccio Busoni, examining the ways in which each engaged Native American source material. Ultimately she places them on a spectrum, identifying MacDowell's engagement as cursory and appropriative while demonstrating that Busoni studied Native American music closely and employed not only melodies (which he reproduced as faithfully as he was able) but also narrative structures drawn from his sources. Knyt additionally uses her approach to focus attention on ethnologist Natalie Curtis-Burlin, thereby centering a woman in the discussion of music by white male composers. While Knyt restricts her comments to the historical Indianist movement, I recommend also exposing students to the work of Dylan Robinson, who addresses more recent attempts to synthesize Western and Indigenous music-making practices in his book *Hungry Listening*. Robinson contrasts "inclusionary music," which requires Indigenous artists to conform to classical modes of musical presentation, with "Indigenous+art music," wherein a true synthesis of traditions is achieved.[6]

My own chapter pairs well with Knyt's, since I, too, am interested in what happens when a Western art music composer borrows from a vernacular tradition. In "Examining Vernacular Borrowings to Denaturalize Western Art Music: The Case of 'Hoe-Down'," I theorize the "composer's ear" as a standardizing mechanism that strips non-classical musical material of all features not recognized and valued in the Western art music frame. My work is rooted in my experience as a classically trained cellist on the one hand and an old-time fiddler on the other. I teach and perform in both traditions, which equips me to evaluate encounters between them. There is a stark disjunct in aesthetics, forms, and musical thinking between Euro-American concert music and Southern Appalachian fiddling as both a historical and contemporary practice. When students interrogate this divide, they gain remarkable insights into the unspoken values that characterize Western art music composition and performance. Like Knyt and Jiang, I am also fascinated by the limits of staff notation as a tool for transcribing music from outside the classical tradition.[7] I consider two transcriptions of William Stepp's "Bonaparte's Retreat" (the tune Copland borrowed for his ballet), both of which were made by competent musicians exercising extreme care, yet which differ in many respects. My chapter contains all of the materials necessary to teach this specific work, but hopefully also paves a path for taking a similar approach with the music of any composer who draws from vernacular sources.

Part II: Teaching Blended Musics

The chapters in this section concern artists who collaborate across stylistic boundaries or draw from cross-cultural sources in their own creative practices. Each considers a unique example of blended music-making the participants in which have varied backgrounds, motivations, and relationships to integrated styles. In examining these cases, the authors reveal their rich pedagogical potential and suggest ways in which to incorporate this material into the classroom.

The first two chapters, by Varshini Narayanan and Alaba Ilesanmi, complement each other well. The authors take on the disparate topics of Indo-jazz fusion and Afrobeat, yet they make related arguments concerning how these musics should be taught in the classroom. Both note that students are often prone to evaluate musical examples in terms of "authenticity" and dismiss non-Western musics that seem to have been corrupted by Western influence. It is essential for instructors to confront this response head-on, leading students to understand both that cultural purity is a myth and that hybridization results from the self-conscious actions of autonomous artists. All music is hybridized, and hierarchies based on so-called authenticity must be dismantled. Narayanan and Ilesanmi also both address what the latter terms "origin listening," or a listening practice that seeks to identify foreign influence. Narayanan suggests moving away from the binary of retentions versus culture loss, while Ilesanmi proposes "an approach to origin listening that can reveal the postcolonial realities of African music-making and ownership." Although Ilesanmi notes that origin listening is more likely to reveal our preconceptions about what African music should sound like than to uncover legitimate information, he believes the practice can be productively employed in the classroom under careful guidance.

Narayanan writes from a deeply personal perspective as a first-generation diaspora musician with training and experience in opera, jazz, and Carnatic music. Their musical practice transcends categories of fusion or hybridity, which suggest the bringing together of fully formed musical styles. Instead, Narayanan draws from their own experience and study of other Indian-American artists to theorize "hyphenation"—in which "multiple influences are intertwined from the outset, leading to a creative process and a musical product that stage a dialogue between cultures and genres from the moment of their inception"—as a framework for understanding the work of diaspora musicians. Their chapter, "Music of the Hyphen: Diaspora Music as Process and Product," takes as a case study the debut album of Indian-American mridangist Rajna Swaminathan, created in collaboration with both jazz and Carnatic musicians. Narayanan's analysis of the album demonstrates an approach that they unpack in pedagogical comments. They criticize the simplistic binary of assimilation versus appropriation while attending to the political nuances of cross-cultural borrowing. Throughout the chapter, they ask incisive questions—twenty-three in total—that instructors can in turn pose to their own students to guide meaningful encounters with hyphenated music.

In "African-Focused Approaches to Teaching African Popular Music in Western Classrooms," Ilesanmi emphasizes the process of indigenization by which styles are embraced, reimagined, and creatively deployed by African musicians. He also addresses the intercontinental, intercultural, and intracultural interactions that characterize African societies and musics. After outlining his approach, Ilesanmi applies it to the study of Fela Anikulapo-Kuti (1938–1997), the composer and bandleader who originated Afrobeat. He details a pedagogical exploration of Kuti's biography and music in ways that center African indigeneity and ingenuity, positioning Kuti as an artist who drew from diverse sources as they suited his needs. While the identification of origins can reveal Kuti's process, students must go further to understand the pervasive "Africanness" of his music.

Gregory Reish's wide-ranging meditation on hybridization in *son jarocho* draws together threads from this section and the first. In "Por ti seré: Jarocho Fusion and Revivalism in 'La Bamba'," Reish embarks on a familiar and often-taught episode in the history of U.S. popular music: Ritchie Valens's adaptation of a Mexican (or, more accurately, Veracruzan) folk song into the 1958 hit "La Bamba," a transference commonly addressed in textbooks to affirm the multicultural origins of rock 'n' roll. While Reish himself has employed the tactic of inviting students to contrast Valens's hit with a performance of the song in the *son jarocho* tradition, he sees serious dangers in this approach. Such a comparison can reinforce misguided notions of authenticity versus commercialism, while at the same time reducing folk traditions to mere source material for popular or art music production centered in the U.S. Instead, Reish suggests grappling with *son jarocho* on its own terms. His detailed cultural history of the tradition, which reveals it to have been hybridized and contested long before Valens came on the scene, contains all of the information necessary for an instructor to pursue this topic in the classroom. Reish outlines an alternate historical trajectory for "La Bamba," one driven by *son jarocho* musicians who reimagine the song and tradition from within, and that bypasses any influence from U.S. rock 'n' roll. By constructing an Indigenized narrative illustrated by recordings that are immediately available through streaming services, Reish effectively decenters U.S. popular musicians and audiences as he traces the transformation of the song's sound and significance into the present day. His framework for approaching cases of intercultural transference can also be applied to other teaching contexts across courses in popular music, jazz, and art music.

Part III: Training Global Musicians

The chapters in this final section emphasize training in performance skills, although the approaches outlined apply to a range of pedagogical settings. All of the authors are primarily music scholars, and much of their work takes place in music history classrooms. However, each addresses the challenges and opportunities that arise when inviting students to acquire competencies in a tradition that falls outside the confines of Western art music.

In his chapter "From Brazilian Worship Houses to a U.S. College: Recontextualizations of Afro-Brazilian Religious Music and Movement," Marc Gidal considers how the meaning of Afro-Brazilian religious music changes as it moves between three contexts: worship in Brazil, folkloric performance in the U.S., and workshops and courses housed within his own public liberal arts institution. Gidal makes the point that all of these settings recontextualize performance and religious practices that have their roots in West Africa; the process of recontextualization begins before the music leaves Brazil. In the U.S., he considers how the folkloric troupe Ologundê translates Afro-Brazilian worship music for presentational and educational purposes. Jailton "Dendê" Macedo, who founded Ologundê after witnessing "a lot of fake stuff" being offered to U.S. audiences, aspires to a high degree of authenticity, yet the process of recontextualization changes the form and meaning of the music and dance all the same. Gidal reports on workshops presented by Ologundê to students at his college, reflecting on tensions that arose during the events and the challenge of providing students with adequate historical and cultural background to inform their embodied experience with Afro-Brazilian music and dance. Finally, he considers the Brazilian Percussion Ensemble he co-founded at his institution. Although the polyrhythms taught in the ensemble bear rich religious and political significance, students tend to understand them in purely musical terms—the inevitable result, Gidal observes, "of teaching music for Carnival and Candomblé in a secular educational setting through percussion instruction rather than gradual enculturation within an Afro-Brazilian cultural community that includes singing, movement, ritual frames, spiritual functions, or social-political activism."

Gidal provides all of the necessary detail, complete with transcriptions and videos, that an instructor will need to explore Afro-Brazilian worship music in the classroom setting. At the same time, he presents a model for considering the role of recontextualization in understanding any musical practice, and his approach can be applied to other traditions. It is essential that we recognize higher education itself as a context that shapes the meaning of *all* the music we teach and practice.

In his chapter "Crossing Over Popular and Classical Traditions through Musical Theater," Alex Bádue considers the need for singers and instrumentalists to become comfortable with diverse styles and performance contexts. Although he is teaching music history courses, Bádue seeks to prepare performers for work in the current market, which increasingly requires flexibility and breadth of experience. Bádue leads students to interrogate the differences between opera and musical theater and to consider how the two can be effectively blended. These differences are nebulous. They can concern musical forms, singing styles, marketing tactics, and reception, but it has always been impossible to make definitive statements about either practice. Additionally, the divide between opera and musical theater has long been racialized, as evidenced by the phrenological terms "highbrow" and "lowbrow." The study of crossover, therefore, must engage with racist ideas about musical value that have had currency in the past and remain prevalent today.

Like the other authors in this volume, Bádue shares enough detail about his readings, listening examples, and classroom activities for other instructors to replicate his approach with minimal difficulty. He also provides complete assignments for final projects in a pair of appendices. He reports that students in his classes revised their audition packages, tackled new literature in their applied study, and took on crossover performance projects as a result of their experiences, all of which supports his argument that the study of musical theater and crossover has an essential place in the music history curriculum.

The final chapter, by Christopher J. Smith, turns the focus almost entirely to performance. Although Smith is a musicologist by training, he has for many years been directing a vernacular music ensemble at his institution. In "The Anti-Colonial Conservatory: The Case of the University 'Folk Band'," he outlines his philosophy and approach in detail, arguing that an ensemble of this type can challenge the "exclusionist and unjust system of access" that characterizes higher education in music. Smith acknowledges both the benefits and challenges of integrating vernacular practices into the college music department. On the one hand, access to vernacular music-making can democratize learning and empower students while helping them to develop valuable skills as musicians. On the other hand, the neoliberal environment of higher education threatens to distort and erode the aesthetic, organizational, and political values of vernacular practices. The instructor who seeks to bring vernacular music into the conservatory, therefore, must acknowledge the impossibility of fully reconciling vernacular pedagogy with the structures of a college music department and strive to resist conformity. "The incorporation of vernacular idioms within the conservatory," writes Smith, "must not come at the cost of eroding those idioms' core priorities."

In the course of making his argument, Smith surveys the practices of "folk bands" at institutions in Helsinki and Buenos Aires before turning to his own ensemble. None of the programs described is preoccupied with the faithful reproduction of historical instrumentation, tunes, or styles. Instead, each dismisses concerns about "authenticity" and sets out to imagine what forms vernacular music-making might take in the present day. Smith's approach departs from expected models in many ways—he provides participants with notation, for example, in an effort "to meet student musicians where they are"—while adhering to the core principles of vernacularity as he understands it. Smith's ensemble functions within a fictional multiverse that is reinvented and expanded by each cohort of students, allowing them to explore new possibilities for imagining "folk music." At the same time, the multiverse narrative intersects with real-world histories, repertoires, and practices, encouraging students to investigate the threads that tie their work to existing traditions. The result is a liberating, imaginative experience that cultivates new musical skills and ways of thinking.

Conclusion

The chapters in the volume range across a great deal of territory, but each takes the negotiation of values—whether musical, social, or pedagogical—as its central theme. As such, each author has advice on how the reader can lead students to recognize, question, and affirm their own values. Music is a contested field. Diverse traditions do not sit comfortably with one another, and skills gained in one field are not effortlessly applied to another. By confronting the myth that music is a universal language, the practitioners of which are prepared to communicate with one another no matter what their backgrounds, instructors can help students to situate their knowledge and recognize the cultural specificity of their practices and skills. Navigating stylistic boundaries requires a thoughtful guide, but it is a journey worth taking.

Notes

1 In his recent monograph, Philip Ewell criticizes the notion of "Western civilization," revealing it to be "a nineteenth-century human construct meant, in very large part, to secure and enshrine white-male dominance in the academic study of music" (Ewell, *On Music Theory*, 55). While acknowledging the mythological status of "Western civilization," I use the phrase "Western art music" in this introduction and my chapter—as do many of the other authors—as a recognizable shorthand for "performance-oriented, notated repertoire belonging to a tradition originating in Europe," or what is often termed "classical music." The fact that the two leading college textbooks in my field are titled *A History of Western Music* (Norton) and *The Oxford History of Western Music* bears witness to the sustained currency of this terminology.
2 Although he never uses the terms "colonization" or "decolonization," Loren Kajikawa's analysis of music departments in the U.S. underscores the key concerns of pedagogues who pursue decolonial strategies (Kajikawa, "The Possessive Investment in Classical Music," 157-8).
3 Walker, "Towards a Decolonized Music History Curriculum," 5, 17.
4 Figueroa, "Decolonizing 'Intro to World Music'?" 40.
5 For empirical accounts of music history curricula in the early twenty-first century, see Seaton, "A Survey and Some Questions," 23; Baumer, "A Snapshot of Music History Teaching to Undergraduate Music Majors, 2011–2012," 32–35; and Walker, "Towards a Decolonized Music History Curriculum," 16.
6 Robinson, *Hungry Listening*, 69.

7 Glenda Goodman's article on early transcriptions of Native American song by European colonizers, "Sounds Heard, Meaning Deferred: Music Transcription as Imperial Technology," is accessible to undergraduates and makes a fine companion to the material in both my and Knyt's chapters.

References

Baumer, Matthew. "A Snapshot of Music History Teaching to Undergraduate Music Majors, 2011–2012: Curricula, Methods, Assessment, and Objectives." *Journal of Music History Pedagogy* 5, no. 2 (2015): 23–47.

Ewell, Philip. *On Music Theory and Making Music More Welcoming for Everyone.* Ann Arbor: University of Michigan Press, 2023.

Figueroa, Michael. "Decolonizing 'Intro to World Music'?" *Journal of Music History Pedagogy* 10, no. 1 (2020): 39–57.

Goodman, Glenda. "Sounds Heard, Meaning Deferred: Music Transcription as Imperial Technology." *Eighteenth-Century Studies* 52, no. 1 (2018): 39–45.

Kajikawa, Loren. "The Possessive Investment in Classical Music." In *Seeing Race Again: Countering Colorblindness across the Disciplines*, edited by Kimberlé Williams Crenshaw, Luke Charles Harris, Daniel Martinez HoSang, and George Lipsitz, 155–74. Oakland: University of California Press, 2019.

Robinson, Dylan. *Hungry Listening: Resonant Theory for Indigenous Sound Studies.* Minneapolis: University of Minnesota Press, 2020.

Seaton, Douglass. "A Survey and Some Questions." In *Proceedings: The 87th Annual Meeting, 2011*, 23–26. Reston: The National Association of Schools of Music, 2012.

Walker, Margaret E. "Towards a Decolonized Music History Curriculum." *Journal of Music History Pedagogy* 10, no. 1 (2020): 1–19.

Part I
Denaturalizing Western Art Music

1 European Art Music is an Ethnic Music

Fraying the Edges in a Music History Classroom

D. Linda Pearse and Sandria P. Bouliane

The idealization of European art music, resulting from a pedagogical, performance, and music historical tradition that emerged in the nineteenth and twentieth centuries, is still dominant in the canonization of musical works with closely circumscribed narratives.[1] Traditional historiographies demarcate strict boundaries that suggest fixed European identities and generate narratives of European art music that are often essentialist and oblivious to its ethnic contexts.[2] Within this framework, Western Europe's dominance and religious orientation are both assumed and unquestioned, and the relations and entanglements of its music with the world beyond its fluctuating borders are rendered invisible.

We, the authors, speak different languages, come from different intellectual traditions, and work in different institutional environments. Pearse was trained in English- (Canada and USA) and German-language (Germany and Switzerland) environments. She works at an undergraduate institution, Mount Allison University, situated within an English scholarly community. Early studies in piano, music theory, and jazz were followed by training in and professional performance of orchestral trombone and early Baroque music (sackbut), including the creation of intercultural projects, and PhD studies in musicology. P. Bouliane was trained in both French and English in Canada. She works within a French-language scholarly community at Université Laval. Early training included classical piano instruction and musicological study of European art music, but her main research focus is on the cultural history of music in Québec, including popular music, during the first half of the twentieth century.

Our shared pedagogical and epistemological interests *and* our differences have brought us together. We find ourselves on a path to a multi-vocal approach to research that actively displaces "one's habitual and comfortable standpoints away from a dominant position, in order to provide space for what seem like alien understandings and experiences."[3] Within a period of significant social and disciplinary change, we are energized by attempts to decolonize and engage meaningfully with social justice. Marginalized groups are asserting their rights, making their voices heard, and insisting that their integrity as human beings be fully recognized and valued. This context has led us and other scholars and educators in a broad range of disciplines (including musicology) to rethink pedagogies and curricula.[4]

We contend that European art music can be productively regarded as an ethnic music. It can be approached using theoretical frameworks that reveal it to be just one music of many, provided that these frameworks reveal its messy boundaries—its entanglements and overlaps with other musics. These approaches decenter Europe and show that European art music never existed in isolation. They make it clear that rigid concepts of Europe, nation states, and cultural identities are flawed. For example, European art music is connected to oral traditions that reveal its inseparability from a variety of improvised and informal practices. Its stylistic developments and expressive aims derive from engagement and movement across political, cultural, and religious borders and its interactions with migrating populations. And it responds to shifting power dynamics between Europe and other regions, exposing its vulnerability and dependency.

In the process, we expose alternate pathways—ones that need not be prescriptive but that open up new horizons.[5] We value and draw on existing Europe-centered narratives, but at the same time, put these in conversation with scholarship that disrupts and reframes them. By showing that European art music was fraught and complex in its social interactions and meanings, we will discuss the concrete applications of different approaches developed within our experiential teaching practice.[6] We aim to fray the edges of what is often a clearly delineated object, revealing early European art music's cultural complexity and exposing its entangled ethnic identity. In doing so, we consider two case studies that explore: 1) the intertwined histories of the troubadours and the Qiyan (11th–13th centuries), and 2) music's multifaceted participation in encounters between Europeans and Ottomans (16th and 17th centuries).

Theory and Methodology

Shahjahan et al. (2022) critically analyze decolonial approaches to curriculum and pedagogy (DCP) and provide an overview of the important threads emerging from this wave of literature.[7] Their work points to decolonial approaches as an emergent paradigm, underscoring the mounting pressure in academia to shift from dominant embedded paradigms (e.g., modernism, postmodernism, neocolonial) toward diverse global, glocal, and decolonial ones.[8]

While we are not suggesting that we are decolonizing the study of Western European art music *per se*, we notice that these approaches for actualizing DCP resonate strongly with our own:

1) "probing the positionality of knowledge within curriculum";
2) constructing inclusive curricula that decenter dominant knowledge systems; and
3) fostering relational strategies that emphasize "the collaborative nature of knowledge production."[9]

These resonances prompt a second observation: our contribution unfolds synchronously and non-linearly with this wave of literature. Across several countries, languages, and institutions, scholars are embracing new theoretical horizons that critically expand our fields of knowledge and intersect in a rhizomatic, complex, and multidirectional manner. To quote Neal Allar in his work on Glissant: "works of different authors may entangle with and mutually influence each other ... without the author (yet) recognizing what has occurred."[10] We wish to add our own tendril to the multi-voiced entanglements that characterize this rich time of epistemological and ontological exploration.

We diverge from the canon by adopting theoretical frameworks that engage alternate historical perspectives.[11] And we consider music that is standard in the curriculum, but present it in new ways:

1) *diversifying* sources to include perspectives that encompass the movement and exchange of people and music across borders;
2) *reframing* European art music to account for shifting power dynamics over time; and
3) *decentering* the idea of cultural or religious identity as distinct and bounded, by considering musicians whose music and lives express complexity and defy labels.[12]

Using this methodology, we develop classroom activities and strategies that engage students in a co-production of knowledge. We prioritize critical thinking about gender, cultural and religious encounter and identity, and oral versus written traditions, in addition to more standard composer biographies, performance practices, and score study (when applicable).

Pedagogical Approaches

As instructors of undergraduate music history courses, we engage with ever-increasing spans of historical time, expanding geographical regions, and a greater variety of musical genres, pushing and extending our expertise into less familiar terrain that can produce discomfort for both instructors and students. As the authors confront our individual *terra incognitae*, we employ a historiographical approach that makes alternate manifestations of music historical narrative possible and defensible. In doing so, we consider our subject from multiple perspectives, carve out distance from it (temporal, geographical, or linguistic), and reflect on the production of knowledge.[13] It is through these efforts that historiography allows us to connect the music of the past with our present understanding.

Through increasing student interaction with course content, we aim to consolidate their acquisition of skills and enrich their perception of the material by fostering connections with their own experiences as musicians, listeners, and students of the twenty-first century. The balance between lectures and active pedagogy, between reception and production of content, is key. We aim to show how active learning strategies can be compatible with the demands of intellectual rigor that are sought at the university level.

a. Threshold Concept Theory.[14] Threshold concepts are core ideas that are conceptually challenging; once understood, these concepts transform the students' perception of the subject. Threshold concept theory emphasizes process over outcomes and lends itself to repeated use in different contexts. We apply historiography as a threshold concept to a variety of situations. The repetition interrupts embedded historical narratives, making them visible, and provides an entry point to critical thinking through which students become sensitized to historiographical issues.

b. Learning Portfolio/Flipped Classroom. We use online learning portfolios to organize activities in ways that encourage student interaction with each other and the instructor. In addition to other activities and assessments, students upload summaries of classes and assigned readings, and build creative content (e.g., a recording of a performance, a comparative analysis of readings, a score analysis, a concert critique, or an interview with a musician). The students provide extended and respectful written responses to the online entries. This flipped approach ensures that students dialogue productively during class time because their readings, summaries, and commentaries are posted prior to the class for which readings are assigned.[15] As a result, more class time is devoted to close reading, peer mentorship, listening, and active participation.

c. Close and Critical Readings. We incorporate accessible scholarly readings to foreground different critical approaches, putting them in productive conversation with standard texts. The following prompts offer one possible strategy for close readings in class that encourages critical evaluation: What is the author's perspective? From what location are they writing? What evidence and/or primary sources are they using? Who is the intended audience? What is the author's aim? How does each text center or decenter assumptions about European music? How do the readings/objects reveal contrasting perspectives or produce different knowledge?

Our case studies raise different historiographical questions and require distinct approaches: they are temporally far apart (the Middle Ages and late Renaissance) and engage musical traditions that leave diverse sources and traces. Yet in each, a standard narrative that centers European knowledge production is juxtaposed with narratives that complement, challenge, or disrupt it.

Case Studies[16]

Intercultural encounters emerging from population displacement and conflict offer opportunities for disrupting implicit narratives of European dominance. They complement the remarkable existing scholarship on early European art music and reveal the constantly shifting nature of Europe's borders, and the (at times) surprising fragility of Europe on the global stage. The accounts of interlocutors, travelers, and those inhabiting blurred identities within conflict zones can productively muddy otherwise clearly delineated ideas about cultural and religious identities. These encounters allow instructors to make historiographical readings of standard texts not only formative but also exciting. For both case studies, we provide, in boxed text, a sample of teaching materials, pedagogical strategies, and prompts to guide class discussions and illustrate our methodology. We present multiple approaches and activities with the expectation that pedagogues will choose from among them, adapt and supplement them with their own ideas, and not necessarily adopt all within a course.

Music and Bodies in Motion: Blurred Borders and Identities

Several difficulties arise when teaching medieval music history, particularly when most students misunderstand key concepts. The first concerns the medieval period, pejoratively called the Middle Ages, which is often perceived as an unchanging *dark ages* even though it extends over 1000 years, longer than any other Western musical period. This reductive approach renders musical practices of this vast period intelligible, but in doing so, obscures their diversity and richness.

Reinhard Strohm's chapter, "'Medieval Music' or 'Early European Music'?," supports a more detailed and nuanced approach, challenging the traditional tripartite periodic organization of Antiquity–Middle Ages–Modern Era, and offering a more representative terminology and a less hegemonic historical division. Although Strohm's refined nomenclature, *Early European Music*, is more adequate and precise, it introduces a second potentially challenging concept for students: that *Europe* is not a fixed entity. Students often misunderstand that the borders of what is called Europe have fluctuated over time, and that European countries or regions of the past cannot be blindly associated with the political and economic organization of the present. As teachers, we need to make students aware that the Middle Ages contain many sub-periods, and that these change over time and within constantly shifting political and cultural regions of Europe.

Early European Music is traditionally articulated by four main events: the standardization of Roman liturgical chant; the establishment of neumatic notation; the importance of the Notre-Dame School composers for the growth of polyphony; and the advent of notated secular music. The result is a flawed premise: that medieval music is European, Christian, and literate. This framework generates a simple linear narrative that permits this series of developments to be linked coherently (albeit problematically). Yet it is this same simplicity that makes this narrative an excellent starting point for reframing European art music by engaging students in its historiography.

Pedagogical Plan #1 In class: 20-minute Think-Pair-Share learning activity:[17]

To increase awareness of existing conceptual borders	• What happens to *art* or *classical* music if we say that Europe, as we know it today, did not exist? • What insights can we acquire if we focus on a musical practice or genre without presupposing its geopolitical or religious boundaries? • What happens if we consider music whose musical trace is non-existent or has not survived?

This case study opens up the standard narrative, disrupting the idea that the troubadours were "the earliest and most significant exponents of the arts of music and poetry in medieval Western vernacular culture."[18] In doing so, we engage with admittedly thorny issues: unlinked fragments of space and time, locations with fluctuating designations, and, in large part, a non-notated musical tradition. As a result, we reposition the troubadours as one actor among many, including women, and we widen the geographical scope beyond France and the Christian world to include the Muslim Iberian Peninsula.

La pensée complexe, or *complex thinking*, as developed by Edgard Morin, serves as a threshold concept.[19] Approaching a system or a phenomenon in its complexity allows us to embrace paradoxes and understand that several competing rationales can coexist—at the same time linked and separated.[20] The foundations of this theory are expressed in the work of Reynolds on medieval Iberian music:

> even the term 'hybridization' falls short, and labels such as Christian, Jewish and Muslim hinder rather than help in reaching an historically accurate understanding of the Iberian Middle Ages. We must instead begin thinking in terms of 'complex genealogies.'[21]

European Art Music is an Ethnic Music 21

To address troubadour love song, Morin's approach invites us to stop looking for infallible proof of an Arab, goliard, liturgical, or folkloric influence (or the absence of one), and instead to focus on the contacts, encounters, and crossovers that flourished in each place and time.

Pedagogical Plan #2	*Close reading and comparison of texts assuming three distinct positions:*
To engage with contrasting meanings across specialized scholarship without undermining the rigor and integrity of the authors	1 – Limiting the Arab influence • Zink, *Les troubadours*, 35–62. 2 – Endorsing the Arab influence • Robinson, *In Praise of Song: The Making of Courtly Culture*, 273–83. 3 – Pushing "the discussion beyond the severely limiting paradigm of 'influence'"[22] • Reynolds, "Music in Medieval Iberia," 236–238. • Brogniet, "L'influence des poètes arabes préislamiques," 9–15. *Additional prompts:* What are the arguments and sources deployed to support each position? What makes the concept of influence so useful in history? Is it possible to prove the influence of one music on another?

We consider the Qiyan (enslaved Iberian singing girls and women) as a way to explore the roots of troubadour love songs in the vernacular poetry. Because the Qiyan were "a key institution in the so-called Golden Age of Arabic music (Abbasid period, 8th–13th centuries) both in the East and in the West," they offer "a unique opportunity for the study of gender, slavery, and social relations during the medieval period."[23]

The need to include more women's voices in the history of music is beyond dispute. But it is also important to demonstrate that the study of a non-Christian region that existed over a thousand years ago must be approached without imposing a contemporary conception of Spain. By paying attention to shifting borders, the movement of people, and the oral circulation of works, such as vernacular and/or courtly love songs, we can consider the al-Andalus's enslaved singing women together with Guillaume IX (1071–1126), the Duke of Aquitaine, also recognized as the first troubadour.

From the eighth to the fifteenth century, al-Andalus stimulated the development of new cultural and economic centers in southern Spain (i.e., Cordoba, Grenada, Seville) that were in constant interaction and competition with cities from the north and east. Also known as Islamic Spain, al-Andalus is often considered a model of multiculturalism—or at least a crucial location for the import, exchange, and export of scientific, philosophical, and cultural production.[24] These comings and goings were contingent on power relations: boundaries shifted through the circulation of music and musicians, free and enslaved. The 1064 Battle of Barbastro (also known as the Siege or Crusade of Barbastro) is one example of a major event that brought Christians and Muslims, from varied locations, into contact, confrontation, and encounter.[25]

Pedagogical Plan #3	*In-class lecture on two themes:*
To strengthen research skills and draw on students' language abilities	1. al-Andalus: geographic area (711–1492) 2. Battle of Barbastro: European conflict (1064) **In-class activities:**
To emphasize the need for contextualization in order to avoid shortcuts and reductionism To observe how a better understanding of a historical region or conflict affects our comprehension of the history of music	1. Lecture on contextualization and complexity: Morin, "Restricted Complexity," 14–16. 2. Small-group research on and discussion of themes 3. Sharing of group exchanges and learning in plenary 4. To increase the number of authorial perspectives, students search for articles according to their individual language skills. The perspectives across scholarship in different languages will vary according to student language background (i.e., students may be fluent in Arabic, Spanish, French, English, etc.).

After a brutal victory, one of the conquerors of Barbastro, Guillaume VIII (1025–1086), returned to France with thousands of prisoners, including many Qiyan.[26] This displacement of Qiyan to the courts of southern France, including Aquitaine, has led researchers such as Lombezzi to compare the song texts of troubadours with those of Andalusian-Arabs, hypothesizing "a contamination due to intertextuality and interdiscursiveness, if not direct contact," given that Guillaume VIII was the father of Guillaume IX, the troubadour.[27]

In exploring the similarities between these song traditions, the instructor faces complex linguistic barriers, including dialects of Occitan, Mozarabic, and classical Arabic. Students' inability to read original texts without the aid of translations and interpretations can productively heighten their awareness of the vast historical and cultural distance that separates them from their subject, making historiography transparent.

The disproportionate number of sources available for one topic compared with another is also instructive. The princely, amorous, and warlike life of Guillaume IX was well documented and reported even in his time, and many biographies and studies have followed since. But for the few Qiyan that we know of, the corpus is much more fragmented and scattered. These constraints compel us to consult different kinds of sources and adopt alternate approaches.

Pedagogical Plan #4	Lecture on the Qiyan, key elements:
To highlight issues surrounding the availability and interpretation of primary sources	• historical records about the Qiyan were written by men and for men • historical records about enslaved musicians were written by authors that did not share their social condition • there is no surviving musical notation from the Qiyan In addition to the references already mentioned, the lecturer may wish to review the following materials: Menocal, *The Ornament*, 94–106; Richardson, "Singing Slave Girls"; and Nielson, "Visibility and Performance," 75–81. Class discussion: types of historical documents that can reveal information about music by women and/or women under slavery. Examples include: • accounts of the sale and commodification of enslaved people • descriptions of physical and musical qualities • appreciation or criticism of a performance • song lyrics • musical instruments owned or played by women and/or enslaved peoples

Rich secondary sources offer a broad range of information on these exceptional women in a format accessible to undergraduate students. Vera Martín-Peñasco takes a feminist approach by revealing the multidimensionality of these musicians in her article "'The Gazelle in the Lion's Claws': The Figure of the Qiyan from the Perspective of the 21st Century. Victims or Empowered?" (P. Bouliane's translation). She argues that the Qiyan are *doubly enslaved*—both women and slaves—yet they are empowered by a certain freedom of action and movement that few women, enslaved or married, were granted. This complex identity is accentuated by their diverse geographical origins and locations, their ethnic origins (Occitan, Arab, and African), and their religious confessions (Muslim, Christian, Moriscos, and Jewish). The Qiyan were selected on the basis of a set of exceptional skills:

> In addition to singing, the training included specialization in different musical instruments with which to accompany themselves, mostly percussion and lute, and could be completed with knowledge of poetry, literature, history, calligraphy, dance, acrobatics, juggling, as well as the strict rules of etiquette and social protocol.[28]

Their specialized training could last up to fifteen years and lead to certification as a music teacher.[29]

A closer look at their experiences exposes surprising contradictions: although they could maintain their own servants and musicians, they always remained the property of a man—an aristocrat, wealthy merchant, or religious official. This paradoxical status resonates with women in other locations who similarly performed music, literary recitations, and other entertainments within a tenuous space at the confluence of slavery and social privilege.[30]

In the absence of a notated tradition, there are few recordings of Qiyan music available, and these recordings hypothetically reconstruct performances based on scant information that engages Qiyan music only indirectly (i.e., either al-Andalusian music is considered broadly or with an emphasis on instrumental or male repertoires).[31] For the music of Guillaume IX there are similar problems, since we lack musical notation for his eleven known songs. Christelle Chaillou-Amadieu notes that across fifteen recordings of his music, reconstructions differ widely: some renditions recite texts instead of singing them, some employ a pre-existing contemporary melody, and others use entirely new music.[32] These processes merge a written art form with an oral tradition, the latter necessarily opening itself to creative interpretation. Students must therefore consider the multi-layered interpretive process that begins with the text manuscript and moves through many stages before arriving at a recording or performance.

Pedagogical Plan #5	*Close reading before class on historical performance practice:*
To make cultural assumptions and biases visible through active listening To go beyond the limits of a non-trained ear	1. On the reconstruction of past musical practices and on modern performances of "medieval" Andalusian music: • Reynolds, "The Re-Creation of Medieval Arabo-Andalusian Music," 176–177, and 185–188. 2. On recordings of Guillaume IX's songs and on historical performance practice and re-creation: • Chaillou-Amadieu, "Les exécutions musicales de Guillaume d'Aquitaine," 9–11, and 14–20. **In-class activities: close listening to historically informed performances:** • Small groups discuss and compare recordings of Arabo-Andalusian and songs by Guillaume IX, with a focus on the instruments, voices, and rhythm. See suggestions in Reynolds, 189, and Chaillou-Amadieu, 12. **After class:** students write reflections based on class discussions in their learning portfolios.

The Qiyan offer rich possibilities for classroom teaching: to explore the hypothesis of an Arabic origin of the word for troubadour (*tarab* or *darab*) or to compare the poetic similarities between Occitan courtly love songs and the Arabic *zejal*.[33] Born in one place, trained in another, bought here and sold there, polyglots and multi-instrumentalists, the Qiyan's almost nomadic existence forces us to think differently about territories and borders. This path exposes a complex genealogy that weaves the conventional narrative of the troubadours together with more marginalized voices.

Conflict and Encounter: The Battle of Lepanto and the Ottomans

European music of the late Renaissance and early Baroque is often considered within a self-referential framework that acknowledges unfolding Protestant–Catholic tensions and divisions, bookended on the one side by the Protestant Reformation and the Catholic Counter-Reformation, and on the other, the Thirty Years' War.[34] This standard narrative is punctuated by the idea of innovation at the turn of the seventeenth century in Italy, spurring developments in dramatic music (e.g., madrigals, *Commedia dell'arte*, and early opera), that then spill over into sacred music (e.g., masses, motets).[35] This narrative, however, is entirely circumscribed by the dynamics of a Europe in tumult during a religious crisis within Christianity. Events beyond Europe that might interact with music production (both secular and sacred) are largely ignored. As a result, European perspectives on European music center European knowledge within a unified (albeit multifaceted and enticing) lens. Similarly, a consideration of predominantly Christian perspectives centers Christianity as the only religion of relevance to an understanding of European music.[36]

The motet, for example, is a Latin-texted sacred work that has been widely studied. Giovanni (1557–1612) and Andrea Gabrieli (1532/1533–1585) were major motet composers in Venice in the late sixteenth century; their work is discussed in many standard texts.[37] A traditional teaching approach applied to the motet imparts core skills in music analysis, and an understanding of musical texture, compositional process, terminology, venues, and performance practice.

Pedagogical Plan #1	
To develop close reading skills and heighten awareness of authorial perspective, contextual scope, and the relationship between evidence and knowledge production	**Written reflection before class**: read Taruskin and Gibbs, *History*, 172–74, and Rothenberg and Holzer, *Anthology*, 192–205; listen to G. Gabrieli's motet, "In ecclesiis"; discuss elements of the music using terminology introduced in the reading; describe its religious and political context. **20-minute Think-Pair-Share learning activity**:[38] • What evidence do the authors consider? • What are the central ideas that emerge from this focus? (e.g., the notated score, virtuosity, church music-making, Counter-Reformation Italy) • Whose perspective is centered in this reading?

Yet within this framework, a narrative of *influence* results: dramatic genres influence sacred ones, Protestant and Catholic music-making influence each other, and developments in Italian music influence European music north of the Alps. But just as Reynolds notes that *influence* is "too facile a paradigm" to describe cultural interactions in medieval Iberia, it also falls short at the turn of the seventeenth century in Europe and the Mediterranean.[39]

In the late sixteenth century, the Ottoman Empire was a well-organized, multicultural, and artistically rich society with a fierce military and ever-expanding land possessions.[40] It was arguably more powerful than the confessionally fractured and subsequently weakened Europe with which it battled both on maritime fronts in the Mediterranean and along land borders in central Europe. European responses to the Ottoman threat are documented in descriptions of sounds, artwork, celebrations, and in music, pointing to a profound European anxiety that can be productively explored within the music classroom.[41] This narrative reveals other strands of Europe's history: not a confessionally fractured Europe on the brink of war, or a dominant Europe extracting resources from the New World, but a Europe that is terrified and vulnerable. When these seemingly disparate strands are brought together, the multifaceted production of European music unfolds within a *complex genealogy*: one that accounts for Protestant–Catholic tensions, colonization, *and* a fearful response to a more powerful Other.

To explore a music that unfolds within turbulent conflict and across multiple borders within the classroom, we consider the well-documented Battle of Lepanto (1571), a major conflict between Europeans (the Holy League) and Ottomans as part of the War of Cyprus (1570–1573). Studying a motet created in response to the Christian victory in this battle shows how music participated in a broad discourse that extends far beyond the boundaries of the notated parts. Following the close reading of A. Gabrieli's motet, "Benedictus Dominus Deus Sabaoth" (1587), we thus broaden the temporal and cultural scope to account for different (and at times contradictory) perspectives, involving students in a critical consideration of historiography.[42]

| **Pedagogical Plan #2** To deepen the understanding of how an expanded temporal scope can influence historical narrative To consider music's role in the public mediation of conflict | **Written reflection before class:** listen to and discuss elements in the score of "Benedictus Dominus Deus Sabaoth"; read Fenlon (below).

Close reading and comparison of texts with distinct focuses:
1 – On the notated score and local Venetian context
• Taruskin and Gibbs reading from Pedagogical Plan #1 above
2 – On music composed in response to conflict from a Venetian perspective
• Fenlon, *The Ceremonial City*, 175–78 (Holy League Victory), 179–80 (celebrations, music)
3 – On a context beyond Europe, one that includes battles with the Ottomans
• Fenlon, *The Ceremonial City*, 158–62 (background on the War of Cyprus)

Additional prompts: How does the choice of evidence in each passage shape the knowledge produced? How does our understanding of the triumphant Venetian response change with the broader perspective provided in the third reading? (i.e., fear response). How does this music participate in conflict? How do the celebrations perpetuate ideas about the Other? |

The War of Cyprus, the larger war in which the Holy League was defeated by the Ottomans, expands this context by showing that Lepanto was the only win in an extended conflict that the Holy League lost.[43] Broadening the temporal scope further, we observe that the War of Cyprus was nestled within a series of skirmishes between Ottomans and Europeans, bookended by the loss of Constantinople in 1453, and the second Siege of Vienna in 1683. Through this process of contextualization, Europe's assumed dominance on the global stage is reframed. A weakened Europe is frightened by the Ottomans' military power and by the threat to its religious autonomy, and at the same time, it is fractured by its own interior confessional divisions. It is engaged in a self-propelled psychological struggle informed by a centuries-long inherited narrative of fear that is carried from generation to generation through various media, including music.

With this layered approach, students apply a historiographical lens repeatedly to the same polychoral motet, yet from different perspectives (i.e., considering the motet narrowly, as a notated work; the motet as a social expression of celebration, composed in response to the win at Lepanto; and the motet as an expression of desperation when viewed within the larger war that the Holy League lost). In doing so, we push back on standard framings of religious conflicts that unfold *within* Europe to consider how European music responds to conflicts *beyond* Europe, encompassing religious tensions with a diverse and multicultural Islamic society. We show how evidence of contact across borders can illuminate the oftentimes invisible contexts of European musical practice.[44]

A problem emerges: this approach is informed by European perspectives, without the balance provided by an Ottoman lens. What types of music might the Ottomans have used to express military power and to inculcate emotional passion on the battlefield? Eric Rice provides an accessible history of Janissary (*mehter*) music, identifying its salient features and including a transcription and analysis of a representative early twentieth-century *mehter* composition, "Ceddin Deden" by Ismail Hakki Bey (1883–1923).[45] Ottoman artworks depicting Janissary musicians in battle allow art to sound in the absence of a notated Ottoman music tradition.[46] European artwork depicting Janissary bands on the battlefield underscores Europe's impression of Ottoman military might.[47] Taken together, these works offer insights into the form, instrumentation, sounds, and emotional impact of Ottoman music used in warfare.

Yet another lens is provided by Mehmet Ali Sanlıkol, whose work is informed by Ottoman primary sources and supported by different evidence.[48] A comparison of Sanlıkol's and Rice's authorial aims and perspectives reveals Rice's primary focus on the incorporation of Janissary music within European music, and his referential frame of "Western ears": he centers European music by analyzing *mehter* music using Western musical frameworks and terminology. In contrast, Sanlıkol centers Ottoman musical culture within Istanbul, accounts for a broader use of *mehter* music that extends beyond military music, and draws more heavily on Turkish scholarship. The accompanying recording provides useful examples for class listening and discussion.

Following this plan, students learn to think critically by reading scholarship written from different perspectives. Moving from the notated music to a local context, then a global one, makes explicit the ways in which scholars' choices about evidence and framework influence the production of knowledge.

Pedagogical Plan #3 To introduce the concept of perspective through readings on Ottoman music To understand how music mediates and participates in conflict by considering different cultural lenses	Written reflection before class: read Rice, "Representations of Janissary Music," 46–56; Sanlıkol, *The Musician Mehters*, 49–53, 61–63; listen to one or two selections from tracks 2–8. Instructor materials for artwork: Bowles, "Turkish Military Bands," 536–39; Pirker, "Pictorial Documents," 2–6; Sanlıkol, *The Musician Mehters*, 74–86. In-class activities: 1. Lecture on Janissary bands: connections with artwork; review Rice's discussion of traits of *mehter* music; compare with Sanlıkol's discussion of *harbi*. 2. Discussion: 20-minute Think-Pair-Share activity,[49] close reading and comparison of the bibliographies and authorial perspectives of Rice and Sanlıkol; choose and discuss one of the assigned Sanlıkol recordings. *Additional prompt:* Compare and contrast the ways in which *mehter* music and the motet by A. Gabrieli mediate and participate in conflict.

Yet we encounter another problem: the bounded terms of *Ottoman* and *European* circumscribe a rigid conception of cultural identity that is oftentimes more porous than these words suggest. Osman of Timisoara's riveting memoir captures his harrowing life as an Ottoman and Muslim soldier, slave, Parisian-trained pâtissier, prisoner, polyglot, and eventual diplomat in Istanbul.[50] His treatment as a prisoner provides an important counter to European narratives: brutalities were committed by Ottomans and Europeans alike. The text provides fascinating insight into the complexity of cultural identity (e.g., Osman escapes from the Habsburgs only to encounter an Istanbul in which he feels foreign. Is he Ottoman, or European, or both?).[51]

The physical journeys of musicians and music can reflect a similar fluidity, blurring borders otherwise considered fixed. The Polish-born 'Alī Ufukī / Wojciech Bobowski (c. 1610–c. 1675) was captured and sold to the Ottoman palace in Istanbul, where he subsequently worked as a musician, composer, physician, and interpreter to the Sultan.[52] At court, he created a fascinating compendium of music that includes transcriptions of Ottoman music in Western notation:

bearing testimony to the multicultural intellectual life in mid-17th-century Istanbul ... [it] contains texts relating to music, linguistics, medicine, current events, food, art, etc. as well as songs in at least 10 languages, often intermingled on the same page.[53]

Pedagogical Plan #4 To expose the complexity of cultural identity and, in tandem, the complexity of music that partakes of more than one culture To disrupt and make visible frameworks that center European perspectives	Written summary before class: Haug, "Critical Edition," 112–13. In-class activities: 1. Group reading of excerpts from Casale, *Prisoner of the Infidels*, 19–22 and 54. 2. Small-group work reviewing the online manuscript Turc 292.[54] 3. Discussion: compare Osman and Ufukī's biographies (both were prisoners) and identities (both inhabited two cultures); Ufukī's transcription of Istanbul court music. *Additional prompts*: How are Osman's and Ufukī's cultural identities blurred? What difficulties arise when transcribing music created within an Ottoman oral tradition to a Western notated one?

Ottoman music's modal melodic structure—based on scales (*maḳāmlar*) determined by final (*karār*) and pitch collection (*perde*)—can be discussed alongside what students have learned earlier in the semester about Western music's modes and melodic structures.[55] Through Ufukī, we consider the transliteration of non-notated musical traditions to European notated music in ways that resonate with other examples of non-notated or improvised music considered across the course.[56] Ufukī, like Osman, is culturally and musically entangled.

A final pedagogical segment can focus on listening and reading liner notes as a way of engaging with the performance practices of earlier musics.

Pedagogical Plan #5 To become sensitive to issues of historically informed performance practice	Written reflection before class: Listen to and critically reflect on two of three recordings.[57] In-class activities: 1) Listen together to two tracks from the suggested recordings (students' choice); 2) Break out into several smaller groups to review the liner notes for each; 3) Reflect together on the performance practice of these works (consider early notation, instrumentation, performance styles, etc.). *Additional prompts*: How many stages of transliteration occur between the Ottoman performances that Ufukī heard and these modern recordings? What issues of performance practice arise when performing this music today?

What becomes obvious through this process of reading across texts and exposing complex genealogies is that recorded examples and theoretical and practical descriptions of Ottoman music-making—no matter how problematic the transmission from the source—disrupt the dominant discourse of European perspectives. This approach exposes the malleability of historical narrative and at the same time equips students with critical thinking skills useful for historical investigation.

Conclusion

Institutions, colleagues, and even students can be highly resistant to perspectives that challenge the prestige and elite positioning of European art music. By probing this positioning, the training, livelihoods, and professional value attached to it are also brought into question. In order to navigate this sensitive terrain, and to create respectful and thoughtful dialogue about curricular and pedagogical change, we consider the emotions that underlie these responses.

William Cheng's work on the humanizing and dehumanizing potential of emotional attachments to music explains why music lovers and musicologists resist criticism of the music they listen to and study.[58] How can we continue loving European art music without perpetuating embedded and reductive narratives? We agree that love is a necessary part of successful teaching, and we are aware of our own attachments to specific musics. This awareness points to the importance of our multi-voiced approach, encouraging us to consider European music from multiple perspectives.

We are not asking students or musicologists to stop loving European music—we are opening up the concept of what *Europe* and *music* are. We consider the ways in which European music is embedded in global conflicts by probing the positionality of knowledge, including diverse sources, and considering identity and borders as fluid. We disrupt the canon to be more inclusive and account for complex genealogies, and we adopt comparative frameworks that elaborate European music within its ethnic context. It is not so much a question of creating new knowledge, but more one of rearticulating that which is already accessible.

Modifying course content to account for a decolonial framework goes hand in hand with a re-evaluation of pedagogical approaches. Active learning strategies facilitate collaborative knowledge production and engage students in challenging conventional wisdom, mobilizing theoretical frameworks, and making historiography transparent. The repeated application of the historiographical lens across case studies further deepens student experience and confidence with critical reading.

Recent scholarship points to new directions for a European music history pedagogy, one that engages meaningfully with race, colonization, and global histories.[59] But conflict and encounters are also important entry points for deeper considerations of gender, power, class, and performance practice. This short foray into the worlds of the Qiyan and the Ottomans suggests multiple directions for further exploration. Engaging European art music within a larger world opens up a multitude of paths to fray the edges of the music history classroom.

Notes

1 We thank Julie E. Cumming (McGill University) for insightful comments made on an early draft of this chapter. This research was undertaken, in part, thanks to funding from the Canada Research Chairs Program and, in part, thanks to funding from the Social Sciences and Humanities Research Council of Canada.
2 See Attas, "Strategies for Settler Decolonization"; Bergeron and Bohlman, *Disciplining Music*; Clark, "Uncovering"; Goehr, *The Imaginary Museum*; Haefeli, "Does Music Evolve?"; Haefeli, "If History is Written"; Hess, "Decolonizing Music Education"; Korsyn, *Decentering Music*; Levitz, "The Musicological Elite"; Walker, "Towards a Decolonized"; Walker, P. Bouliane, and Pearse, "Challenging Embedded Coloniality."
3 Chen, "Western Music History," 12.
4 For example, Bloechl, "Race, Empire, and Early Music," 106, calls for inclusive histories that consider the "migration patterns and interactions of composers, performers, and instrument makers to and from Europe, colonial centers, and non-colonized powers"; see Attas and Walker, "Exploring Decolonization," for context within Canada.
5 Our work is informed by scholarship that aims to make music history courses more inclusive; see Clark, "Uncovering."
6 On historiography, see Goehr, *The Imaginary Museum*; and Tomlinson, "Monumental Musicology." On pedagogy, see Briscoe, *Vitalizing*; Clark, "Uncovering"; Conway and Hodgman, eds., *Teaching Music*; and Natvig, ed., *Teaching Music History*.
7 Shahjahan et al. ("'Decolonizing'") argue that the meanings, actualizations, and challenges of DCP are contextual, suggesting political and epistemological consequences that point to an emergent field of decolonial studies. They googled the word "decolonization" and received 6 million hits in 2020; we did the same on June 12, 2022, and received more than 9.5 million hits in English, and 3.2 million using "*décolonisation*" in French.
8 We do not think that societies have ever arrived at a postcolonial state and do not include it in our list of embedded paradigms.
9 Shahjahan et al., 11–12; the fourth approach to actualization is to strengthen "collaborations between community institutions, and larger sociopolitical movements." Our approaches do not resonate strongly enough with this approach to warrant its inclusion.
10 Allar, "Rhizomatic Influence," 3.
11 At least half of our course content comprises music created or performed by women, people of color, or music from locations outside of Western Europe. While our goal is not to remove standard content, a necessary consequence of including different musics will be the exclusion of others. Locke's articulation of how to engage non-canonic works and multiple perspectives within a music history classroom has been influential for our pedagogical approaches; see Locke, "Chopin."

12 Like Clark, "Uncovering," 4, we do not want to get rid of the survey course. We aim to make the canon, its conception, and its limits transparent to our students.
13 Foucault, "Questions of Method."
14 Kent, "Threshold Concepts"; Meyer, "'Variation.'"
15 For inviting students into the process of research, see Beckerman, "How can you teach." On learning portfolios, see Cassidy, "Learning Portfolios"; White, "Student Portfolios."
16 These case studies are presented in truncated form in a French-language article with the addition of a third study on the Tenshō era embassy to Portugal, Spain, and Italy, 1582–1590; see P. Bouliane and Pearse "Rencontres interculturelles."
17 The three-step class discussion (Think-Pair-Share) facilitates class dialogue on assigned readings or material presented in class: students first think on their own (2 min.), then pair up with a classmate (5–8 min.), before being asked to interact with the whole class (10 min.). See also: McGill, "Ideas for Instruction."
18 Stevens et al., "Troubadours, trouvères."
19 Complexity is central to Morin's work. See, Morin "Complexité restreinte, complexité générale"; *Penser l'Europe*; and "Restricted Complexity."
20 In "On Complexity," Morin presents three principles for addressing complexity; the first is called *dialogic*, which allows "us to maintain duality at the heart of unity," 49.
21 Reynolds, "Music in Medieval Iberia," 253.
22 Reynolds, "Music in Medieval Iberia," 236.
23 Vera Martín-Peñasco, "'La gacela en las garras,'" 45 (trans. P. Bouliane); follow with Reynolds, "Qiyan," 101.
24 Robinson, "In Praise of Song"; Menocal, "The Ornament of the World."
25 Sénac and Corbera, *1064, Barbastro*.
26 Lombezzi, "Ibn Ḥazm," 2–3; Lévi-Provençal, "Les troubadours," 24.
27 Lombezzi, "Ibn Ḥazm," 1.
28 Vera Martín-Peñasco, 49 (P. Bouliane translation).
29 Guardiola, "La figure de la kayna," 78; Navarro de la Coba, "Evidencias y registros," 62.
30 Dunbar, *Women, Music, Culture,* describes Japanese Geisha and Indian Devadasis.
31 Reynolds, "Re-Creation."
32 Chaillou-Amadieu, "Les exécutions musicales."
33 Lévi-Provençal, "Les troubadours," 22; Bec, *Le Comte de Poitier,* 38–51.
34 See Taruskin and Gibbs, *History*, 166–70, 223–24; Burkholder et al., *History*, 213–40, 337–41.
35 Varwig, *Schütz*, addresses the problematic nature of a fixation on innovation at the turn of the seventeenth century by applying a historiographical lens.
36 Although the influence and presence of other religious traditions are sometimes acknowledged, they are usually positioned as peripheral to European musical practices.
37 For example, see Taruskin and Gibbs, *History*; Burkholder et al., *History*.
38 See endnote 18.
39 Reynolds, "Music in Medieval Iberia," 253.
40 For a comprehensive history that considers the weakened position of Europe, see Finkel, *Ottoman Empire*; and Howard, *Ottoman Empire*.
41 Özyurt, *Die Türkenlieder*.
42 On the use of motets following Lepanto, see Bryant "Liturgy"; Fenlon, *Ceremonial*; Fenlon, "Memorialization"; and Ignesti, "Ippolito Baccusi," 260–75; for a score, see Arnold, ed., *Andrea Gabrieli*.

43 Finkel, *Ottoman Empire,* 164, argues that the Ottomans considered the War of Cyprus as a win and the Battle of Lepanto as an insignificant defeat. The Venetians gave up land and made payments to the Ottomans of 300,000 ducats; Finkel, 160–61.
44 See Fichtner, *Terror*, 9–71; Howard, *Ottoman Empire*, 174–75. A similar approach can consider music composed in response to the second Siege of Vienna (1683); see Rawson, "Suffering and Supplication." Using an apocalyptic theological lens, Rawson argues for composers' intentional setting of anti-Turkish crusader texts to amplify support for war on religious grounds.
45 Rice, "Representations," 45–57; for *mehter* music, see Sanlikol, *The Musician Mehters*; for a general reference, see Goodwin, *The Janissaries*.
46 See Pirker, "Pictorial Documents," 2–6; Sanlikol, *Musician Mehters*, 74–86.
47 See Bowles, "Turkish Military Bands."
48 Sanlıkol.
49 See endnote 18.
50 Casale, *Prisoner of the Infidels*, 53–54.
51 Casale, 19–22.
52 Haug, "Critical Edition," 109–110; for a thicker consideration, see Haug, *Ottoman and European Music*.
53 Haug, "Critical Edition," 110.
54 Ufukī, "Mecmua Ou Allbum de Poésies Turques."
55 Haug, "Critical Edition," 112–13.
56 Earlier in the course, we consider improvisation and its connection to the compositional process of notated polyphony, as well as the difficulties in determining how musicians improvised in the past. See Canguilhem, "Improvisation"; Canguilhem, "Singing Upon the Book"; Cumming and Pearse, "Historical Pedagogy"; Cumming and Schubert, "Origins"; Schubert, "From Improvisation."
57 For recordings, see Constantinople and Tabassian, "Fath-e bâb"; Golden Horn Ensemble, *Ali Ufki*; and Galata Mevlevi, *The Music of Islam*.
58 Cheng, *Loving Music Till It Hurts*.
59 For example, Zecher, "The Çengî," examines French and Ottoman accounts that describe the musicking of professional non-Muslim women performing in Ottoman gender-bending theatrical contexts; her work could be considered adjacent to gendered performance in early opera. Other examples include Orden, ed. *Seachanges*; Spohr, "'Mohr und Trompeter'"; Wilbourne and Cusick, *Acoustemologies*; and online resources such as Zanovello and Honisch, "Inclusive Early Music"; and Heller, "Towards a Global Baroque."

References

Allar, Neal A. "Rhizomatic Influence: The Antigenealogy of Glissant and Deleuze." *Cambridge Journal of Postcolonial Literary Inquiry* 6, no. 1 (January 2019): 1–13. https://doi.org/10.1017/pli.2018.25.

Arnold, Denis, ed. *Edizione nazionale delle opere di Andrea Gabrieli*. Vol. 11. Milan: Ricordi, 1988.

Attas, Robin. "Strategies for Settler Decolonization: Decolonial Pedagogies in a Popular Music Analysis Course." *Canadian Journal of Higher Education* 49, no. 1 (April 2019): 125–39. https://doi.org/10.7202/1060827ar.

Attas, Robin, and Margaret E. Walker. "Exploring Decolonization, Music, and Pedagogy." *Intersections: Canadian Journal of Music* 39, no. 1 (2019): 3–20.

Bec, Pierre, *Le comte de Poitiers, premier troubadour. À l'aube d'un verbe et d'une érotique.* Montpellier: Presse de l'Université de Montpellier-III, 2004.

Beckerman, Michael. "How Can You Teach What You Don't know? ... And Other Tales from Music History Pedagogy." In *Vitalizing Music History Teaching*, edited by James R. Briscoe, 3–18. Monographs & Bibliographies in American Music, no. 20. Hillsdale: Pendragon Press, 2010.

Bergeron, Katherine, and Philip V. Bohlman, eds. *Disciplining Music: Musicology and Its Canons.* Chicago: University of Chicago Press, 1992.

Bloechl, Olivia A. "Race, Empire, and Early Music." In *Rethinking Difference in Musical Scholarship*, edited by Olivia A. Bloechl, Melanie Lowe, and Jeffrey Kallberg, 77–107. Cambridge: Cambridge University Press, 2014.

Bowles, Edmund A. "The Impact of Turkish Military Bands on European Court Festivals in the 17th and 18th Centuries." *Early Music* 34, no. 4 (2006): 533–59.

Briscoe, James R., ed. *Vitalizing Music History Teaching.* Monographs & Bibliographies in American Music, no. 20. Hillsdale: Pendragon Press, 2010.

Brogniet, Éric. "L'influence des poètes arabes préislamiques sur la naissance de l'amour courtois chez les troubadours de langue d'oc." Brussels: Académie royale de langue et de littérature françaises de Belgique, 2017. http://www.arllfb.be/.

Bryant, David Douglas. "Liturgy, Ceremonial and Sacred Music in Venice at the Time of the Counter-Reformation." PhD dissertation, King's College, University of London, 1981.

Burkholder, J. Peter, Donald Jay Grout, and Claude V. Palisca. *A History of Western Music*, 9th edn. New York: W. W. Norton & Company, 2014.

Canguilhem, Philippe. "Improvisation as Concept and Musical Practice in the Fifteenth Century." In *The Cambridge History of Fifteenth-Century Music*, edited by Anna Maria Busse Berger and Jesse Rodin, 149–63. Cambridge: Cambridge University Press, 2015. https://doi.org/10.1017/CHO9781139057813.015.

———. "Singing Upon the Book According to Vicente Lusitano." *Early Music History* 30, no. 1 (2011): 55–103.

Casale, Giancarlo, trans. *Prisoner of the Infidels: The Memoir of an Ottoman Muslim in Seventeenth-Century Europe.* Oakland: University of California Press, 2021.

Cassidy, Alice. "Learning Portfolios: Creative Connections Between Formal and Informal Learning." *Collected Essays on Learning and Teaching* 3 (2010): 60–66. https://doi.org/10.22329/celt.v3i0.3241.

Chaillou-Amadieu, Christelle. "Les exécutions musicales de Guillaume d'Aquitaine: Entre réécriture et reconstitution." In *Guilhem de Peitieus duc d'Aquitaine, prince du trobar*, edited by Luc de Goustine, 251–64. Moustier Ventadour: Cahiers de Carrefour Ventadour, 2015.

Chen, Jen-yen. "Western Music History as a Teaching Topic in Taiwan: Pedagogy as Transculturation." In *Listening Across Borders: Musicology in the Global Classroom*, edited by James A. Davis and Christopher Lynch, 11–22. New York and London: Routledge, 2022. https://doi.org/10.4324/9780429027215-1.

Cheng, William. *Loving Music Till It Hurts.* New York: Oxford University Press, 2019.

Clark, Alice V. "Uncovering a Diverse Early Music." *Journal of Music History Pedagogy* 11, no. 1 (2021): 1–21.
Constantinople and Kiya Tabassian (director). "Fath-e bâb." *La Porta d'Oriente*, Glossa, GCD. 924501. https://www.youtube.com/watch?v=Qx-gzDq4TZ0.
Conway, Colleen Marie, and Thomas M. Hodgman. *Teaching Music in Higher Education*. New York: Oxford University Press, 2009.
Cumming, Julie E., and D. Linda Pearse. "Historical Pedagogy in the Graduate Musicology Seminar." In *Meaningful Gaps and Reliable Uncertainties: The Unexplored Potentials of Scholarly Reconstruction*, edited by Carmela Barbaro and Gianluca Foschi. Proceedings of the British Academy Series. Forthcoming (expected Winter 2024).
Cumming, Julie E., and Peter Schubert. "The Origins of Pervasive Imitation." In *The Cambridge History of Fifteenth-Century Music*, edited by Anna Maria Busse Berger and Jesse Rodin, 200–28. The Cambridge History of Music. Cambridge: Cambridge University Press, 2015.
Dunbar, Julie C. *Women, Music, Culture: An Introduction*, 3rd edn. New York: Routledge, 2020.
Fenlon, Iain. *The Ceremonial City: History, Memory and Myth in Renaissance Venice*. New Haven: Yale University Press, 2007.
———. "The Memorialization of Lepanto in Music, Liturgy, and Art." In *Celebrazione e Autocritica. La Serenissima e La Ricerca Dell'identità Veneziana Nel Tardo Cinquecento*, edited by Benjamin Paul, 61–78. Centro Tedesco Di Studi Veneziani 14. Rome: Viella, 2014.
Fichtner, Paula S. *Terror and Toleration: The Habsburg Empire Confronts Islam, 1526–1850*. London: Reaktion Books, 2008.
Finkel, Caroline. *The History of the Ottoman Empire: Osman's Dream*. New York: Basic Books, 2005.
Foucault, Michel. "Questions of Method." In *The Foucault Effect: Studies in Governmentality*, edited by Graham Burchell, Colin Gordon, and Peter Miller, 73–86. Chicago: Chicago University Press, 1991.
Galata Mevlevi Music, Sema Ensemble & Sultan Veled, and David Parsons (producer). *The Music of Islam: Mystic Music Through the Ages*. Vol. 14. Celestial Harmonies 103154, 1997.
Goehr, Lydia. *The Imaginary Museum of Musical Works: An Essay in the Philosophy of Music*, Rev. edn. Oxford: Oxford University Press, 2007.
Golden Horn Ensemble. *Ali Ufki (Wojciech Bobowski)*. Sony BMG Music Entertainment, 2009.
Goodwin, Godfrey. *The Janissaries*. London: Saqi Book Depot, 2013.
Guardiola, Dolores. "La figure de la kayna dans les sources musicales." In *Actes du VII Colloque Universitaire Tuniso-Español. Le patrimoine andalous dans la culture arabe et espagnole. Tunis, February 3–10, 1989*, 107–27. Cahier du CERES, série histoire 4, 1991.
Haefeli, Sara. "Does Music Evolve?" The Avid Listener. July 23, 2020. Accessed June 17, 2023. https://theavidlistenerblogcom.wordpress.com/2020/07/23/does-music-evolve/.

———. "If History Is Written by the Victors." The Avid Listener. July 23, 2020. Accessed June 17, 2023. https://theavidlistenerblogcom.wordpress.com/2020/07/23/if-history-is-written-by-the-victors/.

Haug, Judith I. "Critical Edition as Retranslation: Mediating ʿAlī Ufuḳī's Notation Collections (c. 1630–1670)." In *Perspectives on Retranslation: Ideology, Paratexts, Methods*, edited by Özlem Berk Albachten and Sehnaz Tahir Gürçaglar, 107–28. New York: Routledge, 2019.

Heller, Wendy. "Towards a Global Baroque." Music in the Baroque: Companion Website. Accessed June 11, 2023. https://wendyhellerbaroquemusic.com/welcome/towards-a-global-baroque-resources/.

Hess, Juliet. "Decolonizing Music Education: Moving Beyond Tokenism." *International Journal of Music Education* 33, no. 3 (May 2015): 336–47. https://doi.org/10.1177/0255761415581283.

Howard, Douglas A. *A History of the Ottoman Empire*. Cambridge: Cambridge University Press, 2017.

Ignesti, Alessandra. "Ippolito Baccusi and the Musical Culture of North-Eastern Italy." PhD dissertation, McGill University, 2021.

Kent, Sarah. "Threshold Concepts." In *Taylor Institute for Teaching and Learning Guide Series*, 14. Taylor Institute for Teaching and Learning at the University of Calgary. Calgary, AB, 2016. https://taylorinstitute.ucalgary.ca/resources/threshold-concepts; http://www.ucalgary.ca/taylorinstitute/guides.

Korsyn, Kevin Ernest. *Decentering Music: A Critique of Contemporary Musical Research*. Oxford and New York: Oxford University Press, 2003.

Lévi-Provençal, Évariste. "Les troubadours et la poésie arabo-andalouse." *La pensée de midi* 1, no. 1 (2000): 20–25. https://doi.org/10.3917/lpm.001.0020.

Levitz, Tamara. "The Musicological Elite." *Current Musicology* 102 (Spring 2019): 9–49.

Locke, Ralph P. "What Chopin (and Mozart and Others) Heard: Folk, Popular, 'Functional' and Non-Western Music in the Classic/Romantic Survey Course." In *Teaching Music History*, edited by Mary Natvig, 25–41. Abingdon, Oxon: Routledge, 2017.

Lombezzi, Letizia. "Ibn Ḥazm en Córdoba y los rasgos típicos del *topos* del amor." *Al-Andalus Magreb* 27, no. 104 (2020): 1–13. https://doi.org/10.25267/AAM.2020.v27.04.

McGill. "Ideas for Instruction." n.d. Accessed June 17, 2023. https://www.mcgill.ca/skills21/facilitator-guide/plan/ideas-instruction.

Menocal, Maria Rosa. *The Ornament of the World: How Muslims, Jews, and Christians Created a Culture of Tolerance in Medieval Spain*. New York: Warner Books/Hachette Book Group, 2009.

Meyer, Jan H. F. "'Variation in Student Learning' as a Threshold Concept." *The Journal of Faculty Development* 26, no. 3 (September 2012): 8–13.

Morin, Edgar. "Complexité restreinte, complexité générale." *Sciences humaines* 47 (February 1995).

———. *Penser l'Europe*, Rev. edn. Collection Folio/Actuel 20. Paris: Gallimard, 1999.

———. "Restricted Complexity, General Complexity." In *Worldviews, Science and Us: Philosophy and Complexity*, edited by Carlos Gershenson, Diederik

Aerts, and Bruce Edmonds, 5–29. World Scientific, 2007. https://doi.org/10.1142/9789812707420_0002.

Natvig, Mary, ed. *Teaching Music History*. London and New York: Routledge, 2002.

Navarro de la Coba, Dolores. "Evidencias y registros de la mujer como tañedora en al-Andalus e instrumentos musicales relacionados con ellas." In *Mujeres en la música: una aproximación desde los estudios de género*, edited by Maria Angeles Zapata Castillo, Juan Jesús Yelo Cano, and Ana María Botella Nicolás, 59–71. Madrid: Sociedad Española de Musicología, 2020.

Nielson, Lisa. "Visibility and Performance: Courtesans in the Early Islamicate Courts (661–950 CE)." In *Concubines and Courtesans: Women and Slavery in Islamic History*, edited by Matthew Gordon and Kathryn A. Hain, 75–99. New York: Oxford University Press, 2017.

Orden, Kate van, ed. *Seachanges: Music in the Mediterranean and Atlantic Worlds, 1550–1800*. Florence: Villa I Tatti, 2022.

Özyurt, Şenol. *Die Türkenlieder und das Türkenbild in der deutschen Volksüberlieferung vom 16. bis zum 20. Jahrhundert*. Vol. 4. Motive. Munich: W. Fink, 1972.

P. Bouliane, Sandria, and D. Linda Pearse. "Rencontres interculturelles: stratégies pour une pédagogie alternative de l'histoire de la musique." In *Anti-Racist Pedagogies*, edited by Marcia Ostashewski and Meghan Forsyth. *MUSICultures* 50, no. 1 (2023).

Pirker, Michael. "Pictorial Documents of the Music Bands of the Janissaries (Mehter) and the Austrian Military Music." *RIdIM/RCMI Newsletter* 15, no. 2 (1990): 2–12.

Rawson, Robert C. "Suffering and Supplication as Emblems of Power in Music Relating to the 1683 Ottoman Siege of Vienna." In *Music and Power in the Baroque Era*, edited by Rudolf Rasch, 221–36. Music, Criticism & Politics. Turnhout: Brepols, 2018.

Reynolds, Dwight F. "Music in Medieval Iberia: Contact, Influence and Hybridization." *Medieval Encounters* 15, nos. 2–4 (2009): 236–55. https://doi.org/10.1163/157006709X458846.

———. "The Qiyan of Al-Andalus." In *Concubines and Courtesans: Women and Slavery in Islamic History*, edited by Matthew S. Gordon and Kathryn A. Hain, 100–23. Vol. 1. New York: Oxford University Press, 2017. https://doi.org/10.1093/oso/9780190622183.003.0006.

———. "The Re-Creation of Medieval Arabo-Andalusian Music in Modern Performance." *Al-Masāq* 21, no. 2 (August 2009): 175–89. https://doi.org/10.1080/09503110902875442.

Rice, Eric. "Representations of Janissary Music (Mehter) as Musical Exoticism in Western Compositions, 1670–1824." *Journal of Musicological Research* 19, no. 1 (January 1999): 41–88. https://doi.org/10.1080/01411899908574768.

Richardson, Kristina. "Singing Slave Girls (Qiyan) of the Abbasid Court." In *Children in Slavery through the Ages*, edited by Gwyn Campbell, Suzanne Miers, and Joseph C. Miller, 105–18. Athens: Ohio University Press, 2009.

Robinson, Cynthia. *In Praise of Song: The Making of Courtly Culture in al-Andalus and Provence, 1005–1134 A.D.* Leiden: Brill, 2002. https://brill.com/display/title/7599.

Rothenberg, David J., and Robert R. Holzer. *Oxford Anthology of Western Music*, 2nd edn. Vol. 1. 3 vols. New York: Oxford University Press, 2013.

Sanlıkol, Mehmet Ali. *The Musician Mehters*. Istanbul: The Isis Press, 2011.

Schubert, Peter. "From Improvisation to Composition: Three 16th-Century Case Studies." In *Improvising Early Music: The History of Musical Improvisation from the Late Middle Ages to the Early Baroque*, edited by Dirk Moelants, 93–130. 11th Publication of the Collected Writings of the Orpheus Institute. Leuven: Leuven University Press, 2014.

Sénac, Philippe, and Carlos Laliena Corbera. *1064, Barbastro: Guerre Sainte Et Djihâd En Espagne*. Paris: Gallimard, 2018.

Shahjahan, Riyad A., Annabelle L. Estera, Kristen L. Surla, and Kirsten T. Edwards. "'Decolonizing' Curriculum and Pedagogy: A Comparative Review Across Disciplines and Global Higher Education Contexts." *Review of Educational Research* 92, no. 1 (February 2022): 73–113. https://doi.org/10.3102/00346543211042423.

Spohr, Arne. "'Mohr Und Trompeter': Blackness and Social Status in Early Modern Germany." *Journal of the American Musicological Society* 72, no. 3 (December 1, 2019): 613–63. https://doi.org/10.1525/jams.2019.72.3.613.

Stevens, John, Ardis Butterfield, and Theodore Karp. "Troubadours, trouvères." *Grove Music Online*. Edited by Deane Root. Accessed June 16, 2023. https://doi.org/10.1093/gmo/9781561592630.article.28468.

Strohm, Reinhard. "'Medieval Music' or 'Early European Music'?" In *The Cambridge History of Medieval Music*, edited by Mark Everist and Thomas Forrest Kelly, 1177–200. Vol. 2. The Cambridge History of Music. Cambridge: Cambridge University Press, 2018. https://doi.org/10.1017/9780511979866.040.

Taruskin, Richard, and Christopher H. Gibbs. *The Oxford History of Western Music: College Edition*, 2nd edn. New York: Oxford University Press, 2018.

Tomlinson, Gary. "Monumental Musicology." *Journal of the Royal Musical Association* 132, no. 2 (2007): 349–74.

Ufukī, ʿAlī. *Mecmua Ou Allbum de Poésies Turques, ... de La Musique Italienne et Allemande, et La Notation, Quelquefois Avec Transcription, de Chansons Turques...* [Manuscript, 1601–1615]. Bibliothèque nationale de France. Département des manuscrits. Turc 292. https://gallica.bnf.fr/ark:/12148/btv1b84150086.

Varwig, Bettina. *Histories of Heinrich Schütz*. Cambridge: Cambridge University Press, 2011. https://doi.org/10.1017/CBO9781139027007.

Vera Martín-Peñasco, Carmen. "'La gacela en las garras del león.' La figura de las Qiyan desde la perspectiva del siglo XXI. ¿Víctimas o empoderadas?" In *Mujeres en la música: una aproximación desde los estudios de género*, edited by Maria Angeles Zapata Castillo, Juan Jesús Yelo Cano, and Ana María Botella Nicolás, 44–58. Madrid: Sociedad Española de Musicología, 2020.

Walker, Margaret. "Towards a Decolonized Music History Curriculum." *Journal of Music History Pedagogy*, Special Issue: Decolonization 10, no. 1 (2020): 1–19.

Walker, Margaret, Sandria P. Bouliane, and D. Linda Pearse. "Challenging Embedded Coloniality in Music History Curricula." In *DIALOGUES: Towards Decolonizing Music and Dance Studies*, edited by Tan Sooi Beng and Marcia Ostashewski. University of South California, SCALAR Open Access Platform, 2022. https://scalar.me/anvc/.

White, Carmel Parker. "Student Portfolios: An Alternative Way of Encouraging and Evaluating Student Learning." *New Directions for Teaching and Learning* 100 (Winter 2004): 37–42.

Wilbourne, Emily, and Suzanne G. Cusick, eds. *Acoustemologies in Contact: Sounding Subjects and Modes of Listening in Early Modernity*. Cambridge: Open Book Publishers, 2021.

Zanovello, Giovanni, and Erika Honisch. "Inclusive Early Music." 2020. Accessed June 17, 2023. https://www.inclusiveearlymusic.org

Zecher, Carla. "The Çengî: Descriptions of Professional Female Performers in French and Italian Accounts of Travel to the Middle East, 1550–1650." *L'Esprit Créateur* 60, no. 1 (2020): 148–58. https://doi.org/10.1353/esp.2020.0015.

Zink, Michel. *Les troubadours. Une histoire poétique*. Paris: Éditions Perrin, 2017.

2 From Beijing to Paris
Teaching Music of the Global Eighteenth Century

Qingfan Jiang

Introduction

Drawing on the course I recently taught at the Yale Department of Music, "From Beijing to Paris: Music in the Global Eighteenth Century," this chapter aims to show a new approach to integrating global music history into music history courses for undergraduate students. Although the definition of global music history may vary, its rise stems in large part from a reflection on the problematic colonial roots of higher education in the West. Scholars have shown that not only are the foundations of Western universities deeply colonial, but the university curriculum, particularly the music history curriculum, tends to be entrenched in Eurocentrism.[1] In order to combat this Eurocentrism, an increasing number of music pedagogues have begun to reform the undergraduate music history curriculum, reexamining in particular the canon of Western art music, which had been the bedrock of many university music courses. Some take a thematic approach instead of a chronological approach to teaching Western art music, challenging the teleological narrative of progress exemplified by "masterpieces" and "geniuses."[2] Others analyze the canon through a critical lens based on recent studies on race, gender, and sexuality. Still others try to expand the canon to include pieces composed by marginalized musicians.[3] While these methods shed new light on the curriculum, they still place Western art music at the center, implicitly affirming the superior status of music in the European classical tradition. An alternative approach, I propose, is to remove the center-periphery structure that privileges Western art music by situating music in a global context. As Margaret E. Walker claims: "The first step, therefore, must be to contextualize Western art music's history and historiography firmly within a larger framework of critically and globally situated histories of music."[4]

To successfully incorporate global perspectives into the music history curriculum, the instructor needs to address two issues: the role of non-Western music (often termed "world music") within the curriculum and the selection of repertoire. Courses that focus on world music topics help to destabilize the centeredness of Western art music. While these are important to the music curriculum, and can contribute greatly to the decolonization project, some ethnomusicologists who teach world music courses find the current approaches inadequate. Michael A. Figueroa, for example, observes that the inclusion of "Introduction to World Music" in the curriculum "has historically been a blatant act of tokenism."[5] In addition, the separation of world music from Western art music is predicated on the questionable binary between the West and the Rest, a remnant of European exceptionalism developed in the eighteenth and nineteenth centuries.[6] Built on the foundation of world music, global music history seeks to truly recognize the value of music of the non-West in order to address the issue of tokenism. Moreover, it treats Western art music as one expression among many equally respected musical cultures around the globe through juxtaposing music of the European classical tradition with music of other cultures. In practice, no music history course can address every recorded musical culture across the globe. "From Beijing to Paris" thus focuses on two cosmopolitan cities, Beijing and Paris, which serve as two case studies concerning the global transmission of musical knowledge between China and France in the eighteenth century. Analyzing Chinese and French music side by side enables students to make cross-cultural comparisons and, more importantly, it allows them to see how musicians and music scholars in the past interacted across national and cultural boundaries and how their interactions laid the foundation for global artistic exchange that has continued to this day.

The second issue is the selection of repertoire. Music history textbooks have long been expanding the canon of Western art music to include pieces composed by female musicians, people of color, and members of other previously marginalized groups, as well as pieces representing popular music, film music, and other genres.[7] Although such expansion is an encouraging step forward, authors and instructors may find it increasingly difficult to make their textbooks and courses comprehensive. In teaching global music history, trying to cover everything, if even possible, is less helpful than selecting a variety of examples with which the students can develop appropriate skills that they can later apply to music they have not encountered in class. Given the objectives of global music history outlined in the paragraph above, this selection does not need to exclude canonic pieces of Western art music. At the same time, it does need to include additional musical repertoire and historical sources that reflect new developments in the emerging field of global music history. I follow three guidelines in selecting the materials for "From Beijing to Paris": I give equal importance to music practiced in China and music practiced in France; I include a significant amount of primary sources, many of which are newly discovered or have not been used in music history courses; and I introduce texts written by non-musicians to better contextualize music in societies. The musical examples used in "From

Beijing to Pairs" include Chinese court music used in rituals, *qin* music cultivated by the literati, vernacular operas performed at the playhouses in Beijing, secular and sacred music composed by European missionaries in China, selections of Lully's ballets, and operas by Rousseau and Rameau. In order to fully contextualize the musical examples, I assign readings, most of which are primary and archival sources. In teaching global music history, it is particularly difficult to incorporate primary sources because no English-language publication comparable to William Oliver Strunk's *Source Readings in Music History* has been made available on Chinese music. To partly address this difficulty, I translated some of the primary sources originally written in French or Chinese and also borrowed translations done by other scholars. These translations of primary materials allow the historical figures to speak for themselves without too many layers of modern interpretation. By examining the historical sources directly, students are better positioned to investigate the core issues of music history from different, often contrasting, cultural perspectives. Moreover, I include texts authored by non-musicians. Treating music not as an isolated discipline but as one that is deeply linked to other branches of knowledge and is constantly in dialogue with social changes, I draw on the writings of theorists, philosophers, missionaries, travelers, and court officials who exerted an impact on the local and global musical culture no less important than that of the musicians themselves. Such contextualization further helps students to appreciate and understand music that may not be familiar to them.

In what follows, I offer two sample classes: one is text-focused, examining the Kangxi Emperor's study of Western music from both Chinese and European perspectives; the other is music-focused, comparing three musical examples, including Kun opera, Rameau's *tragédie en musique*, and Catholic liturgical music in Beijing. Both classes serve to introduce students to a kind of music they probably have not encountered, shed a new light on Western canonical music they are familiar with, and explore music as a key agent in the global dialogue between the East and the West. In an effort to show how I lead the class as clearly as possible, I include detailed, sometimes perhaps redundant, teaching plans and goals, as well as the questions I raise for discussion and my students' responses. This lecture-seminar class, which runs one hour and fifty minutes each session, is designed for a group of fifteen undergraduate students, most of whom have musical backgrounds.[8] Instructors may freely adapt the teaching materials to meet their particular needs.

Class One: The Chinese Emperor and Western Music

The first sample class aims to reveal the musical and scientific exchange between China and Europe in the late seventeenth and early eighteenth centuries. Instead of framing the global transmission of musical and scientific knowledge as an "introduction" of a superior form of Western culture to the native people of China, this class affords students an opportunity to explore this transmission from three different perspectives: the Chinese imperial court, Portuguese and French missionaries, and European scholars. Through analyzing these different perspectives, this class investigates a set of broader questions concerning the possibilities and limits of cultural comparison in the early modern period and considers how this historical example can enlighten our discussion of the relationship between music and global history today.

Focusing on the figure of Emperor Kangxi (1654–1722, reigned 1661–1722) and his study of Western music, astronomy, and mathematics, which resulted in the compilation of the imperial compendium *Yuzhi lüli yuanyuan* [Origins of Mathematical Harmonies and Calendrical Astronomy, Imperially Composed] (1723), this class uses four primary source readings to explore the reasons behind Kangxi's interest in Western science and its historical consequences in China, as well as in Europe.[9] Before analyzing the readings, I first give students an overview of how Western music made its way into the Chinese imperial court. This overview concentrates on the life journeys of two individuals: Thomas Pereira (1646–1708) and Kangxi. Pereira, a Portuguese Jesuit missionary, arrived in Beijing in 1673 and served the imperial court as a royal astronomer and Kangxi's music tutor. For Kangxi's music lessons, Pereira wrote the treatise *Lülü Zuanyao* [Elements of Music] (ca. 1685), which, along with other treatises on geometry and astronomy authored by the missionaries, was incorporated into the imperial compendium. For the part on Kangxi, I highlight three time periods in his life marked by intense engagement with Western science: 1665–1669, when Kangxi first became interested in Western astronomy; 1690–1695, when he undertook the serious study of Western science in response to the arrival of the French missionaries, including Joachim Bouvet (1656–1730), in China in 1687; and 1713, when Kangxi established the Studio for the Cultivation of Youth Talent, an "academy of science" in charge of drafting and compiling the imperial compendium.

After the overview, my students and I delve into discussion of the four readings. The first two readings—one authored by Kangxi himself and the other by his son, Emperor Yongzheng (1678–1735, reigned 1722–1735)—explain the Chinese court's effort to incorporate Western science. The third reading, a publication by the French missionary Joachim Bouvet, details the lessons Kangxi took with the missionaries. The fourth reading, the preface to *Novissima Sinica* (1697/1699) by Gottfried Wilhelm Leibniz (1646–1716), compares Chinese and European civilizations and advocates for cultural exchange. Students have read all four as an assignment prior to the class. During the class session, we analyze the four readings in this sequence, with key passages highlighted for discussion. The texts quoted below are the selected key passages.

The first reading is a one-paragraph passage from *Shengzu renhuangdi tingxun geyan* [Maxims from My Forebears] (1730), a collection of informal lessons Kangxi gave for the instruction of his sons. In this passage, Kangxi explained why he wanted to study Western science, especially mathematics and astronomy. Like the Western quadrivium that grouped music with arithmetic, geometry, and astronomy, the Chinese scientific tradition combined music, astronomy, and mathematics. Moreover, music was often regarded as the source of the latter two disciplines, and many treatises on mathematics or astronomy included discussions of music. The imperial compendium, not surprisingly, divided the chapters into three sections devoted to these three branches of science. Because of the inseparable link between the three, when Kangxi commented on mathematics and astronomy, it should be understood that his comments applied to music as well.

The Emperor's interest in Western science stemmed from a competition between the Han Chinese officials and the Western missionaries who served at the Directorate of Astronomy in 1668. The test given to both parties was to calculate where the shadow of a gnomon would fall at noon. While the Han Chinese astronomers failed to make the calculation, the missionaries led by Ferdinand Verbiest (1623–1688) accurately predicted the place of the gnomon's shadow. This test not only proved that Western astronomy was more advanced than Chinese astronomy, but it also led to the appointment of Verbiest as the *de facto* director of the Directorate of Astronomy, a position kept by the missionaries into the nineteenth century. Kangxi was fourteen years old when this competition took place. What impressed the young emperor the most was not the missionaries' triumph but the ignorance of the court officials about astronomical matters. As Kangxi later reflected:

> How unfortunate it was that none of the ministers knew anything about calendar computation. I thought, if I knew nothing about the subject how could I judge for myself who was right and who was wrong? That was why I decided to study for myself. I have now compiled into a book the methods for these calculations, and added clear analysis to make it easier for others to study the subject in future.[10]

Focusing on these words of Kangxi, my students and I explore how Kangxi's study of Western science was tied to his imperial rulership. From this discussion, we learn that, personally, Kangxi wanted to master the scientific method brought by the missionaries to satisfy his intellectual ambition, and politically, he used the knowledge of Western science to present himself as a competent judge of the disputes that arose among his multiethnic and multicultural subjects. Moreover, we talk about how Kangxi based the imperial compendium largely on Western science for the purpose of educating the Chinese people, further strengthening his image as a wise and benevolent emperor.

The imperial compendium was finished in 1723, a year after Kangxi's death. Upon its completion, Emperor Yongzheng, Kangxi's son and his successor, authored a preface to this compendium. This is our second reading. By writing the preface to the compendium, Yongzheng demonstrated both his filial piety toward his late father and his attitude toward Western science. In reading the preface, I select two key passages in order for the students to discuss three interrelated questions: How did Yongzheng explain Kangxi's motive to study Western science? How did Yongzheng characterize the Jesuit mission in China? What is the relationship between Chinese and Western science according to Yongzheng? For the first question, we look at the following passage in the preface:

> Records show that in antiquity King Yao [reigned, according to tradition, 2357–2255 BCE] consulted his astronomers Xi and He; King Shun [reigned, according to tradition, 2255–2205 BCE] commissioned Kui as Minister of Music; and the Duke of Zhou [d. 1105 BCE] visited the mathematician Shang Gao. The dynastic histories each contain sections on music, astronomy, number and measure. That knowledge, to be spread to towns, cities and villages all over the land, can be used to maintain the mandate of heaven, to instruct people, to please the spirits and to promote harmony in society. Such is the importance of setting standards. For several decades, my late father the Sagely Progenitor and Humane Emperor, on whom heaven had bestowed a great intelligence, a love of learning and multiple talents, found time from his numerous official commitments to apply himself to the study of music, astronomy and mathematics.[11]

Building on Kangxi's self-representation as a wise and benevolent emperor, Yongzheng pictured his late father as a sage-king who, like the sage-kings in antiquity, studied music, astronomy, and mathematics for the benefit of the people. While Kangxi framed his study of science in the context of dealing with contemporary issues, Yongzheng situated Kangxi's study in a larger historical narrative, aiming to highlight China's own scientific tradition while downplaying the significance of the missionaries' contributions.

The second passage allows us to investigate the remaining two questions about Yongzheng's view of the Jesuit mission and the relationship between Chinese and Western learning:

> With its perfect order and harmony, our nation has acquired such great power and prestige that European countries in the Far West have paid tribute by presenting their knowledge of technology,

carefully cultivated over generations and contained in impressive treatises and tables. My late father took all the works into consideration and settled their final shape in such a way that what is lost from our ancient knowledge through the passage of time or through poor selection is restored, that what is clumsy and obscure in the Western works is rectified, and that the completed compilation is clear and coherent...This [imperial compendium] is not only a gift from the late emperor but also a culmination and a completion that surpasses previous ages and reveals the eternal laws for future ages. Anyone wishing to create an accurate calendar and standardize weights and measures will find in this work a source of universal truth and sagely knowledge.[12]

Yongzheng assumed that what drove the missionaries to China was their respect for the "great power and prestige" of the empire. In other words, the Jesuits' establishment of their mission in China was an act of admiration and not an act of conquest in terms of religious conversion. Although Yongzheng likely knew the religious motives of the missionaries, in this preface, a document to be circulated throughout the empire, he chose to bypass the religious basis of the Jesuit mission altogether in favor of an age-old narrative predicated on China's civilizing influence on foreign nations. Indeed, Yongzheng described the missionaries' teaching of Western science and technology as the presentation of tribute gift. The word "tribute" referred to the tributary system China had practiced with its neighboring countries. In this system, tributary nations like Korea and Vietnam sent ambassadors to China who presented gifts to the emperor in exchange for diplomatic peace and military protection. In the eyes of Yongzheng, these "European countries in the Far West" were no different from nations like Korea and Vietnam, and—like them—should submit to the superior culture of China. For the third question, my students and I focus on this phrase in the passage: "in such a way that what is lost from our ancient knowledge … is restored, that what is clumsy and obscure in the Western works is rectified." Speaking of the significance of the imperial compendium, Yongzheng summarized its double objective to both restore China's ancient knowledge and rectify the errors in Western knowledge. Importantly, Yongzheng saw Western science through a critical lens: he did not accept it wholeheartedly, nor did he reject it completely; rather, he strategically selected what was useful and discarded what was not. Finally, we discuss the meaning of "universal truth" in the last sentence of the passage. Yongzheng argued that the compendium would benefit not only Chinese people but humanity in general. Imperial ambition aside, this "universal truth" revealed Yongzheng's belief in the compatibility of Chinese and Western science and a certain openness toward foreign knowledge.

For the third reading, we turn from the emperors to the missionaries by examining the monograph *Portrait historique de l'empereur de Chine presenté au roy* (1697), authored by the French Jesuit missionary Joachim Bouvet, who instructed Kangxi on Euclidean geometry, and widely known by its contemporary English title, *The History of Cang-Hy*. This monograph is important to understanding the scientific dialogue between Beijing and Paris: Bouvet was one of the five French Jesuit missionaries dispatched to China by Louis XIV (1638–1715, reigned 1643–1715). These missionaries, referred to as the "King's mathematicians," were also trained scientists. Although, like the two previous readings, the *History of Cang-Hy* focuses on Kangxi's study of Western science, it was written not from the emperors' perspective but from the missionaries' perspective and intended not for people in China but for readers in Europe.

In order to understand these differences, with a focus on Bouvet's unique characterization of Kangxi and his interest in Western science, my students and I look at the following passages:

> During the space of two years, Father Verbiest instructed [Kangxi] in the usefulness of the best of the mathematical instruments...It was also about the same time, that he took first to our music, under the tuition of Father Pereira, who not only composed an entire treatise of music, but also caused several European instruments to be made for the Emperor's use; upon some of which, he taught him to play some tunes.[13]
>
> Such was [Kangxi's] eager desire to attain to the perfect knowledge of these things, that nothing was able to prevent or hinder his resolution...and if it happened sometimes that we had not the good fortune to give him a clear idea of the matter at that time, he would not grudge to defer the further explication of it, to another time, a convincing instance of his most admirable patience and attention.[14]

Bouvet painted two images here: one of the missionaries themselves and one of Kangxi. By stating how Verbiest and Pereira "instructed" Kangxi in mathematics and music, Bouvet unmistakably identified the missionaries as teachers. By contrast, he characterized Kangxi as a student: while he praised the Emperor's "eager desire" and "most admirable patience and attention," these qualities showed Kangxi as a good student and not as a powerful and wise emperor capable of correcting the errors in Western science. Indeed, juxtaposing Kangxi's and Yongzheng's accounts and Bouvet's description, we see a reversal of the hierarchy within which the Chinese court and the European missionaries were situated: whereas according to Kangxi and Yongzheng, Western scientific knowledge was a tribute presented to the all-powerful Chinese emperor, according to

Bouvet, it was sophisticated learning imparted by the missionaries to the ignorant Chinese. In short, what had been interpreted as a master-servant relationship became, under Bouvet's pen, a disciple-teacher relationship.

Bouvet's book and other missionary publications regarding China had a huge impact on how Europeans conceived of the oriental world. Thanks to the missionaries' propaganda, it was no surprise that China, and later India, held the most fascination for European scholars such as the philosopher and mathematician Gottfried Wilhelm Leibniz. In fact, Leibniz was a friend of Bouvet's and had been corresponding with the missionary for over ten years. The fourth reading my students and I analyze is thus an excerpt from the preface to Leibniz's *Novissima Sinica* [The Latest News from China] (1697/1699), in which he compared China and Europe.

We first look at the passage that traces how the Jesuit missionaries influenced Leibniz's view of Kangxi's study of Western science:

> I remember the Reverend Father [Claudio Filippo] Grimaldi, an eminent man of the same Society [of Jesus], telling me in Rome how much he admired the virtue and wisdom of this prince [Kangxi]. Indeed (passing by, if I may, the comment on his love of justice, his charity to the populace, his moderate manner of living, and his other merits), Grimaldi asserted that the monarch's marvelous desire for knowledge almost amounted to a faith. For that ruler, whom eminent princes and the greatest men of the empire venerate from afar and revere when near, used to work with Verbiest in an inner suite for three or four hours daily with mathematical instruments and books as a pupil with his teacher.[15]

Like many other scholars in Europe, Leibniz relied almost exclusively on Jesuit reports to make his judgment about Kangxi and China as a whole. Here, he learned from Claudio Filippo Grimaldi (1639–1712), a colleague of Verbiest and Pereira, about this emperor and his interest in Western science. Like Bouvet, Leibniz praised the exceptional diligence of Kangxi, which was not expected from an emperor who oversaw a vast empire like China. Besides diligence, Leibniz enumerated Kangxi's other merits such as his love of justice, benevolence, and modest living style. Following Bouvet, Leibniz also characterized Kangxi as a pupil and Verbiest, a Jesuit missionary, as his teacher, acknowledging the value of Western science and affirming the hierarchical relationship between the Emperor and the missionaries.

Leibniz, however, offered a more nuanced analysis of the historical significance of Kangxi's incorporation of Western knowledge into the Chinese system. In the following passage, we explore the differences between Bouvet's and Leibniz's accounts:

> [Kangxi] seems to me to have had individually much more foresight than all his officials, and I take the reason for his superior judgement to be that he combines European [culture] with Chinese…So, while understanding the learning of his own people to begin with, and moreover, not being a bad judge when he first received a taste of European knowledge from Father Ferdinand Verbiest of Bruges in Belgium, of the Society of Jesus, a pupil of Johann Adam Schall of Cologne—which perhaps no one in his empire had previously received—his foresight and his grasp of affairs can only elevate him above all other Chinese and Tartars, exactly as if on a pyramid of Egypt a European steeple should be placed.[16]

Unlike Bouvet and other missionary-tutors at the imperial court who placed Western science far above Chinese science, Leibniz did not consider Chinese learning inferior or irrelevant to the pursuit of human knowledge. Rather, he boldly advocated for the necessity of learning from both cultures. Using the metaphor of a European steeple built on the top of an Egyptian pyramid, Leibniz made it clear that the greatest merit of Kangxi consisted of his openness to and embrace of the knowledge taught by both the Chinese masters and the European missionaries. Through recognizing Kangxi's merit, Leibniz ultimately tried to persuade his European readers to actively search for new knowledge coming from the East. It was no coincidence that Leibniz, through his correspondence with Bouvet, learned about hexagrams—figures used in divination practices as recorded in the Chinese classic *Yijing* [The Book of Change]—and made connections between the hexagrams and the mathematical concept of calculus.[17]

After analyzing the four readings individually, I raise a couple of broader questions that consider the readings as a whole:

1. What role did music play in this global exchange of scientific knowledge?
2. If you were Emperor Kangxi, would you study Western science?
3. Did the four authors embrace a global perspective? What constitutes a "global" perspective?

The three questions invite students to explore global music history at a deeper level. The first question allows students to see music not as an isolated discipline but as a branch of science closely linked with mathematics and astronomy in both Chinese and European contexts. For this reason, it is necessary to situate the transmission of music knowledge in the broader scientific dialogue between China and Europe. The second question flips the Eurocentric narrative by encouraging students to look at this dialogue from a Chinese perspective. Investigating the motives behind Kangxi's study of

Western science challenges the Eurocentric assumption that Western science and technology are inherently superior and should be emulated by people in other parts of the world. It also grants agency to non-European peoples, allowing the Chinese to voice their opinions. The third question affords students an examination of "globalism" through a critical lens. Although all four authors exhibited a certain degree of openness toward foreign knowledge, most of them arranged a hierarchical order that placed their own cultural traditions at the top. Moreover, the so-called "global" perspective they adopted was quite limited: it neither looked at the Self and the Other on equal terms nor did it fully recognize the diversity and complexity of the world's cultures. Leibniz, for example, proposed a Sinocentrism in addition to Eurocentrism, bypassing the Islamic world and India, which lie between the extremes of Eurasia. Even for us living in the twenty-first century, our "global" perspective is often filtered through personal experiences, cultural biases, and media exposure. Considering historical examples of global interaction enables students to critically engage with global musical encounters and awakens in them a sense of global citizenship.

Class Two: Operas in Beijing and Paris

The second class focuses on three musical examples that exemplify the diverse operatic styles prevalent in eighteenth-century Beijing and Paris. The first example is an excerpt from *Peony Pavilion*, arguably the most influential Kun opera in China in the seventeenth and eighteenth centuries, enjoyed by elites and commoners alike. The second is the conclusion of Act 4 of the celebrated *Hippolyte et Aricie* by Jean-Philippe Rameau (1683–1764), a canonical work of Western art music that has been included in anthologies of Western music history. The third example is drawn from Catholic liturgical music used in Beijing that was heavily influenced by both Kun opera and seventeenth- and eighteenth-century European music. This liturgical music, notated by the French missionary Jean-Joseph-Marie Amiot (1718–1793), demonstrates the fusion of Chinese and Western music and is key to our understanding of musical integration across national and cultural boundaries. By analyzing and comparing these examples, students will learn to articulate the differences and similarities between Chinese and European operas, describe canonical works of Western art music from a multi-cultural perspective, and explain the potentials and limitations of cross-cultural exchange.

The class is divided into three sections aligning with the three different musical examples. In each section, I first give a brief introduction to the historical context of the musical example. Students and I then listen to the musical example and analyze its key features. Next, we read together short textual passages related to the musical example and discuss a set of broader questions.

Before delving into *Peony Pavilion*, I introduce my students to the history of Kun opera and the different venues in eighteenth-century Beijing at which people watched performances of Kun and other regional genres of opera. Originating in the sixteenth century, Kun opera developed in the literati circle and gained enormous popularity in the subsequent two centuries, becoming a nationally celebrated dramatic genre. The playhouses, commonly known as "tea gardens," were indoor commercial theaters that frequently staged Kun opera performances. Situated along the south border of Beijing's Inner City, the playhouses attracted audiences from both the Manchus, who mostly resided in the Inner City, and the Han population of the Outer City. Although the imperial court forbade high officials, especially those who were Manchus, to attend performances at the playhouses, many of them sneaked into the playhouses regularly, testifying to the popularity of Kun opera. Besides the educated elites, wealthy merchants and the urban poor also frequented the playhouses, though each had a different type of seat in accordance with their social rank. As a rule, women were barred from entering the playhouses.[18] This background information helps students to understand the social foundations that gave rise to Kun opera. Indeed, some essential characteristics of Kun opera, such as boys assuming female roles on stage, were inextricably linked to the social restraints imposed on women in general.

We then turn to *Peony Pavilion* (1598), which recounts the love between Du Liniang, daughter of an official in the Southern Song dynasty (1127–1279), and Liu Mengmei, a young scholar. Like many elite women, Du was not allowed to step out of her chamber without her parents' permission. One day in spring, however, Du secretly went to the garden and was enchanted by the beautiful scenery. As she fell asleep in the garden, Du dreamt of a young scholar by the Peony Pavilion and fell in love with him. Shortly after her visit to the garden, Du died broken-hearted because she was not able to find her beloved in real life. Three years later, the young scholar Liu Mengmei visited the temple where Du was buried. Wandering in the garden, Liu came across Du's portrait and began calling Du's name. In a magical moment, Du came out of the picture as a ghost and the couple reunited. The next day, Liu opened Du's coffin. Having won the sympathy of the Lord of the Underworld, Du was reincarnated, and the couple lived happily ever after. During the class, we watch an excerpt from *Peony Pavilion* that shows the couple's first encounter in Du's dream (YouTube link: https://youtu.be/pV3AclcOcSs). This excerpt has two parts: Du's soliloquy, in which she laments the passing of spring and reveals her hidden desires, and the dialogue between Du and Liu that sparks passion in their hearts. Because for most of my students, it is their first time to watch Kun opera, we examine both the musical and extra-musical components of the excerpt in great detail.

I first ask my students if they have noticed anything in the music that is different from the Western operas they have listened to. The most apparent difference is the voice of the male singer who plays the role of Liu Mengmei. His voice is in the same register as female singers, and some students compare his voice to that of European countertenors. Besides register, Kun opera singers use a vocal technique that projects a brighter tone in contrast to the deeper and rounder tone employed in Western opera. The melodies of Kun opera tend to be melismatic, which is why even a short sentence is often stretched over a long period of time. They also have few motivic repetitions and unequal phrase lengths. Despite the complexity, most of the melodies are not composed anew but drawn from a pre-existing collection of tune types, to which the author of the opera adds new lyrics. Some students also note the different performing style: the flute, which doubles the singer's melody, is slightly out of sync with the voice on the first note. This is because Kun opera singers often emphasize the initial consonant of a word, and the flute player helps them by playing a trill-like figure on the first note just before the entrance of the voice. In addition to melody, we also talk about harmony and meter in Kun opera. Harmony as a deliberate organization of vertical sonorities is absent in Kun opera, and although most of the music is in duple meter, there is less of a distinction between strong and weak beats. Last, we discuss the role of the orchestra. Composed of a flute that doubles the voice, plucked-string instruments that provide the accompaniment, and a percussion section (gongs, cymbals, and wooden clappers), the orchestra serves to support the voice, introduce new characters onto the stage, and underscore dramatic actions.

In terms of extra-musical elements, we focus on costumes, staging, and bodily movement. Kun opera singers often use elaborate costumes and stylized facial make-up to communicate the different social statuses of the roles—a lady as opposed to a maid, for example—and the different types of characters, such as Wusheng, a martial male role-type, and Wensheng, a male role-type used for scholars and bureaucrats. In contrast to eighteenth-century European opera, Kun opera has simple staging with few props, which draws the attention of the audience to the singers themselves. Another difference is the incorporation of dance in Kun opera. Singers' movements are strictly choreographed to reflect their inner thoughts and emotions, as demonstrated by the excerpt from *Peony Pavilion*, in which much of the two singers' interaction is conveyed through their graceful movements and subtle eye contact. On the whole, the example of *Peony Pavilion* not only introduces students to a new style of opera but also acquaints them with a different kind of musical aesthetic that privileges subtlety, elegance, and the slow unfolding of musical events. Most importantly (at least where my own students are concerned), it enables them to see Western canonical operas, particularly Rameau's *Hippolyte et Aricie*, which we will analyze below, in a new light.

I select Rameau's *Hippolyte et Aricie* as an example of French opera in eighteenth-century Paris. Because many of my students have studied this piece in their survey classes, I briefly remind them of Rameau's contributions as an opera composer: recognized as one of the most important French composers after Lully, Rameau continued the tradition of *tragédie en musique*, in particular its five-act structure, the use of characters from Greek mythology, and the inclusion of dances and choruses. Rameau, however, differed greatly from Lully in his employment of colorful orchestration that vividly depicts natural phenomena such as earthquakes and thunderstorms. My students and I then watch the conclusion of Act 4 (YouTube link: https://youtu.be/FIoE8Yr-a1E), which centers on the main hero Hippolytus's battle with a sea monster and his stepmother Phaedra's illicit love and guilt for Hippolytus's death. I ask my students to imagine themselves as Chinese living in eighteenth-century Beijing who, upon their visit to Paris, watch Rameau's opera for the first time Which aspects of the opera would appeal to you and which would not? The first thing they notice is that the orchestra plays a much more significant role than in Kun opera. At the beginning of the excerpt, the strings and flute depict the scene's roaring wind and tumultuous sea through rapid scales. Unlike the flute in Kun opera, which doubles the melody, the orchestra here serves not to strengthen the voice but to set the stage. When the singers enter, they use a kind of vocal production that aims to project dramatic tension rather than to display refined elegance, as in Kun opera. This dramatic tension is closely linked to the use of dissonant harmonies, especially in Phaedra's lament. Compared to the music of Kun opera, which is largely based on the pentatonic scale, the saturation of diminished fifths and sevenths in Rameau's opera would sound rather complicated and disorienting to Chinese audiences. Another component that sets this French opera apart is its use of a chorus. Although Kun opera also includes choruses, they are not prominently featured, nor do they employ a rich harmonic language. With regard to extra-musical elements, the stage of Rameau's opera is decorated more elaborately, with a considerable number of props and background scenery that depicts Hippolytus's engagement with the sea monster in a fairly realistic manner. In addition, singers mostly rely on their voices to convey their emotions; while they also use hand gestures, no dance steps are as carefully choreographed as in Kun opera. Overall, students find Rameau's opera to be very different from *Peony Pavilion*: the one depicts a dramatic sequence of events, the other patiently tells a love story through subtle movements and soft, elegant voices.

After analyzing *Peony Pavilion* and *Hippolyte et Aricie*, my students and I read together a passage that shows how Chinese in the eighteenth century reacted to hearing European music, as observed by a French missionary in China:

> I only saw in their faces a cold and inattentive air, which made me believe that nothing I had played moved them. One day, I asked them how they found our music and begged them to tell me what they thought frankly. They answered me in the most polite way possible that "our songs are not made for their ears, nor their songs for our ears. It is not surprising that they do not feel the beauties [of our songs] as they do those of their nation..."[19]

The observer, Jean-Joseph-Marie Amiot, was also a musician. Shortly after he arrived in China, he played for a group of Chinese elites some of Rameau's harpsichord compositions as well as Michel Blavet's (1700–1768) flute pieces. The quote above describes how these Chinese elites responded to Amiot's performance. In an effort to maintain politeness, the Chinese expressed their indifference toward European music. My students and I talk about the reasons behind this indifference. To be sure, there is undeniably a vast distance between Chinese music and French music, as reflected in the two operas. In fact, one student even questioned the categorization of Kun opera as opera, given how little in *Peony Pavilion* could be readily recognized as opera in the Western art music context. Indeed, cultural barriers often frustrate efforts to appreciate and understand foreign music. Both the Chinese in the eighteenth century and my students in the twenty-first century find it difficult to fully recognize the aesthetic and artistic values of unfamiliar music. Despite rapid globalization, appreciating music from a global perspective is no easy endeavor and may not even be possible. Yet instead of staying in our comfort zone, perhaps we should strive to acknowledge the limitations of our own perspective and try to engage with unfamiliar music on its own terms as closely as possible.

In order to delve deeper into the issue of intercultural understanding/misunderstanding, we read two passages from Rameau's two music theory treatises, in which he talked about Chinese music theory and how it related to one of his own theoretical discoveries. I ask my students to read them with two questions in mind: what kind of assumptions did Rameau make about Chinese music and extra-European music in general? What is the purpose of Rameau's study of Chinese music?

> The Chinese, like Pythagoras, derive their [musical] systems from the triple progression [progression of 5ths]. They only have five notes in their Lu, which apparently means system, scale, or mode. One Chinese musician gives the five notes in this sequence: G, A, B, C#, D#, E#, one of the most defective scales that one can imagine. But another author gives this scale, which corresponds to our scale except

for two missing notes: G#, A#, C#, D#, E#. This scale can be transposed to G, A, C, D, E. Mr. Dupleix gave me a "barbarous organ" from the Cape of Good Hope as a gift, on which all Chinese melodies copied in Father du Halde's book could be played. This proves that the second scale had been practiced in China for a long time…[20]

I must add to the aforementioned facts that the Chinese propose the progression of 5ths, called the triple [progression], until its thirteenth term, which they follow in their system of music still more regularly than Pythagoras did, and the Chinese lived even before the establishment of the Egyptians. Here is the 5th much celebrated everywhere, even before any question of geometry was raised. We will also see that this 5th constitutes harmony and its most natural progression, from which follows the melody.[21]

Rameau learned about Chinese music theory from Amiot, who sent a treatise on Chinese music to Paris, the manuscript of which was then circulated among a group of music scholars. What Rameau stated above is in fact not entirely accurate, though we do not know if Rameau or Amiot made the mistake because the original manuscript has yet to be found. In any case, Rameau concluded that the Chinese had two kinds of scales. One, to use modern terminology, was the whole-tone scale, and the other was the pentatonic scale. In order to test whether the Chinese used the pentatonic scale, Rameau played Chinese folk melodies on an instrument imported from the Cape of Good Hope. Here, Rameau made two assumptions. He assumed that Chinese music, like European music, used a pitch-oriented musical system and that scale, rather than rhythm, timbre, etc., was at the core of Chinese music theory. Additionally, he assumed that musical cultures of the non-West were more or less the same, and thus it was justifiable to play Chinese folk melodies not on a Chinese instrument but on one that had originated in southern Africa. The second paragraph tells us why Rameau studied Chinese music. One major claim Rameau made as a music theorist was that harmony, based on the progression of 5ths, preceded melody. In an effort to prove that the progression of 5ths had a long history, Rameau turned to Chinese music and used its pentatonic scale, which was derived from the progression of 5ths, as evidence. Rameau studied Chinese music not for its own sake, but to corroborate his own theory of harmony. Given the limited information about Chinese music in eighteenth-century Paris, Rameau might not have realized how he made biased assumptions about it for self-serving purposes. Yet his example allows us today to become more aware of and avoid similar pitfalls in cross-cultural studies. Finally, I ask my students to compare Rameau as a composer and as a theorist. While there is very little trace of Chinese elements in Rameau's compositions, he linked Chinese music theory to one of his most important theoretical concepts. In other words, while in practice Rameau acknowledged diverse musical cultures and favored his own above others, in theory he believed in a universally valid system that underpinned French and Chinese music alike. This discrepancy shows the gap between theory and practice in the West's appropriation of music of the East. It remains interesting to explore how European composers and theorists coped with the polarity of universality and diversity in their compositions and theoretical output.

To conclude the class, I invite my students to listen to a third musical example: the Lord's Prayer sung at Catholic churches in eighteenth-century Beijing (YouTube link: https://youtu.be/5Eo9XYDDmH0). This piece was included in the collection of Catholic liturgical music compiled by Amiot titled "musique sacrée." The texts of the liturgical music, some in Chinese and some in Latin, were drawn from the Daily Exercises (1601) prepared by an earlier generation of missionaries and Chinese converts. In 1779, Amiot sent the "musique sacrée" to Paris along with some Chinese folksongs to educate his French compatriots about the musical culture of China and the missionaries' contributions to it. Upon listening to the Lord's prayer, I ask my students to describe its musical style. Many of them are surprised to find that it resembles the excerpt from *Peony Pavilion*. Indeed, the Lord's Prayer, like Kun opera, uses a flute to double the voice and a wooden clapper to mark the beats. Moreover, the melody is melismatic and contains very little motivic repetition. There are, however, notable differences: unlike the Kun opera excerpt, the Lord's Prayer is sung by a group of singers, and in order to achieve some degree of unity between the voices, the beats are more strongly felt than those in *Peony Pavilion*. After analyzing the music, my students and I discuss the reasons why the missionaries in China would employ the style of Kun opera to compose music for the Catholic churches. Many of them point out that music here functioned as a bridge between Chinese and European Catholic cultures. Borrowing elements from Kun opera helped to attract potential Chinese converts who were familiar with this musical style. Indeed, at the peak of the Catholic mission in China around 1705, there were 200,000 Chinese converts, and music did play a role in the religious conversion.[22] I then show my students the notation of the Lord's Prayer, a unique experiment that combined Chinese and European systems (see Figure 2.1).

When Amiot sent his collection of sacred music to Paris, he notated the pieces using both Chinese gongche notation and European staff notation. In gongche notation, the characters, which indicate the different pitches, are laid vertically from right to left and top to bottom, just like the Chinese writing system. In Amiot's version, however, they are laid horizontally and from left to right, consistent with European writing convention. Moreover, Amiot carefully placed these characters adjacent to the staff notation to show the corresponding pitches in the European system. Thus, the first

Figure 2.1 Jean-Joseph-Marie Amiot, *Tainzhu jing*天主經 [The Lord's Prayer] in "Mélanges sur la Chine et les Chinois," Bibliothèque nationale de France, Paris (F-Pn). Reproduced from gallic.bnf.fr

character in the first measure, "Liu六," indicates that the word "Zai在" should be sung to the note *sol* (in a movable-do system), and the second character, "Wu五," indicates that the second beat of the word "Zai在" should be sung to the note *la*, while the word "Tian天" should be sung to "Liu六," the note *sol* again.

This Lord's Prayer, along with its notation, exemplifies an attempt to fuse Chinese and European music. We discuss the historical significance of this fusion to conclude the class. It is true that Amiot's notation experiment was never popularized. It did not prompt French musicians to study Chinese music and its gongche notation beyond a small circle of enthusiasts, nor did it alter musical education in China apart from a small group of church musicians. Despite his best intentions, Amiot often felt frustrated in his attempts to convey European ideas to the Chinese and vice versa. He expressed this frustration upon finishing his French translation of the *Art of War*: "How can I be sure, moreover, that after my exchange with the Tartar and the Chinese, and after my assiduous readings of works written in their languages, my own ideas have not absorbed something of the climate in which I have lived for so many years, and that my own language is not a type of impenetrable jargon for a Frenchman living in his own country?"[23] Amiot's frustration notwithstanding, a number of students remark that the Lord's Prayer, more than Orientalist operas they have listened to, such as Mozart's *Abduction from the Seraglio* and Puccini's *Madama Butterfly*, genuinely acknowledges Chinese and European musical traditions without degrading either. Indeed, while biased assumptions often plagued the Sino-Western musical dialogue, as shown by Rameau's writing on Chinese music, Amiot's case demonstrates that there were attempts to respect, understand, and translate a foreign musical language, and such attempts should not be overlooked in our study of global music history.

Conclusion

This chapter demonstrates a new way to teach global music history in the college classroom through two sample classes that foreground the musical dialogue between Beijing and Paris in the eighteenth century. The first class examines the Kangxi Emperor's interest in Western music and other sciences through four historical accounts, revealing the different and often conflicting cultural motives of the Chinese court, the Portuguese and French missionaries, and European scholars like Leibniz. The second class uses three musical examples drawn from the Chinese and French operatic repertoires to show the fruits and limitations of music appreciation across the cultural boundaries. Both classes employ a new pedagogical approach that aims to fulfill three objectives. First, it shows that music history courses do not need to strictly adhere to the divide between the West and the Rest. Instead, Western art music and Chinese music (in this case) can be jointly studied. In juxtaposing the two, students are encouraged to analyze Western music from a Chinese perspective and to challenge the assumed universality of Western aesthetic and artistic standards. Second, this approach highlights music that travels between places. The examples of Kangxi's study of Western music and Rameau's study of Chinese music show that music, like other commodities and ideas, can be transported to different places, and that while this transcultural journey often sparks clashes between civilizations, it also inspires assimilation and integration. How music travels and how it affects its new cultural context are precisely the key questions of global music history. Third, it uses historical examples of global music travel to shed light on the current discussion regarding globalization. Trying to understand cultures other than one's own and see the globe as a unified whole is not a new phenomenon. While we admire the musicians and other historical figures in the eighteenth century for their curiosity and courage to explore new music from other places, we should also critically examine their motives and biases. Such examination allows us to reflect on our own efforts to understand the role of music in the process of globalization and our own contributions to building a more diverse and welcoming society.

This approach can have a wider application beyond teaching music in eighteenth-century Beijing and Paris. Instructors may find the comparative model useful in designing a course that features the musical culture of multiple places. The course may focus on how the music of one place differs from that of another and/or how they have shaped each other. It may explore how local music practice has shifted over time as a result of adopting global influences. It may also analyze how the indigenous people resisted globalizing forces. Instances of both adoption and resistance are part of global music history. For courses that focus primarily on Western art music, instructors may employ a listening experiment that juxtaposes canonical pieces of the West with pieces from a non-Western culture. Such juxtaposition would sharpen students' listening skills and help them better articulate the different kinds of sounds. It would also expand their musical vocabulary and help them recognize the diversity of the world's musical cultures. Finally, instructors may focus on musical fusion that draws from multiple cultural sources. Amiot's collection of liturgical music that combines elements from Kun opera and European music is one example. Particularly for courses on contemporary music, examining the numerous examples of musical fusion would offer us insights into the very process of globalization and the creation and development of an increasingly global community of musicians and scholars.

Notes

1 Bhambra, *Decolonizing the University*, 6; Walker, "Decolonized Music History Curriculum," 1.
2 Gavin Douglas points out that concepts like "masterpieces" are not universal but rooted in particular historical and cultural contexts. Douglas, "Teaching Music History from an Ethnomusicological Perspective," 41.
3 Walker, "Decolonized Music History Curriculum," 3.
4 Walker, "Decolonized Music History Curriculum," 15.
5 Figueroa, "Decolonizing 'Intro to World Music?'."
6 One notable exception is the newly reformed music history sequence at Vanderbilt University's Blair School of Music, which includes the course "Music as Global Culture" that examines both European music and music of other places as part of a global culture. See Lowe, "Rethinking the Undergraduate Music History Sequence."
7 See Paul Gabriel Luongo's discussion of the various editions of *A History of Western Music* and the *Norton Anthology of Western Music*. Luongo, "Constructing a Canon." See also J. Peter Burkholder's response to Luongo's article. Burkholder, "Stewarding a Shared Resource."
8 For information on teaching students with varying musical backgrounds, see Epstein, "Inclusive Pedagogies for Diverse Classrooms."
9 The imperial compendium *Yuzhi lüli yuanyuan* [Origins of Mathematical Harmonies and Calendrical Astronomy, Imperially Composed] is a multivolume book on astronomy, mathematics, and music in both Chinese and Western traditions. It was drafted by Han Chinese and Manchu scholars using the treatises authored by Portuguese and French missionaries as their main source. Emperor Kangxi supervised the drafting process, and the compendium was published by the imperial printing house in 1723, a year after the death of Kangxi. This compendium served as the most important textbook to train young Han Chinese and Manchu mathematicians, astronomers, and musicians in the eighteenth century.
10 Cheung, *An Anthology of Chinese Discourse on Translation*, 134.
11 Cheung, *An Anthology of Chinese Discourse on Translation*, 137.
12 Cheung, *An Anthology of Chinese Discourse on Translation*, 138.
13 Bouvet, *The History of Cang-Hy, the Present Emperor of China Presented to the Most Christian King*, 51.
14 Bouvet, *The History of Cang-Hy, the Present Emperor of China Presented to the Most Christian King*, 54-55.

15 Leibniz, *Gottfried Wilhelm Leibniz: Writings on China*, 49.
16 Leibniz, *Gottfried Wilhelm Leibniz: Writings on China*, 49.
17 Swetz, "Leibniz, the Yijing, and the Religious Conversion of the Chinese."
18 Goldman, *Opera and the City*, chapter 2.
19 Amiot, *Mémoire sur la musique des Chinois tant anciens que modernes*, 2–3; my translation.
20 Rameau, *Code de musique pratique ou méthodes pour apprendre la musique*, 191–192; my translation.
21 Rameau, *Origine des sciences*, 2; my translation.
22 Hsia, *A Companion to Early Modern Catholic Global Missions*, 362
23 Parr, *The Mandate of Heaven*, 69.

References

Amiot, Jean-Joseph-Marie. *Mémoire sur la musique des Chinois tant anciens que modernes*. Paris: Nyon l'aîné, 1779.
Bhambra, Gurminder K., Dalia Gebrial, and Kerem Nişancıoğlu, eds. *Decolonizing the University*. London: Pluto Press, 2018.
Bouvet, Joachim. *The History of Cang-Hy, the Present Emperor of China Presented to the Most Christian King*. Translated by Jodocus Crull. London: F. Coggan, 1699.
Burkholder, J. Peter. "Stewarding a Shared Resource: A Response to Paul Luongo." *Journal of Music History Pedagogy* 12, no. 1 (2022): 37–45.
Cheung, Martha P. Y., ed. *An Anthology of Chinese Discourse on Translation*. Vol. 2. London: Routledge, 2017.
Douglas, Gavin. "Some Thoughts on Teaching Music History from an Ethnomusicological Perspective." In *Vitalizing Music History Teaching*, edited by James R. Briscoe, 27–43. Hillsdale: Pendragon Press, 2010.
Epstein, Louis Kaiser, Taylor Okonek, and Anna Perkins. "Mind the Gap: Inclusive Pedagogies for Diverse Classrooms." *Journal of Music History Pedagogy* 9, no. 2 (2019): 119–72.
Figueroa, Michael A. "Decolonizing 'Intro to World Music?'." *Journal of Music History Pedagogy* 10, no. 1 (2020): 39–57.
Goldman, Andrea S. *Opera and the City: The Politics of Culture in Beijing, 1770–1900*. Stanford: Stanford University Press, 2012.
Hsia, Ronnie Po-chia, ed. *A Companion to Early Modern Catholic Global Missions*. Leiden: Brill, 2018.
Leibniz, Gottfried Wilhelm. *Gottfried Wilhelm Leibniz: Writings on China*. Translated by Daniel J. Cook and Henry Rosemont Jr. Chicago: Open Court, 1994.
Luongo, Paul Gabriel. "Constructing a Canon: Studying Forty Years of the Norton Anthology of Western Music." *Journal of Music History Pedagogy* 12, no. 1 (2022): 1–36.
Lowe, Melanie. "Rethinking the Undergraduate Music History Sequence in the Information Age." *Journal of Music History Pedagogy* 5, no. 2 (2015): 65–71.
Parr, Adam. *The Mandate of Heaven: Strategy, Revolution, and the First European Translation of Sunzi's Art of War (1772)*. Leiden: Brill, 2019.

Rameau, Jean-Philippe. *Code de musique pratique ou Méthodes pour apprendre la musique*. Paris: l'imprimerie royale, 1760.

———. *Origine des sciences*. Paris: Sébastien Jorry, 1761.

Swetz, Frank J. "Leibniz, the Yijing, and the Religious Conversion of the Chinese." *Mathematics Magazine* 76, no. 4 (October, 2003): 276–91.

Walker, Margaret E. "Towards a Decolonized Music History Curriculum." *Journal of Music History Pedagogy* 10, no. 1 (2020): 1–19.

3 "Song of the Spirit Dance" and Native American Songs
Teaching about Appropriation in Late Nineteenth- and Early Twentieth-Century Symphonic Compositions

Erinn E. Knyt

When Antonín Dvořák (1841-1904) suggested in the 1890s that Native American songs could contribute to a national style of music in the United States, he drew attention to melodies that had recently become of interest to ethnologists, anthropologists, and composers.[1] Yet Dvořák, like many composers in the late nineteenth or early twentieth centuries, primarily appropriated the melodies and placed them into Western classical forms without deep knowledge of Native American song or customs.[2] At the same time, another contemporaneous composer, Ferruccio Busoni (1866-1924), sought to educate himself about Native American song and to derive formal, harmonic, and stylistic characteristics from the songs. This is evident in several of his pieces based on Native American melodies including his *Indianisches Tagebuch* II, BV 269 (*Gesang vom Reigen der Geister*, 1915) for strings, six wind instruments, and timpani. His unique treatment of forms was more closely aligned with traditions of narration and song than the works of his contemporaries. If Busoni altered the music of the Native American people, he also sought to make minimal changes to the melodies he used and to set them in a manner that preserved or reflected their rhythms, meters, contours, intervals, and harmonic ambiguity. In addition, he composed his own melodic material in imitation of Native American song. A sparse, driving, and sometimes dissonant style, in turn, became characteristic of Busoni's writing. This approach was fostered by a detailed study of Native American music and culture conducted through lengthy discussions and as-yet unpublished correspondence with pianist, anthropologist, and ethnologist Natalie Curtis-Burlin (1875-1921).

This chapter positions Busoni's pieces within the broader "Indianist" movement of the 1880s-1920s, including in relation to symphonic works more commonly covered in music history courses, such as Dvořák's Symphony No. 9 "From the New World," Op. 95, or MacDowell's Orchestral Suite No. 2 ("Indian"), Op. 48. As such, it not only contributes new knowledge about lesser-known compositions, about the life and career of an important woman ethnologist, and about the music of

DOI: 10.4324/9781003415954-5

Native American people, but also aids discussions concerning music normally excluded from music history surveys as well as about an evolution of approaches within the "Indianist" movement from uninformed appropriation to a more profound engagement with the culture, ideas, and styles.

This research, in turn, could enrich music history classroom discussions, which frequently focus on Dvořák's "New World" Symphony without providing more detailed information about songs and traditions of the Native American people that he invoked. The chapter suggests approaching the topic in the classroom by teaching about Native American song traditions and comparing those to various symphonic compositions from the era that reveal a spectrum of approaches toward the use of Native American song. It proposes having students compare early anthropological and ethnological source materials, analyze scores, listen to recordings of Native American music, and look beyond the canon for course content.

"Indianist" Movement

Any class exploring Dvořák's "New World" Symphony, or the early twentieth-century symphony, would benefit from investigating Native American song traditions and the history of the so-called "Indianist" movement in classical music, which lasted from around 1890 to 1920. Students will quickly learn that many members of this movement perceived Native American people as "other" or "inferior" and held a colonizing attitude characterized by support for appropriating Native American melodies and placing them within Western classical forms and harmonies.[3] Following are a few key points to be shared during a lecture. Alternatively, the professor could ask students to learn about the material by looking at and analyzing the source materials on their own.[4] Some of the original early recordings of Native American voices might also be played in class, but it should be noted that recording technology, mainly wax cylinders, were not able to adequately capture the instrument timbres or larger ceremonial events in sound.[5] In addition, in some instances, subjects were not willing to share their sacred rituals with outsiders.

The "Indianist movement" in classical music was tied to a sense of cultural evolution and a romantic nostalgia for nature that related to discontent with urban modernity. In many cases, classical composers, mostly white men from Europe and the United States, had little interaction with Native American people and no interest in the original context of the music. They often appropriated the melodies as a means to portray "otherness" in music. A few such U.S. composers include Edward MacDowell, Arthur Farwell, Charles Cadman, John Comfort Fillmore, Henry Gilbert, Amy Beach, Frederick Burton, and Thurlow Lieurance.

Many of these composers obtained melodies from the early scholarly fieldwork of musicologists, ethnologists, or anthropologists, especially Theodore Baker or Alice Fletcher. While these scholars did important work in preserving the melodies of Native American communities whose traditions were being oppressed and suppressed by the U.S. government at the time, their published texts do not contain extensive information about the cultural context.[6] Moreover, their work reflected a commonly held and mistaken viewpoint that Native American cultures were generally undeveloped or unsophisticated.

By examining some of these texts directly, students can examine firsthand what late nineteenth- and early twentieth-century composers encountered and can understand how the texts guided their thinking. In some cases, these texts represent the only exposure the composers had to Native American music. Baker's text, "Über die Musik der nordamerikanischen Wilden" [On the Music of the North American Indians], for instance, uses the offensive term "Wilden" to describe Native American people. Moreover, as the field was just emerging, he did not yet have the ethnomusicological tools to accurately transcribe many of the melodies he notated. Baker also restricted his research to members of the Seneca nation in western New York and students at the Training School for Indian Youth in Carlisle, Pennsylvania, who had already been acclimatized to Western culture. Finally, Baker's text, which included German translations of song lyrics, encouraged the decontextualization of Native American music from its social and cultural meaning by giving the notes primacy over cultural information; Baker's analyses centered on scales, organology, and performance practices rather than upon discussion of the context.

Fletcher's works, which were based largely on communities in Omaha, also included some disturbing early twentieth-century biases and notions of cultural superiority. Her *Indian Story and Song from North America* (1900) contains some orally passed down stories, many in first person narrative form, as well as numerous songs that are harmonized by John Fillmore using Western harmonies.[7] Yet unlike Baker, Fletcher knew Native American people intimately and unofficially adopted and mentored the son of an Omaha Chief, Francis La Flesche, as an adult, which aided his career as an ethnologist.[8] Fletcher began her transcription work in 1892 based on live performance, but by 1895 she was recording using a graphophone, eventually working together with La Flesche to create notated transcriptions.

Unfortunately, the published transcriptions contain little indication of instrumentation, but some of the surviving recordings provide hints about the instruments, as muffled sounds of percussion or other instruments can be heard faintly in the background on some of the wax cylinders.[9] It would thus be worthwhile to supplement examination of these printed sources

"Song of the Spirit Dance" and Native American Songs 65

with a general overview of instrumentation, song types, and uses of music in Native American culture, along with historical recordings. This would help acquaint students with exposure to the sounds of Native American song and also provide insight into the difficulties early ethnologists encountered when transcribing and recording the music.

Symphonic Works Based on Native American Melodies

After providing an overview of Native American songs, ethnological approaches, and the source materials available to composers in the later nineteenth or early twentieth centuries, a music history professor might demonstrate the spectrum of approaches used by the early-twentieth-century symphony composers in responding to these Native American melodies. Approaches range from appropriation, to imaginative but uninformed evocations, to a deeper absorption of ideas as well as a more profound engagement with the material in its cultural context. When teaching about these pieces, it would be useful to ask students to read some of the composers' writings on the topic (some of which are cited here in the endnotes) and to have students compare/analyze quoted material with the finished composition. Following is a case study comparing symphonic works by three contemporaneous composers. The material presented here can be drawn upon for lectures or used to generate productive learning activities in which students complete their own investigations based on the source materials. Such assignments could be designed for undergraduate or graduate students.

An early example of appropriation can be found in MacDowell's Orchestral Suite No. 2 (1892).[10] Source readings show that the connectedness of Native American people to nature was important for MacDowell, who was interested in depicting landscapes in his music. Yet, MacDowell considered Native American people to be less developed, and he frequently applied descriptors to them that today would be considered overtly racist, such as "barbaric." Even so, he idolized what he perceived as the free and natural state of the Native American people. It offered an imaginative escape, yet not one that MacDowell wanted to experience in real life. When invited to travel west, MacDowell complained about perceived hardships required by the journey: "I'd like to do that, but it is a long way to go, and besides I'm afraid I couldn't stand the food and the beds. I'm not used to roughing it."[11]

MacDowell considered writing a tone poem about Henry Wadsworth Longfellow's *The Song of Hiawatha* as early as 1887.[12] Longfellow's book is in itself a romanticized and largely fictional account of the lives of Native American people, and it is hardly surprising that MacDowell's earliest completed composition based on Native American melodies was

66 *Erinn E. Knyt*

an imaginative and romantic programmatic depiction of Native American traditions. That piece, his Orchestral Suite No. 2, contains five movements:

I. Legend
II. Love Song
III. In War Time
IV. Dirge
V. Village Festival

When quoting from Native American sources, MacDowell appropriated them both musically and contextually, often recasting the emotions to better fit a Western mindset. MacDowell's primary exposure to Native American song was through Baker's text, and each of the movements uses melodies from Baker's text related to its theme. For instance, MacDowell chose an "Iowa love song, sung by young warriors when out riding" for the "Love Song" movement. The "Dirge" movement, which was one of MacDowell's favorites, features Baker's transcription of the "Kiowa Song of a Mother to Her Absent Son."

Instead of considering the original context of the song, MacDowell focused on universal feelings of loss, transforming a text about *absence*, perhaps the result of a hunting expedition, into one about *death* and *loss*:

> "Of all my music," he confessed at the time, "the 'Dirge' in the 'Indian' suite pleases me most. It affects me deeply and did when I

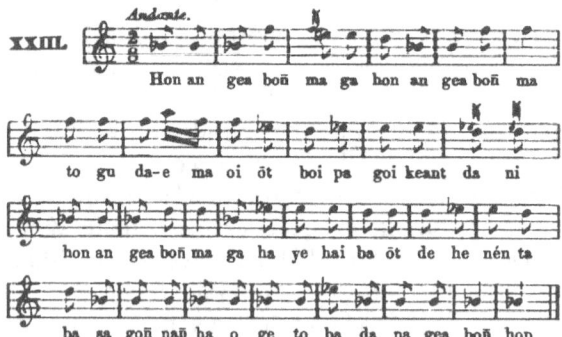

Figure 3.1 Theodore Baker's transcription of the "Kiowa Song of a Mother to Her Absent Son."

was writing it. In it an Indian woman laments the death of her son; but to me, as I wrote it, it seemed to express a world-sorrow rather than a particularised grief."[13]

MacDowell also used generic musical markers to signify grief, such as descending-second "sigh" motives and a *langsam* tempo. A horn positioned behind the stage evokes a sense of wide-open geography and aural distance. The melody itself is fragmented in MacDowell's "Dirge" movement, even as it is harmonized with traditional diatonic chords. The initial measures of the movement, for instance, include fragments of the Native American melody emerging in the strings while the winds and brass play an extended drone. Any harmonic implications, along with the original ornamentation, are ignored in MacDowell's setting, thereby obscuring the unique aspects of the melody, even as repetitive rhythms in the strings serve to evoke a generic sense of "otherness."

Overall, MacDowell's Suite No. 2 sounds like a romantic tone poem. The "Legend" movement features horn calls and open string lines, conjuring a vast landscape. The "Love Song" movement is pastoral and features the various wind timbres. The third movement, "In War Time," depicts a war between two different cultures by means of contrasting melodies, one of which is a Native American melody transcribed by Baker. The "Dirge" is solemn, while the "Village Festival" features playful melodies on the piccolo and other wind instruments.[14]

MacDowell represents the "otherness" of the Native American people generically with repetitive rhythms and startling accents that contrast with his unmarked Western classical style. In the opening movement, "Legend," the opening melody derives from an Iroquois harvest festival song transcribed by Baker, but MacDowell sets it using Western orchestral instruments. Since he was working from Baker's single-line melody transcription, it is likely that he did not even have any awareness of traditional Native American instruments. In addition, he chose not to include voices or text.

It is not the melody alone that conveys a sense of "otherness" within the orchestral texture and timbres, but rather MacDowell's inserted rests between staccato notes in the clarinets and bassoons and pizzicato in the low strings, as well as upward swooping notes. In addition, there is the frequent repetition of fragmented melodic motifs and a descending anapestic rhythm coupled with driving rhythms. MacDowell's "othering," using stereotyped rhythmic and textural features, reflects his disturbing belief that Native American music was inferior. The composer, for instance, wrote that the repetitive rhythms in some Native American music were reflective of a less developed culture and people. He expressed these ideas in shockingly disparaging writings, such as the following:[15]

Example 3.1 MacDowell, Suite No. 2, Op. 48, IV: Dirge, mm. 1–7.

To the primitive savage mind, the smallest rhythmic phrase is a wonderful invention, therefore it is repeated incessantly. Add to that a certain joy in mere sound, and we have the howl, which certainly follows the sequence of nature[;] for a thunderclap, or the phenomenon of echo, is its prototype, being a loud explosion followed by a more or less regular sequence of minor reverberations.[16]

Dvořák's ninth symphony, by contrast, represents an imaginative evocation of Native American music. Dvořák held the music and culture of Native American people in high regard. Despite this, any kind of cultural exchange in terms of music was limited, and his famed Symphony "From the New World" represents a romanticized view of Native American people without a deep understanding of their music or culture.[17] It is possible that before coming to the United States, Dvořák read an article in *Dalibor* magazine written by his friend, Václav Juda Novotný, which included a few transcribed melodies by Native American people. After Dvořák arrived in the United States, where he stayed from 1892–1895, he had two encounters with Native American people. He likely attended a Buffalo Bill Wild West Show in New York in spring 1893 at the invitation of Jeannette Thurber, director of the National Conservatory of Music, but there is no record of personal interactions with Native American people at that time. The show recreated dances and tribal warfare by Oglala Sioux, Crow, Cheyenne, Arapaho, and Shoshoni great plain communities for a white audience. His second encounter with Native American people took place in Spillville Iowa in the summer of 1893 when he met Kickapoo Chief Big Moon, who was traveling with a multi-tribal medicine show designed to make money by selling medicinal herbs. The Native American people Dvořák encountered at Spillville were part of different communities, including Algonquin, Siouan, and perhaps Caddoan; thus, the music they performed would have been representative of the eastern woodlands and plains traditions but could have been adapted for the show. The performers were also marginalized people desperately trying to make a living. Dvořák was also exposed to Alice Fletcher's *A Study of Omaha Indian Music* in June 1893.

After the encounters in Spillville, Dvořák wrote a few chamber works that incorporated some of the Native American melodies and drum rhythms he heard there and which he had transcribed himself.[18] Yet Dvořák adapted the themes to a Western classical style of writing and to Western classical instruments. Moreover, despite these encounters, his music exhibits little attempt to represent the melodies and rhythms authentically. In fact, composed as it was in New York in 1893 (completed in May 1893) before his time in Spillville, his famous "New World" Symphony does not even quote from any Native American music. Instead, the second and third movements are tone poems based on Longfellow's *Hiawatha*, and the music is a portrayal of sounds he associated with an imagined U.S. landscape and Native American people.[19]

Since Dvořák did not quote directly from Native American melodies in his "New World" Symphony, there is no direct appropriation. However, he mimicked the style and spirit based on his very limited understanding of the music of the Native American people.[20] The connection to the Longfellow text is substantiated by an interview with Dvořák that appeared the day of the premiere of the symphony (Dec. 15, 1893):

> The second movement is an Adagio. But it is different to the classic works in this form. It is in reality a study or a sketch for a longer work, either a cantata or an opera which I propose writing, and which will be based upon Longfellow's "Hiawatha." I have long had the idea of someday utilizing that poem. I first became acquainted with it about thirty years ago through the medium of a Bohemian translation. It appealed very strongly to my imagination at that time, and the impression has only been strengthened by my residence here. The scherzo of the symphony was suggested by the scene at the feast in Hiawatha where the Indians dance, and is also an essay I made in the direction of imparting the local color of Indian character to music.[21]

Dvořák intended the scherzo movement to depict the dance of Pau-Puk-Keewis, while the larghetto represented Hiawatha's wooing scene in Longfellow's text. Michael Beckerman argues that Dvořák focuses less on the actual wooing between Hiawatha and Minnehaha than on Hiawatha's journey, which frames the wooing. The tenth chapter of the *Song of Hiawatha* tells of Hiawatha's fears about courting a member of the Dakota community, since he was a member of the Ojibway community, as well as his hopes that the union would bring about peace. The wooing scene is then framed by two journeys—Hiawatha's journey to the land of the Dakotas and Hiawatha and Minnehaha's joint journey back to the land of the Ojibway. The homeward journey of the two lovers features descriptive discussions of nature, such as birds and the sun. Beckerman's reading of the movement notes that, like Longfellow's poem, the music contains three main sections. The opening, with seventh chords in open tenth positions, suggests expansiveness. The use of the English horn over low drones also evokes pastoral landscapes and vast open plains. The middle section, by contrast, features two instrumental voices—the oboe and flute—in unison over tremolando strings, signifying the union of the two warring communities. Even so, Becker resists a literal correlation between the poem and music, suggesting instead that Dvořák was primarily responding to the images of the poem. Beckerman argues that the music depicts the landscape the lovers saw as they journeyed home. For instance, the trilling in the woodwinds could be seen as reflecting trilling birds. Thus, the symphony is steeped in Western classical symphonic references to literary depictions of Native American people and an imagined landscape without explicit reference to the actual musical sounds or traditions of Native American people.

Students will profit from comparing these approaches with Busoni's portrayal of Native American song in his *Gesang vom Reigen der Geister* (Song of the Spirit Dance). If MacDowell appropriated Native American melodies into a Western classical idiom and Dvořák created his own imaginative portrayal of Native American culture in symphonic form, Busoni sought a deeper engagement with the music in his *Gesang* for chamber orchestra.

Busoni, an Italian-German composer, first visited the United States (mainly Boston and New York) from 1891 to 1894, and thus he was in New York when Dvořák was writing his "New World" Symphony. It is likely that he was aware of Dvořák's ideas about Native American music, and he heard Dvořák's "New World" Symphony and compositions by other Indianist composers.[22] However, Busoni was primarily drawn to the music of Native American people during his subsequent stays in the United States (1910, 1911, and 1915).

Busoni became deeply interested in Native American music beginning in 1910 after one of his former harmony pupils, Curtis-Burlin, shared her research and ideas about Native American and African American music with him. In March 1910, Mahler conducted Busoni's *Turandot Suite*, BV 248 in New York, and Curtis-Burlin, who was attending the concert, subsequently gave Busoni a copy of her *Indians' Book*. Although Curtis-Burlin had studied harmony with Busoni in New York in 1893 and was an accomplished pianist, she eventually devoted her life to transcribing and preserving the music of Native American communities. After she visited the Southwest around 1900, she was captivated by the land and people. Her first lengthy work was *Songs of Ancient America* in 1905. The *Indians' Book* followed in 1907. The latter was a lengthy (572-page) book with about two-hundred transcriptions of Native American songs, with text in the original languages, as well as English translations. The book also included numerous descriptive drawings and photographs.[23] Curtis-Burlin's research was an act of preservation, as the Federal Bureau of Indian Affairs did not want Native American people speaking and singing in their own language during the assimilation period (until about 1920). Curtis sought to transcribe the songs as faithfully as possible, so, unlike Fletcher, she refrained from harmonizing or embellishing the melodies. Also, unlike the books by Fletcher and Baker, Curtis-Burlin's writings include extensive cultural context for the melodies, which are from eighteen different communities. Her book includes detailed background information and cultural information relayed directly from the perspective of Native American people, who willingly shared their stories with her because she had gained their trust. Curtis collected Hopi and Navajo songs as early as 1902, and by 1903 she was making use of an Edison cylinder in her work. Unlike some of her predecessors, Curtis-Burlin, who was born into a wealthy New York City family, did not consider Native American people as inferior, but rather, as less privileged, even if she still held some outdated evolutionary views. She sat on dirt floors and lived among Native American people, and they in turn shared their cultural traditions, stories, and songs, which she recorded in her book.[24]

Curtis-Burlin subsequently directly disseminated the melodies to composers and conductors, such as Busoni and Leopold Stokowski. Curtis-Burlin felt strongly that Native American music should not be adapted to Western classical idioms. Instead, there needed to be an exchange in which Western classical music was altered in response to the Native American melodic contours and rhythms. Busoni came to uphold these views as well, following numerous lengthy conversations with Curtis-Burlin. Curtis-Burlin was highly critical of earlier pieces that she felt reflected the "old" world more than the "new." She believed that Busoni was the first to undertake a deeper engagement with the ideas:[25]

> To me it was of course peculiarly interesting to see how the intrinsic character of Indian music, on which the work is built, compels its own treatment, remaining unalterably Indian, standing out with its own sharp rhythmic and melodic outline on the background of the composer's thought like sculptured bass-relief. And this, of course, was Busoni's own ideal in regard to this work. Before he put pen to paper he said that he would not overlay the Indian themes with any feeling of European culture nor "develop" them according to the usual standards of composition. He wished to regard them as individual musical entities which should develop through the composer *according to their own nature and character.*[26]

Their discussions in person and in numerous letters about the music of Native American people involved extensive consideration of both culture and music. In one letter, Curtis-Burlin protested the common practice of harmonizing native American melodies with a harmonium or piano. She also criticized the colonizing attitude of many musicians who thought they had to "teach" Native American people and to alter the music. Moreover, she acquainted Busoni with the ethnological work and music of other contemporaneous scholars to enrich his studies on the topic. Although she sent Busoni specific notated melodies she thought would interest him, it is not clear whether or not she shared any sound recordings with him as well.

Unlike MacDowell and Dvořák, Busoni also beheld the U.S. landscape. Although he was rushed from city to city on concert tours, he saw the United States from east to west while traveling, primarily by train.[27] Busoni admired the connectedness of Native American people to nature, and he believed that he had a better understanding of their music after seeing the country from coast to coast. His many letters describe his impressions of deserts, mountain chains, plains, and red rocks.[28] It was only after his travels that ideas for his first published work based on Native American themes began to take shape.[29]

In addition, Busoni had several personal encounters with Native American people outside of organized shows or commercialized events in which he discussed their music and ideas. It is possible that he heard some of their songs in these settings, but he did not mention that in his letters. He described one personal encounter in a letter to his wife in March 1910. After the interaction, he stated that he deemed Native American culture superior and more inventive than that of white Americans in several ways, including in terms of sound or timbre. He also admired their spirituality and praised their use of language:

I spoke to a Red Indian woman. She told me how her brother (a talented violinist) came to New York to try and make his way. "But he could not associate his ideas with the question of daily bread." How much good it does one to hear of such a sentiment in the United States! Then she said that her tribe ought to have an instrument something like this: A hole should be dug in the earth and strings stretched all round the edges of it. I said (in the spirit of the Red Indians): An instrument like that ought to be called 'the voice of the earth" She was quite enthusiastic about this. [...] The Red Indians are the only cultured people who will have *nothing to do with money* and who dress the most everyday things in beautiful words. How different is a business man from Chicago compared with this![30]

When using Native American melodies in his compositions, Busoni considered the culture and ceremonies, as well as the forms and musical characteristics. He was critical of Dvořák and others who had ignored these factors: "It is absurd to make a Symphony with Indian melodies, after the Leipzig model (like Dvořák), or a Meyerbeer-ish opera (like Herbert's recent one). It needs a great deal of study to get inside the Indian life." [31]

Busoni initially struggled to discover a way to draw upon Native American music while preserving its unique contours, intervals, and forms. Busoni's first attempt was a short piano piece, *Indianisches Erntelied,* which was completed on a ship as he left the United States on April 12, 1911. Busoni went on to compose three more significant works based on Native American melodies, including his piece for orchestra, the *Gesang vom Reigen der Geister*.[32]

Busoni did not simply appropriate Native American melodies when he composed with them. He also changed his own compositional style in response, and he recorded his thoughts in a discussion of "absolute melody." Busoni wrote about how melodies contain latent harmony and moods of feeling, as well as suggestions of timbre. He believed it was the job of the composer to discover the harmonic implications of each melody. Thus, he did not want to force Native American melodies into Western classical harmonies but rather to derive any latent harmonies, however unconventional, from the implications of the melodies:

The Red Indians are passing by, and thoughts begin to move. Today, I began putting down some thoughts about the melody again. Perhaps they will interest you. [...] Absolute melody: A row of repeated ascending and descending intervals, which are organized and move rhythmically. It contains in itself a latent harmony, reflects a mood of feeling. It can exist without depending on words for expression and without accompanying voices. When performed, the choice of pitch or of instrument makes no alteration to the nature of its being. Melody, independent at first, joined the accompanying harmony subsequently, and later melted into inseparable unity with it. Recently it has been the aim of polyphonic music, which is always progressing, to free itself from this unity.[33]

While such ideals are inherently European, they nevertheless represent a more respectful and educated approach toward the music of Native American people than was typical during Busoni's lifetime.

Busoni's letters to pupils and colleagues also indicate how a deep study of Native American music and culture influenced his compositional style, including his approaches to form and meter. In a letter from 1913, Busoni revealed that he had progressed from trying to force the melodies into a Western classical rhapsody form, instead utilizing a loose collection of movements to better reflect the source material.[34] In a letter to Hugo Leichtentritt, he not only described the overall structure of his *Indianische Fantasie* for piano (1914) but also noted how he alternated between two time signatures to reflect the natural rhythmic shape of the melodies. Busoni also sought to incorporate the Native American melodies without modification and then layer in other musical material derived from the distinctive rhythms, meters, contours, and intervals of Native American song.

Busoni selected a single Pawnee spirit dance as the basis of his *Gesang*. Curtis-Burlin stated that it would be hard to understand the spirit dance without first knowing about the suffering of Native Americans brought about by the slaughtering of buffalo and the building of the railroad. Native American people were confined on reservations, fed rations, and transported against their will.[35] Curtis-Burlin noted in her book that this particular piece referred to a dance created in response to a prophet's call (a Paiute, in western Nevada in 1888) for peace and harmony.[36] However, some felt threatened by the new dance. The agent in charge of the Dakota community felt particularly threatened, and brought in extra troops. Frightened, one member of the Dakota community fired a weapon, and this led to the massacre of about 300 Dakota people.

Busoni would have been drawn to this account of a prophet and the unification of communities through music and dance, as well as the message of pacifism. He saw in the Native American belief system a oneness between nature, culture, music, and life—something he had long sought in his own life. Busoni, a pacifist, set this song of war and peace while in exile during the First Great War, so it probably had personal significance for him as well.

In his musical setting, Busoni sought to achieve the harmony described by the Paiute prophet in musical terms. He finished the piece before departing for Europe in 1915 and tried it out in Zurich with the Tonhalle Orchestra on Oct. 28, finishing the score on Dec. 30. Busoni intended it to be a companion piece to his other orchestral works from around the same time, such as the *Berceuse élégiaque*, BV 252a, and the *Nocturne Symphonique*, BV 262.

"Song of the Spirit Dance" and Native American Songs   75

Without resorting to generic musical markers of "otherness," Busoni sought to write a symphonic piece that brought Native American and Western classical musical traditions into co-existence. The dance Busoni selected for his *Gesang* is chorale-like in its regularity of phrase and simplicity of rhythm and phrase shape. Yet instead of forcing the melodic quotation to conform to traditional Western classical harmony, Busoni quoted the melody nearly verbatim and altered his own musical writing to conform to the suggestions of the melody. Busoni presents the melody beginning in measure 38 of his *Gesang*, after an extended chromatic introduction characterized by rising scales and descending chromatic figures that are passed from one instrument to the next. The rising scalar material in the introduction is based on intervals from the melody and foreshadows its unveiling in measure 38.

It is notable that when Busoni presented the melody almost in its entirety in the first strophe, he set it in unison in the woodwinds, thereby drawing attention to it. It is possible that he chose woodwinds to approximate the timbre of the flute used in some Native American songs. Harmonic polyphony in the strings, which sounds separate because of the difference in color, functions simultaneously but independently, and chord choices derive from the simultaneity of lines.

At the same time, material following the melody also derives directly from and varies the melody in a through-composed succession of textures. An ostinato in the bass also reflects the melody and is followed by quasi-canonical three-part writing in a contrapuntal texture so prized by Busoni. The composer subsequently introduced his own pentatonic melody that nevertheless derives from the pitches of the Native American melody.

The Native American melody centers on E but lacks a third scale degree, suggesting modal ambiguity, and Busoni, correspondingly, alludes to G major and E minor/minor, shifting deftly between harmonies using the plurisignificance of pitches. This modal ambiguity is reflected in the introduction, for instance, which suggests E minor, but cadences on E major in bar 34. At bar 56, the melody is transposed up a half step to F. As Colin Davis explains, Busoni also superimposes fourth and fifth related harmonies, such as in measure 54–77, when Busoni establishes C/F pairs and D/G pairs and G/D, Eb/Bb, and E/B pairs.[37] Such relations help establish a sense of openness of sound and interval in line with the landscapes known by the great plains communities, which the Pawnee community once roamed.[38] The harmonies, similarly, form a rapid succession of triads in unrelated key that nevertheless are related to the melody; this disembodied language is derived from the Native American melody.

Conclusions

When teaching "Western art music," it has been common to focus on traditional symphonic works using a Western stylistic lens without providing due respect to other traditions that informed that music. This chapter has sought

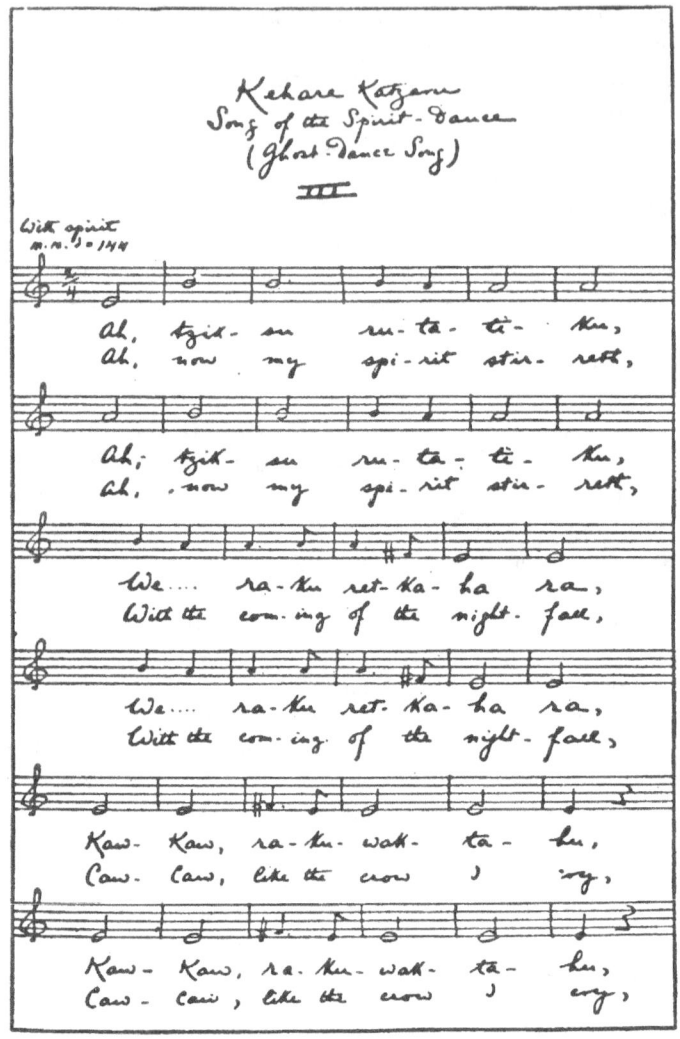

Figure 3.2 Pawnee "Ghost Dance," part I. Transcribed by Curtis-Burlin.

to introduce a more complex perspective on intersections between Western classical symphonic music and Native American melodies in the late nineteenth and early twentieth centuries. It reveals a spectrum of practices ranging from uninformed appropriation in the case of MacDowell to a deeper study of the music and culture in the case of Busoni. In addition, it seeks to introduce students to the melodies of Native American communities.

The pieces discussed in this chapter reflect the complicated and conflicted ways these musics came together at one point in history. And while one could summarily dismiss all late nineteenth and early twentieth century

"Song of the Spirit Dance" and Native American Songs 77

Example 3.2 Pawnee "Ghost Dance" quotation by Busoni in *Gesang vom Reigen der Geister*.

attempts to make use of the melodies in symphonic literature as racist and colonizing, it is also true that Dvořák helped recognize the great significance of Native American and African American melodies in ways that still resonate today.[39] In addition, Busoni found a way to use the melodies in more respectful ways than was common in his era. To see those traditions

78 Erinn E. Knyt

Example 3.2 (Continued)

as co-existing—as different yet equally valued—was what Busoni sought in his music. Busoni heard novel music and also sought to represent a culture of valor, pride, ceremony, and oneness with nature that he so admired. While all of these attempts fall short of true exchange or collaboration, at the same time, some reveal a respectful coming together of different cultures that was uncommon at the time.

Yet this chapter seeks to go beyond merely studying Busoni's historical attempts to engage with the music of a marginalized people. It also seeks to recenter Native American music in the music history classroom when students engage with primary sources and study varied preservation attempts. This chapter does not seek to erase the troubling parts of music history but rather to expose students to the songs of a marginalized and oppressed people and to demonstrate ways that Native American music intersected with and were appropriated in canonic classical repertoire. I have specifically suggested having students study the early published transcriptions of the music of Native American people as presented in ethnological source material, to read through some of the early texts about Native American music and culture, to listen to early sound recordings, and to compare and contrast these with a broader spectrum of roughly contemporaneous symphonic works in order to better understand the range of techniques classical composers used to respond to Native American songs at one moment in history.

The material here could be profitably taught and then discussed in a class session or two at the graduate or undergraduate levels. Depending on time constraints and the goals of the class, it might be profitable to simultaneously supplement the material discussed in this chapter with reference to opera and to Native American classical composers as well. In particular, students could compare and contrast Victor Herbert's *Natoma* (1911), a grand opera, with Zitkála-Šá's (1876-1938) *The Sun Dance Opera* (1913), which combines late Romantic classical styles with the music of the Sioux and Ute communities. Alternatively, students might appreciate supplementing the historical material discussed in this chapter with more recent examples that illustrate a richer musical exchange, such as the compositions by Louis Ballard (1931-2007). For instance, the class might compare the earlier symphonic pieces discussed in this chapter with Ballard's orchestral sketches, *Scenes from Indian Life* (1964). Teaching this material can help students better understand why and how these musical styles merged at one point in history, while at the same time acknowledging little-studied traditions that informed classical music in significant ways. In addition, it is possible to show the difference between historical approaches toward Native American melodies and more recent ideals characterized by deeper musical exchange and collaboration.

At the same time, the approaches suggested here, which include an exploration of the source material of Native American people could be used to help expand the music history curriculum. Margaret Walker claims that an important decolonizing step is "to contextualize Western art music's history and historiography firmly within a larger framework of critically and globally situated histories of music."[40] This chapter proposes decentering some of the canonic content by placing pieces normally taught in a music history survey in dialogue with musical communities regularly excluded from music history classes. The more inclusive pedagogical methods proposed here go beyond a tokenist addition of pieces by underrepresented composers while at the same time acknowledging and critiquing the role that colonizing attitudes have had in excluding a study of some music communities. As Kimary Fick has recently noted: "Western art music privileges white, cisgender, male composers through systems of power and oppression inherent in our histories and canons."[41] Talking about, listening to, and studying these systems of oppression helps students identify and recognize ways that the musics have been marginalized, and in that way, helps dismantle the systems of power that have been upheld for so long in the music history classroom. Discussing not only the source materials, but also the origins of the "Indianist" movement and why so many ethnologists like Curtis-Burlin felt compelled to preserve the materials due to the systemic oppression of Native American people contributes to these goals.

In addition, this chapter calls for engagement with original and unabridged source materials from Native American communities and an exploration of how those sources were preserved by early ethnologists. In this way, the chapter also promotes deeper engagement with primary source documents in line with some of the strategies proposed by Timothy Cochran and Blake Howe, such as studying original sources in context and with critical inquiry.[42] Cochran argues: "To become effective classroom tools, primary sources require intentional pedagogical strategies that break down these assumptions, build interpretation skills, and raise awareness of where sources come from and how they contribute to the production of knowledge."[43] This chapter proposes doing this by exploring where the sources came from and how they contributed a growth of knowledge about Native American music.

Moreover, these pedagogical strategies could be usefully applied to other repertoires.[44] For instance, any class on Dvořák's ninth symphony might also cover African American music in addition to Native American songs. Alternatively, even if a professor chooses not to teach about MacDowell, Dvořák, and/or Busoni's symphonic pieces, similar approaches, could, for instance, be used to engage with other pieces that quote from and appropriate non-canonic music from Asia, the Americas, or Africa. Such pieces could be decentered through engagement with primary source materials from marginalized repertoire, discussions of cultural context for those sources, and critical discussions about appropriation and colonizing value systems. For instance, such discussions could also help decenter pieces like Giacomo Puccini's *Madama Butterfly,* which has also been included in major music history anthologies without due consideration for the cultures represented so inaccurately in the opera even as they are woven into Eurocentric treatments of form and musical language.

"Song of the Spirit Dance" and Native American Songs 81

As Douglass Seaton has eloquently argued, professors can teach "off of" the canon by teaching "music *in* history."[45] This involves more than consideration of a historical survey of "masterpieces;" it requires consideration of music in culture by recentering the previously marginalized communal music making that made these pieces possible. As Stephen Meyer has noted, "cultural associations of particular musical sounds are always in a state of flux" and "teaching across difference allows us to demonstrate our engagement with the vital issues of cultural identity that are shaping our world."[46] Teaching historical music today requires both acknowledgment of how that music was shaped by the cultural identifiers of that period as well as acknowledgment of the meanings of those identifiers in the present, a task this case study has sought to model.

Notes

1. A shorter version of this paper was presented at the Teaching Music History Day conference on June 11, 2022. I am grateful for audience comments, including from Louis Epstein, Eric Hung, and Esther Morgan-Ellis.
2. Disclaimer: this chapter includes quotations of historical source material that contain terminology deemed offensive today. This chapter does not condone that language but includes it in its original context to document the thinking and practices of a past era.
3. A professor might assign Browner, "Breathing the Indian Spirit," for use in undergraduate surveys or a graduate seminar.
4. Citations to primary source materials and to secondary literature are included in the reference section.
5. Some of the recordings made by Alice Fletcher and Francis La Flesche can be accessed online through the Library of Congress. The few sound recordings based on the work of Natalie Curtis-Burlin are not readily available online but can be accessed at the Archives of Traditional Music Collections, Indiana University.
6. Another important ethnologist was Frances Densmore (1867–1957).
7. Fletcher (1838-1923) lived on a Sioux reservation in 1881. She also worked with the Omaha, Pawnee, Arapaho, Cheyenne, Chippewa, Ponca, and Winnebago communities. Together with her adopted son, La Flesche, Fletcher published *The Omaha Tribe* in 1911 and she also wrote 46 monographs on ethnological topics.
8. After Fletcher travelled to Omaha in 1881, she met Francis La Flesche and encouraged him in his ethnological pursuits. He came to live with her in a mother-son relationship. If Fletcher, who was 20 years his senior, never legally adopted La Flesch, she fulfilled that role until her death. La Flesch, in turn, helped Fletcher with translations and other ethnological work.
9. Native American performers regularly used an assortment of percussion instruments, such as drums and rattles. Melodic instruments included flutes (similar to a recorder), whistles, and (occasionally) some string instruments, such as the Apache violin or the Yaqui violin.
10. MacDowell drew upon Native American melodies in the following compositions:

    Second ("Indian") Suite, Op. 48 (1892)
    Sonata Tragica, Op. 45 (1893)

Woodland Sketches ("From an Indian Lodge," Op. 51 (1896)
Indian Idyl, Op. 62 No. 6 (1902)

11 For more information, consult the Edward MacDowell Papers, 1880-1967 at the University of New Hampshire.
12 MacDowell, (letter in Marian MacDowell's hand) to Henry E. Krehbiel, December 1897, Music Division, Library of Congress; quoted in Irving Lowens, 55.
13 MacDowell, Interview, 14.
14 The piece was first performed in New York City on January 23, 1896 by the Boston Symphony Orchestra.
15 MacDowell, *Critical and Historical Essays,* 141–2.
16 Ibid.,141–142.
17 Dvořák primarily observed and recorded melodies without understanding their original contexts or meanings. Moreover, Dvořák's understanding of race relations might have been limited by his own experiences as a Czech composer, where primary concerns about difference mainly involved language and religion.
18 Pieces by Dvořák that quote from Native American melodies include the following:

Quintet in E-Flat Major (1893)
String Quartet in F Major (1893)
Indian Lament in G Minor, Op. 100

19 Dvořák expressed some of his ideas about the importance of Native American songs here: Dvořák, "Music in America,"433.
20 Clapham, "Dvořák and the American Indian," 12.
21 Dvořák, quoted in Beckerman, 2.
22 Busoni, letter of March 9, 1911 (Kansas City) to Gerda Busoni, in *Letters to his Wife,* 186-187.
23 Her marriage to painter Paul Burlin in 1917 was a happy one, but she died unexpectedly at the age of 46 in a car accident.
24 Curtis-Burlin actively campaigned for the rights of Native American people, including in communications to President Roosevelt.
25 I am not aware of any acknowledgement of Busoni's work from the Native American community. In reality, Busoni had difficulty getting his *Gesang* performed, unlike his other orchestral works, so neither Europeans nor Native Americans had much opportunity to hear it. Curtis-Burlin, on the other hand, was apparently very much loved by numerous Native American communities, and they were shocked and heartbroken by her untimely death. While we might think of Curtis-Burlin in retrospect as conveying a Eurocentric perspective, her approach was novel for the time in which she lived. Busoni's was too. So there are different historical ways of looking at the music and texts. To read and listen from a twenty-first century perspective is to perhaps miss the point of the novelty of what they were doing in their own time.
26 Curtis-Burlin, "Busoni's Indian Fantasy," 541.
27 He travelled across much of the country in 1910 and from coast to coast in 1911. A letter to his wife from March 4,1911 lists the main cities on his itinerary. Busoni letter of March 4, 1911 to his wife in Busoni, *Letters to His Wife,* 185.
28 Busoni, letter of March 13, 1911 to Gerda Busoni, in *Letters to His Wife,* 187.
29 Busoni, letter of March 15, 1911 to Gerda Busoni, in *Letters to His Wife,* 191.
30 Busoni, letter of March 22, 1910 to Gerda Busoni, in *Letters to His Wife,* 163.
31 Busoni, letter of March 9, 1911 to Gerda Busoni in *Letters to His Wife,* 186-187.
32 The other pieces include the following:

  Red Indian Fantasy, Op. 44 (Fantasia-Canzone-Finale), 1914
  Red Indian Diary Book I: Four Studies on Motifs of the North American Indians, 1915
  Song of the Spirit Dance, Op. 47: Book II of the Indian Diary Study for string orchestra, six wind instruments and timpani, Third Elegy for orchestra, 1915.

33 Busoni, letter of July 22, 1913 to Gerda Busoni, in *Letters to His Wife*, 228-229.
34 Busoni went so far in his admiration of Native American people that he began inventing names for himself: "Your Ferromann, Pappaferro, Mannpappa (which sounds Indian too)" Busoni, letter of March 10, 1911, to Gerda Busoni, in *Letters to His Wife*, 187.
35 Curtis-Burlin, *Indian's Book*, 41.
36 Curtis-Burlin, *Indian's Book*, 42.
37 Davis, "Polyphonic Harmony in Three of Ferruccio Busoni's Orchestral Elegies," 141.
38 The community lived in Nebraska and northern Kansas historically, even if they are headquartered today in Oklahoma.
39 See, for instance: Horowitz, *Dvořák's Prophecy: And the Vexed Fate of Black Classical Music*.
40 Walker, "Towards a Decolonized Music History Curriculum," 15.
41 Fick, "Systems of Power, Privilege, and Oppression."
42 Cochran, "Reading Primary Sources Analytically" and Howe, "Against Abridgement."
43 Cochran, "Roundtable Introduction," 69.
44 Dvořák's recognition of the uniqueness of the music can be attributed to the common practice of using folk melodies as a basis for a national style in terms of rhythm and melody. However, the situation is complicated by the fact that most U.S. classical composers would not be discovering their own roots in the melodies, but rather, the voice of a colonized and subjugated people. The national style of music he thus proposed was one that would have been built out of blood and suppression.
45 Seaton, "Teaching Based 'Off of' the Canon," 192.
46 Meyer, "Teaching Across Difference: Music History Pedagogy in an Era of Polarization," 233.

References

Baker, Theodore. *Über die Musik der nordamerikanischen Wilden*. Leipzig: Breitkopf und Härtel, 1882. Reprinted as *On the Music of the North American Indians*. Translated by Ann Buckley. New York: Da Capo Press, 1977.
Beckerman, Michael. "Dvořák's 'New World' Largo and 'The Song of Hiawatha'." *19th-Century Music* 16, no. 1 (Summer 1992): 35–48.
Browner, Tara. "'Breathing the Indian Spirit:' Thoughts on Musical Borrowing and the 'Indianist' Movement in American Music." *American Music* 15, no. 3 (Autumn 1997): 265–84.
Busoni, Ferruccio. "Letter of August 19, 1913 to Curtis-Burlin, Mus. Nachl. F. Busoni BI, 514, Musikabteilung mit Mendelssohn Archiv. Preussischer Kulturbesitz, Staatsbibliothek zu Berlin."
———. *Letters to His Wife*. Tanslated by Rosamond Ley. London: Edward Arnold & Co., 1938.

Clapham, John. "Dvořák and the American Indian." *The Musical Times* 107, no. 1484 (October 1966): 863–67.
Cochran, Timothy. "Reading Primary Sources Analytically." *Journal of Music History Pedagogy* 9 (2019): 79–89. Accessed January 27, 2023. https://www.ams-net.org/ojs/index.php/jmhp/article/view/285.
———. "Roundtable Introduction: Rethinking Primary Sources." *Journal of Music History Pedagogy* 9: 67–69. Accessed January 27, 2023. file:///Users/eknyt/Downloads/284-Article%20Text-2101-1-10-20190202%20(1).pdf.
Curtis-Burlin, Natalie. "Busoni's Indian Fantasy." *Southern Workman* XLIV, no. 10 (October 1915): 541.
———. *The Indian's Book: An Offering by the American Indians of Indian Lore, Musical and Narrative, to Form a Record of the Songs and Legends of their Race*. Recorded and edited by Natalie Curtis. New York: Harper and Brothers Publishers, 1907.
Davis, Colin. "Polyphonic Harmony in Three of Ferruccio Busoni's Orchestral Elegies." PhD Diss., University of North Texas, 2015.
———. "Music in America." *Harper's Magazine* (1895): 433.
Fick, Kimary. "Systems of Power, Privilege, and Oppression: Toward a Social Justice Education Pedagogy for the Music History Curriculum." *Journal of Music History Pedagogy* 12 (2022): 46–67. Accessed January 26, 2023. http://ams-net.org/ojs/index.php/jmhp/article/view/329.
———. *Indian Story and Song from North America*. Boston: Small, Maynard, 1900.
Horowitz, Joseph. *Dvořák's Prophecy: And the Vexed Fate of Black Classical Music*. New York: W.W. Norton, 2021.
Howe, Blake. "Against Abridgement." *Journal of Music History Pedagogy*. Accessed January 27, 2023. https://www.ams-net.org/ojs/index.php/jmhp/article/view/286.
Lowens, Irving. "New York Years of MacDowell." PhD Diss., University of Michigan, 1971.
MacDowell, Edward. *Critical and Historical Essays*. Edited by W. J. Baltzell. New York: Da Capo Press, 1969.
———. Interview. *San Francisco Chronicle* (January 3, 1903).
Meyer, Stephen. "Teaching Across Difference: Music History Pedagogy in an Era of Polarization." In *The Norton Guide to Teaching Music History*, edited by C. Matthew Balensuela, 224–234. New York: W. W. Norton, 2019.
Seaton, Douglas. "Teaching 'Off of' the Canon." In *The Norton Guide to Teaching Music History*, edited by C. Matthew Balensuela, 184–194. New York: W. W. Norton, 2019.
Walker, Margaret E. "Towards a Decolonized Music History Curriculum." *Journal of Music History Pedagogy* 10 (2020): 1–19. Accessed January 26, 2023. https://www.ams-net.org/ojs/index.php/jmhp/article/view/310.

4 Examining Vernacular Borrowings to Denaturalize Western Art Music
The Case of "Hoe-Down"

Esther M. Morgan-Ellis

A survey of Western art music is certain to include examples of works for which the composer drew inspiration from outside musical traditions. Sometimes, as in the case of Hungarian composer Béla Bartók's engagement with Eastern European and Middle Eastern folk music, the practice of borrowing is examined in terms of musical nationalism, or the modernist compulsion to develop a unique compositional approach. Other times, as with French composer Claude Debussy's imitations of Javanese gamelan, students are told that the composer was looking for new sounds to expand their palette, or was engaging in orientalist practices fashionable at the time.[1] Although composers drawing on vernacular sources have professed various motivations and applied a range of techniques, they share something important in common: when they adapt the borrowed musical material to its new context, they make decisions—conscious or otherwise—about which elements to retain and which to discard. By leading students to critically examine this process, we can reveal the narrowness and cultural specificity of Western art music practices.

In this chapter, I will theorize the "composer's ear" in the context of a specific musical example that is familiar to many students and frequently included in the music history curriculum: the "Hoe-Down" from Aaron Copland's 1942 ballet *Rodeo*. This example includes a relatively straightforward borrowing from the Appalachian fiddling tradition, for Copland's melody is taken from a 1937 recording of "Bonaparte's Retreat" made by Kentucky fiddler William Hamilton "Fiddler Bill" Stepp. Students can immediately recognize that Copland used Stepp's melody and rhythms, but careful listening to the source recording will reveal the many musical elements that Copland passed over—perhaps because he considered them inessential, perhaps because he did not "hear" them at all (a term I will use in both the literal and metaphorical sense), or perhaps because the limitations inherent in orchestral notation and technique made them inaccessible. Introducing students to the practices and values of Appalachian fiddling—oral transmission, tune families, and

DOI: 10.4324/9781003415954-6

idiosyncrasies in performance style, for example—will further expose the gulf between the vernacular and Western art music worlds, even when the same instrument is being used in each context. Ideally, students will come away from the encounter with a heightened ability to evaluate the orchestral tradition "from the outside," as it were, without assumptions of universality.

I will not provide a great deal of detail regarding either Aaron Copland and his ballet or William Stepp. Information on the former is available in most textbooks and on the Internet, and I will cite some recommended sources as I mention relevant details. For a complete biography of Stepp and a detailed account of how "Bonaparte's Retreat" came to be recorded and popularized, the reader should consult Stephen Wade's 2000 article in *American Music*, which is also highly suitable to assign to undergraduates either in part or in full. Wade spent several years tracking down Stepp's neighbors and descendants, piecing together details from archival and ethnographic sources to tell the story of this well-known tune. I will reference his findings frequently as I outline my approach to teaching this topic. However, it is my intent to treat the reader roughly the same as I treat my students, leaving them "in the dark," as it were, until I think the time is right to provide essential information.

The Composer's Ear

When I speak of the "composer's ear," I refer to the process by which someone trained in Western art music makes sense of musical material with the intent of transcribing or adapting it. The composer's ear is constituted by a lifetime of practice in listening critically to Western art music. It is adapted to predominantly homophonic textures, quick to discern between melody and accompaniment. It is likely to "hear" harmonies, even when they are absent (see Erinn Knyt's chapter in this volume for an example). It is predisposed to map unfamiliar material onto standardized patterns of pitch (e.g., diatonic modes, equal-tempered intonation) and rhythm (e.g., pulse, meter), even when these are insufficient. The composer's ear is a superb and finely-honed tool, and I do not mean to disparage it. However, it perceives all music through filters manufactured by and for the Western concert repertoire.

The composer's ear is shaped by and expressed through staff notation. Staff notation reifies the pitch and rhythm patterns referenced above, making them seem natural and inescapable. As the medium through which the composer communicates with performers, staff notation necessitates the shedding of stylistic characteristics, for it is not well-suited to the documentation of style; regarding the fiddle, for example, it cannot represent subtleties of bow speed/pressure/placement, arm tension, or timbre.

I begin by reminding my students that when two people listen to the same music, they do not hear the same thing. Although sound can be quantified in terms of its wave characteristics, our perception of it is infinitely more complicated. What we "hear" is shaped by our experiences as listeners and musicians, which in turn reflect a lifetime of acculturation and practice.[2] In her chapter in this volume, Qingfan Jiang considers the inability of 18th-century Chinese listeners to appreciate French harpsichord and flute compositions; they listened to the same thing as French audiences, but did not "hear" the same thing. This phenomenon is not limited to listeners from different cultural backgrounds. In the course of teaching music appreciation for over a decade, I have been surprised time and again by the gulf that separates my listening experience from those of many of my students. It is not just that we have different tastes and preferences, or different emotional responses; they simply do not hear what I hear.

Although I cannot know exactly what my students hear, I can understand how different it must be because I am aware of how my own perceptions have transformed over time. I remember finding atonal music meaningless and distasteful as a high school student, before experiences in college music history helped me to develop a more productive approach to listening. I also remember the first time I heard a field recording of Appalachian fiddling. As part of a graduate seminar on American music, I watched the 1980 documentary *Homemade American Music*, which features North Carolina fiddler Tommy Jarrell (1901–1985) in the first segment.[3] At the time, I thought the noise he made was simply appalling, and I couldn't imagine how anyone could find value in it. Eight years later I started fiddling myself, and I now enjoy listening to Jarrell more than anything. I've spent countless hours studying his recordings and videos and have learned Jarrell's style directly from his own students, including Kirk Sutphin, James Leva, and Brad Leftwich. In this process, I have (to some degree) transcended the hearing limitations imposed by an education in Western art music and developed a new set of parameters for perceiving and evaluating an alternative musical practice.[4]

Listening to "Bonaparte's Retreat"

I begin this lesson not with Copland but with Stepp. Doing so emphasizes that Stepp is more than grist for the composer's mill. It also provides students with an opportunity to critically assess the limitations of their own hearing, and to begin developing the complex skill of listening to old-time[5] fiddling on its own terms. Stepp's recording, made in 1937 by Alan and Elizabeth Lomax while collecting in Kentucky on behalf of the Library of Congress, is readily available online.[6] "Bonaparte's Retreat" was one of 17 tunes that Stepp played for the pair on October 25 at his Salyersville home. Like most Appalachian fiddlers, Stepp was not a professional musician in the modern sense; although he made some money playing for dances, he supported his family primarily by means of manual labor. However, he had a local reputation for speed and virtuosity on the instrument. As his nephew Arnold McFarland put it, "Now, Bill Stepp hit it at a dog race. I mean he moved along. He fiddled like he meant it."[7] According to his granddaughter, Dorothy Allen, crowds of ten or fifteen people regularly gathered on Stepp's porch to hear him play, especially when the weather impeded work. He often used "Bonaparte's Retreat" to close out his porchfront programs.[8] Alan Lomax, writing to a colleague, described Stepp as "the best fiddler I have heard in Ky."[9]

First, we listen as a class and observe all that we can about the sound object itself. I ask students what they hear, and I specifically encourage them to address each of the typical musical elements in turn. Regarding pitch, does Stepp seem to be playing in tune, or out of tune? Stepp is usually playing two pitches simultaneously; which line is the melody? Can they sing it? What rhythms emerge from the texture? Can they tap or clap them? Does Stepp maintain a steady tempo? How might one describe his timbre? Next, I ask them to consider how their own musical backgrounds might shape their perceptions. If students suggest that Stepp plays out of tune, for example, I ask: *why* does he seem out of tune? Where does your concept of "in tune" come from? Are the pitches consistently placed in each iteration of the melody? If so, does that not indicate Stepp intended to tune them exactly as he did—that they are "in tune"? If students note that Stepp increases his tempo, I ask: is that an "error," or a stylistic feature, or even a key characteristic of the tune itself? (Some commentators have ascribed programmatic meaning to the tempo change, which is present in recordings by various fiddlers, suggesting that we are hearing Bonaparte's hasty retreat sounded in performance.[10])

Next, we map the form of "Bonaparte's Retreat." A single listening should reveal that the tune has two main parts, the second of which is played in both the low and high octaves. These are typical characteristics; most old-time fiddle tunes have a binary structure, constituted of what many traditional musicians call the "course strain" (played on the lower strings) and the "fine strain" (played on the higher strings). Either strain can be transposed by an octave if it fits within the playable range of the instrument. On repeated listening, students might notice that the high variation of the B strain actually has several extra beats, or that Stepp concludes with an A strain—both distinctive characteristics.

Outlining the form of Stepp's performance should lead to other questions. Is this a recording of a fixed composition that is always rendered exactly as captured? Does Stepp stop playing because the tune is over, or for another reason? Stepp plays two low-octave B strains before switching to the upper-octave variation; does that pattern seem to be integral to the tune, or would a different approach—say, alternating the two versions—be equally valid? As students consider these questions, it becomes necessary to provide some contextual information. They need to know, for example, that the Lomaxes used a cumbersome disc recorder that could only capture a few minutes of sound, and that might have been off-putting for the performer.[11] Stepp was demonstrating the tune for outsiders, as evidenced by his exclamation, "Here's the bony part!" It is likely that he would have played it for a longer time and perhaps with greater flexibility for the friends who frequently gathered on his porch in the evenings, or for dancers.

There are additional elements to this performance that students might hear, but that will require further explanation. One concerns tuning. While a violin is most always tuned GDAE (from bottom to top), Appalachian fiddlers use a wide variety of tunings to play in different keys. Stepp plays "Bonaparte's Retreat" in DDAD tuning, which allows him to double up the top-octave D, playing it simultaneously on the top two strings, and to supply a low drone while playing in the lower octave. These characteristics are not incidental, but integral; the tune cannot be played accurately in standard tuning. In addition to facilitating distinctive harmonies produced on adjacent strings, DDAD tuning simplifies the procedure of transposing the B strain to a higher octave, which would otherwise require a difficult string crossing. The tuning might also play a programmatic role; in 1935, folklorist Bascom Lamar Lunsford claimed that the low D string "is supposed to represent the drum in retreat."[12] (The unusual tuning also explains why Stepp always played "Bonaparte's Retreat" last, since it takes time to adjust the strings so radically.) Another element concerns bowing, which is similarly integral, and which produces the rhythms that students might have observed. While classical violinists tend to think of slurs as discrete units, fiddlers think in terms of bowing patterns, which operate on a higher level.

Finally, I ask students how they would go about transcribing this performance for replication by a violinist. Are there elements of Stepp's playing that cannot be represented using staff notation? How might we expect the playing of a classical violinist to differ, even assuming the transcription captures every note and rhythm? What characteristics of this performance cannot be translated to an orchestral context? After considering these questions, we examine two such transcriptions. The first was published in John and Alan Lomax's 1941 collection *Our Singing Country* (see Figure 4.1).[13] This transcription—along with all the rest in the volume—was produced by composer and folklorist Ruth Crawford Seeger, who spent many years listening repeatedly to the Lomaxes' field recordings, intent on capturing every detail to the best of her ability. Her transcription is highly accurate; Harry Bolick and Stephen T. Austin describe her as "one of the foremost

Figure 4.1 This transcription of "Bonyparte," as the Lomaxes identified the tune, was produced by Ruth Crawford Seeger and published in *Our Singing Country* (1941).

composer-transcribers of the twentieth century," noting the skill with which she balanced accuracy and playability.[14] Students, however, should notice certain curiosities. To begin with, Seeger notes the DDAD tuning as "probable," betraying an insecurity with the fiddling tradition. Even in the correct tuning, her transcription is not playable as-is due to the fact that, while she has included drone notes and rhythms, she has omitted the bowings for the melody line. In a footnote on the next page, she confesses that "The bowing [...] could not be determined with sufficient accuracy to allow its notation."

The second transcription comes from a much more recent volume, Clare Milliner and Walt Koken's 2011 *The Milliner-Koken Collection*

Figure 4.2 This transcription of "Bonaparte's Retreat" was produced by Clare Milliner and published in *The Milliner-Koken Collection of American Fiddle Tunes* (2011). Used with permission.

of American Fiddle Tunes (see Figure 4.2). While Milliner was aware of Seeger's work, she created a new transcription directly from the recording itself. Her process, however, was similar; it began with repeated, careful listening, and concluded with three formal reviews of every transcription included in the volume, with Koken's assistance.[15] Like Seeger, Milliner has a background in classical music. However, at the time she began this transcription project, she was deeply immersed in old-time fiddling, giving her an embodied perspective to which Seeger did not have access. She also had different motivations; while Milliner, like Seeger, is concerned with preservation and authenticity, she first began transcribing to facilitate her own playing of the tunes in participatory contexts.

Milliner's transcription is, of course, similar to Seeger's, but there are significant differences, each of which students should be able to quickly recognize and discuss. You might begin by asking your students, how does each transcriber approach the task of representing form, and why do they arrive at different solutions? The answer is that Milliner, as a fiddler writing for other fiddlers, is thinking in terms of an open-ended binary tune with A and B strains, while Seeger set out to represent the entire performance as a self-contained work. Students will also notice pitch and rhythm differences. You might have them follow along with each transcription in turn and debate who got it right; but even more interesting is the question, how can disagreement arise between two such skillful and qualified transcribers? Is there something about the style or sound object that resists notation? The two transcribers agreed on one point: bowings are to be omitted. Like Seeger, Milliner chose not to indicate bowings because it is impossible to derive them with certainty from an audio recording. However, she emphasizes their significance and instructs players to consult the original source. She also believes that the bowings come naturally to a player who executes pitches exactly as the original fiddler did.[16] Finally, Milliner and Koken made the decision to omit all bar lines. This is due to the fact that most of the tunes in their collection are "crooked," meaning that one or both strains has an irregular number of beats. They felt that meter changes in the transcriptions of crooked tunes would be arbitrary, and that if they were going to omit bar lines in the crooked tunes then it was only sensible to forgo them altogether.

From Cabin Porch to Ballet Theater

At this point, I get to drop a bombshell: Aaron Copland (1900–1990) probably never heard Stepp's recording. Instead, he came across Seeger's transcription while searching for a fiddle tune to use in the climactic scene of *Rodeo*, and most likely lifted it directly from her notation. In this respect, we are dealing with two "composers' ears": the literal ear of Seeger, who translated Stepp's performance into notation, and the metaphorical ear of Copland, who sought to capture the sound and energy of fiddling in his score. Copland was certainly no stranger to vernacular tradition, and he sought out both live performances and field recordings of vernacular music-making throughout North America. However, when it came to the work of composing, he preferred to engage with notated transcriptions.[17] As Copland remarked in a 1982 interview, "give me a book of tunes and I'll immediately know what tune attracts me and what one doesn't. [...] I can play a tune out of a book and think: 'Gee, this is a good tune—but I could never work with it.' I can't tell you why exactly."[18] When Copland "listened" to these tunes, therefore, it was through the filters of both notation and an equal-tempered piano.

As a theatrical work, *Rodeo* reflects the collaborative vision of several artists. The leading creative force was dancer and choreographer Agnes de Mille (1905–1993), who wrote the synopsis and presented Copland with a fully developed vision for the ballet, which had been commissioned by the Ballet Russe de Monte Carlo. A complete account of the ballet's conception and contents, suitable for undergraduate readers, can be found in chapter 20 of Howard Pollack's biography, *Aaron Copland: The Life and Work of an Uncommon Man*. After convincing Copland to join in her creative endeavor, de Mille supplied him with her own transcription of the herding song "I Ride an Old Paint" and encouraged him to seek out other tunes.[19] Copland had drawn from vernacular sources in a number of previous works, including his first "frontier" ballet, *Billy the Kid* (1938), for which impresario Lincoln Kirstein supplied him with several anthologies of cowboy songs.²⁰ For the concluding "Hoe-Down" scene, de Mille provided Copland with a detailed outline that included moods, tempos, timings, styles, dynamics, instrumentation, and even measure counts:

> *Introduction—16–24 measures—girl appears.*
> *Pause and silence for about 4 counts while she faces boy.*
> *Dance begins on walk—hit a fiddle tune hard.*
> *Verse and chorus with brass yells and whoops.*
> *Vamps in-between,*
> *long tacet toward close for tap cadenza,*
> *8 measures of frenzy.*
> *Kiss, tacet or pianissimo.*
> *Finale windup—the beginning of the tune again,*
> *curtain comes down as the big promenade starts.*²¹

While "Hoe-Down" features Stepp's tune in the external sections of its ternary form, the central passage includes snippets of the fiddle tunes "Miss McCleod's Reel," "Gilderoy," and "Tip Toe, Pretty Betty Martin," all of which Copland found in Ira W. Ford's 1940 collection *Traditional Music of America*.²² Elizabeth Crist has additionally suggested that he borrowed phrase endings from a version of "Arkansas Traveler" found in the same volume, as well as elements from Ford's guide to accompanying tunes on the piano.²³ (Piano accompaniments, although anachronistic, were a typical feature of folk music publications, since they facilitated domestic performance by literate urban musicians. It is interesting to consider how Copland might have been influenced by this practice.) The ballet was an enormous success when it premiered at the Metropolitan Opera House on October 16, 1942, due in large part to de Mille's evocative choreography and charismatic performance as the Cowgirl. Copland's score, however, was also well received, and went on to win acclaim in its own right as an orchestral suite, *Four Dance Episodes from Rodeo* (1943), which was premiered by Arthur Fiedler and the Boston Pops on May 28, 1943. Copland streamlined "Hoe-Down" to serve as the finale, removing passages that made little musical sense without the accompanying stage action.

Much has been written about the nature of Copland's "Americanist" style, as well as his motivations for developing it. Scholars have repeatedly traced the origins of Copland's musical nationalism to the years he spent in Paris, where he studied composition with Nadia Boulanger and first became aware of a unique "American" cultural identity.²⁴ His interest in vernacular music was later spurred on by his commitment to left-wing politics (folk music is also working-class music) and the Great

Depression, which inspired many composers to abandon lofty experimentation in favor of populist works with broad appeal.[25] The onset of World War II, which set the stage for de Mille's commission, further heightened interest in explicitly "American" concert works, although the ensuing Cold War saw Copland called before the House Committee on Un-American Activities to explain his past ties to Communist organizations.[26]

Ask your students: what did "Bonaparte's Retreat" *mean* to Copland? What did it *mean* to Stepp? The perspectives of these two men, although both white Americans, could hardly have been more different. Copland, the well-educated son of Jewish Russian immigrants, grew up in Brooklyn and spent his formative years in Europe. He had a broad knowledge of music spanning historical and modernist classical works, jazz, popular song, and a variety of vernacular traditions. From these, he borrowed and adapted elements to support his own compositional efforts. Stepp was one of three children born to a prominent white man and Lucinda Stepp, a Nottoway[27] woman who worked as a domestic and prostitute. Stepp's father never acknowledged him, and he lived in a cave with his mother (who was periodically incarcerated for pursuing her trade) until being removed to the care of a local landowner sometime before he was five.[28] As an adult, Stepp worked as a manual laborer and farmer, although surviving family members recall that he "cared little for workaday toil;" music was his one true passion.[29] Like many Appalachian fiddlers, Stepp learned informally from a male relative (an uncle) and spent little time in school. It does not seem that he ever traveled more than a few counties from his birthplace, and it is unlikely that he had much interest in politics. His views were probably quite conservative and generally out-of-step with Copland's. While he would have encountered a variety of popular styles either by means of phonograph recordings or performances by itinerant musicians, he was indigenous to the fiddling tradition, and his activities as a musician were integral to his participation in the local community.[30] Stepp, like many fiddlers, may also have valued the narrative and programmatic associations of "Bonaparte's Retreat," which was widely connected with fictionalized accounts of the military leader—a program that had no significance for Copland.[31]

Problematizing the "Work Concept"

What is "Hoe-Down" from *Rodeo*? Although an in-depth discussion of this question might take some interesting twists and turns (this is a work that has been uncoupled from its dramatic origins, arranged for all manner of ensembles, and resituated in various contexts), it is not controversial to claim that "Hoe-Down" consists of a specific number of metrical units containing specific pitches and rhythms, perhaps assigned to specific instruments, and all brought into concord by the composer Aaron Copland.

What is "Bonaparte's Retreat"? This is a more difficult question to answer. Stepp's is but one version of a tune that has traveled widely by means of oral tradition. Generally speaking, the tune seems to have derived from a family of Bonaparte songs known collectively as "The Island of St. Helena" or "Boney's in St. Helena." However, it has also been connected with an Irish pipe march called "The Eagle's Whistle."[32] Countless versions of "Bonaparte's Retreat" have been and are still played by countless fiddlers, each of whom has altered elements from other sources to suit their own needs, preferences, and playing style. Students will be interested to explore the network of "Bonaparte's Retreat" tunes, more than 60 of which are documented on the website Slippery Hill.[33] These versions include commercial "hillbilly" records from the 1920s, more recent commercial recordings, and field and home recordings made throughout the 20th century. Ask your students: what does it mean to claim that these are all recordings of "the same tune"? Is there an immutable characteristic that constitutes the fiddle tune "Bonaparte's Retreat"? If your teaching space and class size allow, you might divide students into groups and assign each four or five recordings to compare and contrast, with the task of assembling a list of possible "immutable characteristics." When the students come back together, they can share their observations and try to create a master list. Given the great variety in tempos, tunings, forms, phrase lengths, and melodies, however, they will find it difficult to pin down the identity of this tune. The issue is further complicated by the fact that a number of tunes known by different titles also share elements with "Bonaparte's Retreat," such as the Earl Collins's "Miller Boy," also in DDAD tuning.[34]

If taking on the entire catalog of "Bonaparte's Retreat" recordings is too great a task, I recommend comparing Stepp's version with those of Tommy Jarrell (North Carolina, 1901–1985),[35] Gaither Carlton (North Carolina, 1901–1972),[36] Ralph Blizard (Tennessee, 1918–2004),[37] Clyde Davenport (Kentucky, 1921–2020),[38] and The Skillet Lickers (Georgia, active 1926–1931).[39] Students will marvel at the variety represented in these recordings, all of which were made by important and influential Southern fiddlers. Several share elements—left-hand pizzicato, for example—that are absent from Stepp's rendition. Students might also notice that other versions contain irregular numbers of beats in one or both strains (they are "crooked," in fiddlers' parlance), in contrast to Stepp's largely "square" rendition. For a further twist, you might play the 1975 recording by Al Cherney (Ontario, 1932–1989),[40] which reflects Cajun influence and includes a C strain taken from the familiar Tin Pan Alley song "The Streets of Cairo" (James Thornton, 1895).[41]

Exposure to any subset of these recordings should lead students to note a significant idiosyncrasy in Stepp's performance: while all of these fiddlers record "Bonaparte's Retreat" at a stately march tempo, Stepp turns it into a breakdown. In that respect, Stepp's version of "Bonaparte's Retreat" is a singularly poor representative of the tune. Indeed, in her landmark 1975 study of Southern fiddling, ethnomusicologist Linda Burman-Hall selected "Bonaparte's Retreat" for analysis as "as the only surviving widespread example of the slow fiddle-tune not intended for dance music."[42] However, due to Copland's intervention, it is Stepp's dance-tempo version of "Bonaparte's Retreat" that has come to dominate in the American consciousness. When Agnes de Mille instructed Copland to "hit a fiddle tune hard" for the Hoe-Down scene, she demanded a lively dance number; the tempo marking of quarter note = 138 in Seeger's transcription indicated that Stepp's "Bonaparte's Retreat" could fit the bill.[43] Copland's selection of the tune, however, ignores—even erases—its historical development and significance.

Why This Lesson Matters

This lesson promises a range of significant learning outcomes, from the specific to the general. At the very least, it will provide your students with important insights into a well-known piece of music. Hopefully, however, it will also reveal the limitations of both Western art music practices and their own ears, open a window onto a rich vernacular tradition that operates according to principles largely divorced from those of the concert hall, and spark their curiosity—and caution—regarding other cases of cross-cultural borrowing in the Western art music tradition.

The danger of ignorance on these topics is illustrated by a 2000 New York University doctoral dissertation on Copland's *Four Dance Episodes from Rodeo*. In it, the author—a composer—acknowledges that Copland borrowed a tune known as "Bonyparte" (the title used in the Lomaxes' collection), but seems ignorant of the fact that "Bonyparte" is not a unique composition. The author reprints a version that bears limited resemblance to Stepp's, and then credits Copland with reworking the tune into its familiar form. The resulting claims are entirely inaccurate.[44] This error might have been averted with more careful research, but ideally our students will know better than to project the norms of Western concert music onto outside musical traditions. They will know that concepts of "composer" and "work" do not translate effortlessly across cultural boundaries. Students might also be led to question the near-ubiquitous characterization of folk tunes as "simple"—a description applied both by Copland himself and by scholars who analyze his work.[45] While a fiddle tune might seem "simple" after it has been reduced to a sequence of chromatic pitches and metric rhythms, such a perspective is highly limited.

This approach to examining the borrowing process also centers the source tradition, encouraging students to engage with that tradition on its own terms and perceive it as complete, nuanced, and valuable. While I hope instructors will apply the same template to other examples, even this one experience can change the way students think about similar instances. What other misconceptions do we hold about vernacular traditions because of decisions made by ill-informed cultural representatives, whether composers, popular entertainers, or folklorists? How have other attempts to integrate outside influences into Western art music been hampered by the limitations of the tradition and its assumptions? Asking these questions—whether or not we find all the answers—reveals the closely inscribed boundaries of a practice that has long claimed universality.

This lesson might also lead your students to reflect on continuing practices of cross-cultural borrowing and collaboration. In his 2020 monograph *Hungry Listening*, Dylan Robinson considers recent collaborations between classical artists/institutions and Indigenous musicians. He finds that, although Indigenous artists seem to be increasingly included in the concert music scene, they are almost always required to adapt their contributions to classical norms of music presentation and consumption, with the results that "inclusionary efforts bolster an intransigent system of presentation guided by an interest in—and even a fixation upon—Indigenous content, but not Indigenous structure."[46] While Copland and Stepp have long passed away, the questions of why and how Western art music powerbrokers engage with outside traditions and their individual practitioners have never been more pressing.

Although I see no profit in passing moral judgment on Copland's engagement with vernacular musics, it is hard to read about Stepp's impoverished circumstances and not find it at least unfortunate that he never benefited from the widespread and lasting success of "Hoe-Down." How did 1930s-era social, institutional, and legal structures lead to Stepp dying in anonymity and poverty, while the Lomaxes, Seeger, and Copland were able to profit from his genius? How do these structures continue to deny profit to working-class artists today? When Wade visited the 1999 Stepp family reunion, he played the 1937 recording of "Bonaparte's Retreat" for Stepp's descendants in a medley with Copland's "Hoe-Down." For those present, it was a revelation that their ancestor was the source for a famous tune—one they all recognized from its use in Beef Industry Council commercials. However, Stepp's family reacted not with indignation at an act of appropriation, but with pride that their private family heritage had become a part of U.S. heritage.[47]

Stepp's Alternate Legacy

In the world of concert music—and indeed, within mainstream American culture generally—Stepp's legacy begins and ends with his now-ubiquitous version of "Bonaparte's Retreat." This alone would make him a historical figure worth remembering, but it so happens that Stepp's music is very much alive in another sphere: revivalist[48] old-time musicians in the United States and abroad study, play, and celebrate his tunes, keeping them in the repertoire as informal jam tunes, contest numbers, and fodder for the recording studio. In this scene, "Bonaparte's Retreat," although familiar, is not Stepp's most influential tune. This is due in part, certainly, to it's unusual tuning, which makes it inconvenient to play in the jam session setting. Instead, Stepp's "Ways of the World," played in the common AEAE tuning,[49] is in the repertoires of countless jam groups, as is his G tune "The Rebels' Raid," played in standard tuning.[50]

Contemporary old-time musicians have a different use for Stepp's tunes. In the festival and jam scenes, they are vehicles for collective participation. (At the 2022 Appalachian String Band Festival in Clifftop, WV, I believe I heard "Ways of the World" played more often than any other tune, and I played it several times myself.[51]) In contests, skilled players perform Stepp's tunes to exhibit their virtuosity, striving to replicate his speed, precision, and crisp ornamentation. Almost all players learn the tunes by ear, choosing to adhere closely to Stepp's 1937 recordings, simplify his melodies, or add variations as suits their personal ability and preference. Old-time players, who tend to be fanatical about the history of their music, are much more likely than classical concertgoers to know about Stepp and his encounter with the Lomaxes. Their love for the tunes often inspires an insatiable thirst for knowledge about them.

As such, this classroom encounter with Stepp creates an opportunity to introduce your students to an alternate world of contemporary music-making and emphasize the gulf that separates participatory and presentational practices.[52] When Copland used Stepp as a resource, it was for the purpose of integrating regional and programmatic flavor into a set of fixed instructions (that is, notation) to be executed by paid, highly trained performers for an attentive, paying audience. Although "Hoe-Down" continues to be performed in various theatrical and concert contexts, it is always, to put it in the simplest terms, *performed*—a presentational construct that mandates distinct roles for skilled musicians and (perhaps unskilled) auditors. When old-time musicians draw on Stepp, they seek to imaginatively inhabit his playing for the purpose, most often, of engaging directly with other members of a participatory community. In doing so, they aim to replicate not only Stepp's melodies, as Copland did in "Hoe-Down," but his holistic technique, including tuning, bowing, intonation, timbre, and ornaments. They are also likely to value rural settings for music-making, whether front porches or campgrounds. This mode of engagement is not necessarily more authentic or respectful than Copland's. Both composers of art music and present-day revivalists put traditional music to uses that would never have been imagined—and in some cases may well have been disdained—by historical culture bearers. Indeed, revivalists, who are often comparatively wealthy and well-educated, have much more in common with the concert hall elite than with Stepp, an illegitimate child who lived in a cave for five years before entering foster care, rafted logs (and later farmed) to make a living, and never had access to formal education.[53] Instead, "Hoe-Down" and a festival jam session should be understood as representing two distinct lines of historical development, one of which adapts Appalachian fiddling to the presentational values of the concert hall, and the other of which adapts it to the participatory values of revivalist gatherings.

Conclusion: Applying This Lens Across the Curriculum

I have chosen here to focus very closely on a narrow example. I have done so in order to demonstrate the riches that await discovery if this approach is applied to any example of concert music that draws from a vernacular tradition—and these examples are countless. In the Internet era, it is often not difficult to track down recordings of and detailed information about vernacular tunes and traditions, and even brief consideration can greatly enrich student learning. I know less about Eastern European folk music than Appalachian fiddling, for example, but many of Bartók's field recordings are available online, and I always include them in my classroom presentations, whether we are discussing *Romanian Folk Dances* in Music Appreciation or 14 Bagatelles, Op. 6 No. 4 in Music History III. The same types of questions apply in every case: what did the composer take from their source, and why? What did they ignore, and why? What are the music-making values of the source musicians, so far as we can know, and how might they differ from those typical of Western art music? Even five minutes spent interrogating the "composer's ear" can help students to decenter the composer's perspective, denaturalize the practices of Western art music, and glimpse a world of musical practices and values beyond the Western concert hall.

Notes

1 If you are teaching this topic, do not overlook Danielle Fosler-Lussier's excellent open-access textbook *Music on the Move*, which addresses Debussy's engagement with gamelan from multiple perspectives using an approach similar to that which I recommend here (Fosler-Lussier, *Music on the Move*, 27-33).

2. For a summary of cognitive research on this topic, see Morrison and Demorest, "Cultural Constraints on Music Perception and Cognition."
3. Aginsky and Aginsky, *Homemade American Music*, 2:45–7:33.
4. My hearing is, of course, permanently shaped by my classical training, both in ways of which I am aware (e.g. I perceive all melodies in terms of scale degrees) and doubtless in others of which I am not.
5. The term "old-time," although contested, is broadly applied to the repertoire and practices associated with American fiddle and banjo traditions before World War II. For a close consideration of the term's history and connotations, see Reish, "On the Notion of 'Old-Time' in Country Music."
6. Today, most old-time players consult the website Slippery Hill when in search of historical recordings. It is an excellent resource for exploring the legacy both of Stepp and "Bonaparte's Retreat." His recording is available there: https://www.slippery-hill.com/content/bonapartes-retreat-48.
7. Wade, "The Route to 'Bonaparte's Retreat'," 351.
8. Wade, "The Route to 'Bonaparte's Retreat'," 347.
9. Wade, "The Route to 'Bonaparte's Retreat'," 353.
10. Tommy Jarrell, whose related version of "Bonaparte's Retreat" will be considered later, was documented as exclaiming, "That was Bonaparte retreatin' at the end" as he accelerated during his final repetition of the B strain (Milliner and Koken, *The Milliner-Koken Collection of American Fiddle Tunes*, 69).
11. "Making the Recordings," *The Lomax Kentucky Recordings*.
12. Wade, "The Route to 'Bonaparte's Retreat'," 356.
13. A later edition of this volume is currently available for digital borrowing through Internet Archive: https://archive.org/details/in.ernet.dli.2015.158045
14. Bolick and Austin, *Mississippi Fiddle Tunes and Songs From the 1930s*, 18.
15. Clare Milliner and Walt Koken, interview by the author, 13 September 2022.
16. Clare Milliner and Walt Koken, interview by the author, 13 September 2022.
17. Wade, "The Route to 'Bonaparte's Retreat'," 359.
18. Pollack, *Aaron Copland*, 468.
19. Wade, "The Route to 'Bonaparte's Retreat'," 358.
20. Garafola, "Making an American Dance," 127.
21. Copland and Perlis, *Copland: 1900 Through 1942*, 357.
22. Pollack, *Aaron Copland*, 367. A later edition of Ford's collection is currently available for digital borrowing through Internet Archive: https://archive.org/details/traditionalmusic0000ford
23. Crist, *Music for the Common Man*, 142; Ford, *Traditional Music of America*, 22-24.
24. Fauser, "Aaron Copland, Nadia Boulanger, and the Making of an 'American' Composer," 524.
25. Dickstein, "Copland and American Populism in the 1930s."
26. Crist, "Copland and the Politics of Americanism," 277.
27. The Nottoway are an Iroquoian people who continue to live in what is now Virginia.
28. Wade, "The Route of 'Bonaparte's Retreat'," 344–345.
29. Wade, "The Route of 'Bonaparte's Retreat'," 346.
30. With great effort, Wade has traced the rich network of Salyersville musicians who shared not only songs and tunes but family and community ties (Wade, "The Route of 'Bonaparte's Retreat'," 350–353).
31. Wade, "The Route to 'Bonaparte's Retreat'," 353–354.
32. Wade, "The Route to 'Bonaparte's Retreat'," 355.

33 "Bonaparte's Retreat" https://www.slippery-hill.com/taxonomy/term/16 (accessed 8 July 2022).
34 "Miller Boy" https://www.slippery-hill.com/content/miller-boy
35 https://www.slippery-hill.com/content/bonapartes-retreat-45
36 https://www.slippery-hill.com/content/bonapartes-retreat
37 https://www.slippery-hill.com/content/bonapartes-retreat-42. This version comes from Tennessee fiddler Arthur Smith (1898–1971).
38 https://www.slippery-hill.com/content/bonapartes-retreat-7
39 https://www.slippery-hill.com/content/bonapartes-retreat-32
40 https://www.slippery-hill.com/content/bonapartes-retreat-3
41 It appears that this strain originated with Pee Wee King, who added words to the fiddle tune and recorded "Bonaparte's Retreat" in 1950 (Hall, *Hell-Bent for Music*, 152). The "hoochie coochie" strain, as it is often referred to, is now commonly incorporated into the tune.
42 Burman-Hall, "Southern American Folk Fiddle Styles," 55.
43 Wade, "The Route of 'Bonaparte's Retreat'," 358.
44 Young Mi Ha, "Characteristics of Aaron Copland's American Style in Four Dance Episodes from Rodeo," 126.
45 Antokoletz, "Copland's Gift to Be Simple Within the Cumulative Mosaic Complexities of His Ballets," 255.
46 Robinson, *Hungry Listening*, 6.
47 Wade, "The Route of 'Bonaparte's Retreat'," 363–364.
48 I use this difficult and contested term here to indicate individuals who are not enculturated into a musical tradition, but instead discover and adopt it as adults.
49 https://www.slippery-hill.com/content/ways-world-0
50 https://www.slippery-hill.com/content/rebels-raid
51 This video captures a group of musicians playing "Ways of the World" at the 2017 Appalachian String Band Festival: https://youtu.be/MXYxipx7vdU
52 Turino, *Music as Social Life*, 33-36.
53 Wade, "The Route of 'Bonaparte's Retreat'," 345–346.

References

Aginsky, Carrie, and Yasha Aginsky. *Homemade American Music*. Carrie and Yasha Aginsky, 1980. 40 min. https://www.folkstreams.net/films/homemade-american-music.

Antokoletz, Elliott. "Copland's Gift to Be Simple Within the Cumulative Mosaic Complexities of His Ballets." In *Aaron Copland and His World*, edited by Carol J. Oja and Judith Tick, 255–74. Princeton: Princeton University Press, 2005.

Bolick, Harry, and Stephen T. Austin. *Mississippi Fiddle Tunes and Songs from the 1930s*. Jackson: University Press of Missippi, 2015.

Burman-Hall, Linda C. "Southern American Folk Fiddle Styles." *Ethnomusicology* 19, no. 1 (1975): 47–65.

Copland, Aaron, and Vivian Perlis. *Copland: 1900 Through 1942*. New York: St. Martin's Griffin, 1984.

Crist, Elizabeth B. "Copland and the Politics of Americanism." In *Aaron Copland and His World*, edited by Carol J. Oja and Judith Tick, 277–306. Princeton: Princeton University Press, 2005.

Crist, Elizabeth B. *Music for the Common Man: Aaron Copland During the Depression and War*. New York: Oxford University Press, 2005.

Dickstein, Morris. "Copland and American Populism in the 1930s." In *Aaron Copland and His World*, edited by Carol J. Oja and Judith Tick, 81–100. Princeton: Princeton University Press, 2005.

Fauser, Annegret. "Aaron Copland, Nadia Boulanger, and the Making of an 'American' Composer." *Musical Quarterly* 89, no. 4 (2006): 524–54.

Ford, Ira W. *Traditional Music of America*. Hatboro: Folklore Associates, Inc., 1965.

Fosler-Lussier, Danielle. *Music on the Move*. Ann Arbor: University of Michigan Press, 2020.

Garafola, Lynn. "Making an American Dance: *Billy the Kid*, *Rodeo*, and *Appalachian Spring*." In *Aaron Copland and His World*, edited by Carol J. Oja and Judith Tick, 121–47. Princeton: Princeton University Press, 2005.

Ha, Young Mi. "Characteristics of Aaron Copland's American Style in Four Dance Episodes from Rodeo." PhD diss., New York University, 2000.

Hall, Wade. *Hell-Bent For Music: The Life of Pee Wee King*. Lexington: University Press of Kentucky, 1996.

Lomax, John A., and Alan Lomax. *Our Singing Country: A Second Volume of American Ballads and Folk Songs*. New York: The Macmillan Company, 1949.

"Making the Recordings." *The Lomax Kentucky Recordings*. Accessed August 30, 2022. https://lomaxky.omeka.net/lomaxtech.

Milliner, Clare, and Walt Koken. *The Milliner-Koken Collection of American Fiddle Tunes*. Kennett Square: Mudthumper Music, 2011.

Morrison, Steven J., and Steven M. Demorest. "Cultural constraints on music perception and cognition." In *Cultural Neuroscience: Cultural Influences on Brain Function*, edited by Joan Chiao, 67–77. The Netherlands: Elsevier, 2009.

Pollack, Howard. *Aaron Copland: The Life and Work of an Uncommon Man*. Urbana: University of Illinois Press, 1999.

Reish, Gregory. "On the Notion of 'Old-Time' in Country Music." In *The Oxford Handbook of Country Music*, edited by Travis D. Stimeling, 117–40. New York: Oxford University Press, 2017.

Robinson, Dylan. *Hungry Listening: Resonant Theory for Indigenous Sound Studies*. Minneapolis: University of Minnesota Press, 2020.

Turino, Thomas. *Music as Social Life: The Politics of Participation*. Chicago: University of Chicago Press, 2008.

Wade, Stephen. "The Route of 'Bonaparte's Retreat': From 'Fiddler Bill' Stepp to Aaron Copland." *American Music* 18, no. 4 (2000): 343–69.

Part II
Teaching Blended Musics

5 Music of the Hyphen
Diaspora Music as Process and Product

Varshini Narayanan

The opportunity to contribute to a volume on the theme of "navigating stylistic boundaries" struck a deep personal chord for me as someone who has long negotiated themes of borders and crossings, fluidity and multiplicity, reciprocity and, indeed, dissonance in my personal, professional, and artistic lives. As a first-generation diaspora musician who studies and performs alongside other diaspora musicians, questions of ownership and belonging are central to my identity as both an artist and a scholar. What do appropriation and assimilation mean in a context where the boundaries between self and Other are themselves blurred, and where straightforward notions of hybridity are insufficient to capture the multiplicity and perpetual liminality that characterize the diaspora subject? What does it mean to make one's "own" music as someone who identifies equally with multiple cultural and artistic traditions? And what are the tools available to us as we attempt to understand musics that defy categorization and, in doing so, resist established metrics for analysis?

Musicians who work across genres often complicate established theories of hybridity and bi-musicality. When I sing jazz, my scatting draws unmistakably on Carnatic improvisation; my ornaments are born of *gamakka*; the chestiness of my vocal timbre is the result of childhood training in the Carnatic style. When I read Baroque counterpoint, it is the subconscious translation of notes and sequences into Carnatic *swara* that renders Bachian sequences more or less intuitive. Meanwhile, my operatic training has extended my Carnatic range by almost an octave, and my years of experience performing in jazz ensembles lends a certain angularity to my *swarakalpana*. What I describe here is not fusion. It is not a straightforward, superficial, or post-hoc bringing together of Eastern and Western elements. Rather, multiple influences are intertwined from the outset, leading to a creative process and a musical product that stage a dialogue between cultures and genres from the moment of their inception. This chapter considers music and artists that put multiple cultural and aesthetic influences in conversation, suggesting that our focus when teaching and analyzing such musics should be on the quality and nature of the interactions between genres, cultures, and styles. In particular, my research centers around music of the Indian-American diaspora that can be loosely described as Indo-jazz fusion, drawing on my own experiences as a performer in multiple traditions as well as ethnographic interviews with Indian-American artists whose work draws on a variety of musical and cultural influences. Diaspora music reflects a lifelong process of translation through and across disparate traditions that nonetheless results in a cohesive whole.

When music that synthesizes multiple influences is brought into the classroom, the challenge is to accept it on its own terms. Diasporic cultural production has historically been analyzed in terms of assimilation on the one hand and retentions on the other, with even uniquely diasporic art forms portrayed as a balancing act between these two poles. While these concepts are generally outmoded, they still find purchase in popular discussions of diaspora music, as purists lament the "Westernization" of classical forms and diasporic artists find themselves and their music superficially exoticized for the inclusion of home-culture elements. A recent study from Sarah Weiss revealed an intriguing pattern in university students' perceptions of "authenticity" and "hybridity" in world music, with relatively high value assigned to the former and less to the latter; hybridity and authenticity were also considered mutually exclusive, with so-called "pure" (often meaning precolonial) entities deemed more authentic.[1] This approach to description and analysis promotes a misguided notion of the supposed "purity" of more established traditions, and also reinforces a heteropatriarchal discourse that maintains a hierarchical and unidirectional relationship between diaspora and nation.[2] Put more simply, the music that emerges from global communities of artists often involves a more nuanced and agentive process than a straightforward acquiescence to local aesthetic norms.

As such, instructors should be aware of the potential for instinctual value judgments when discussing crossover or fusion musics. Students should be reminded to problematize the very notion of purity that undergirds these snap judgments, and encouraged to consider the reciprocity that informs any cross-cultural encounter even in the face of unequal power dynamics. In the case of the music I analyze here, it is not a matter of identifying Carnatic or Hindustani or even folk "retentions" in Indian diasporic music, but of seeing how multiple starting points lead to something that is at all times both and neither Indian and/nor American. The works of Tejaswini Niranjana and Tina Ramnarine on the Indo-Caribbean provide examples of what it might look like to consider diasporic cultural production on its own terms, with Ramnarine in particular emphasizing the importance of considering historicity alongside newness in our analyses of diasporic forms.[3]

Music of the Hyphen 107

Insofar as the usual theoretical frameworks leave something to be desired, then, the question of how to best describe diaspora music has dogged this project from its outset. While "hybridity" has proven useful for many postcolonial scholars, including Homi Bhabha and Stuart Hall, others such as Paul Gilroy have critiqued the hybridity concept insofar as hybridity presupposes the anterior purity of comprising elements. Meanwhile, "fusion" has acquired a sort of depreciated status among many musicians and is firmly disavowed by the majority of my interlocutors, perhaps in response to the proliferation of shallow and often appropriative genre-blending explorations in popular music in India as well as stateside. Faced with the insufficiency of existing descriptors, I have taken recourse in the long academic tradition of inventing my own. I analyze the music of my diaspora community in terms of "hyphenation," drawing on the orthographic symbol that enacts a simultaneous conjoining and separation of related terms. The hyphen represents my attempt to recuperate fusion as a practice if not a label. It forms a literal bridge that inextricably connects formative parts while articulating a wholeness—a single, unified identity and musical epistemology rather than one comprised of two separate influences—in a manner that forces us to explore the political implications of particular collaborations in search of resonances that go beyond the aesthetic. At the same time, as a line that demarcates a physical separation between constitutive elements, the hyphen embodies a certain irreconcilability that feels equally productive, reflective of the anxieties around authenticity that prove key for any discussion of minority and non-Western musics.

The questions at the heart of this chapter are: what are the theoretical frameworks best suited for classroom discussion of music and musicians that complicate such mainstream yet fraught concepts as ownership, appropriation, and belonging? What does it look like to take such art and artists on their own terms? What does "crossover" mean if we take seriously the idea that multiple cultural and musical influences can spring from and reside within the same source?

Musics with Indian or other Eastern influences are not unfamiliar to the world music and music history classrooms, but our metrics for describing and analyzing such musics are sorely in need of an update. We need to move beyond the pentatonic scales and perfunctory Eastern instrumentation of any number of Orientalist classical works and instead consider that, for artists who can truly claim ownership over multiple cultural forms, every musical tradition carries with it an entirely different way of thinking about melody and rhythm. As we analyze music that resides in the hyphenated space of Indo-jazz fusion, we might ask: what assumptions about melody and structure, rhythm and time, pitch and ornamentation, guide each artist's approach to composition and improvisation? How do

Indian and American elements interact, and with what success? What does it mean to perform in a way that doesn't just *sound* Indian, but *is* Indian, or more accurately, Indian-American? My comments here are limited to Indian and Indian-inspired music, focusing in particular on the music of the Indian-American diaspora; but I believe this mode of analysis is applicable to diaspora musics more broadly, as we continue to consider the ways migrant musicians make a new culture their own while still sounding their native idioms. This approach places performers and their identities at the center of the conversation, analyzing the sounds of the diaspora on their own terms. I begin with a case study that exemplifies hyphenation in both the process and products of diasporic musicking.

Case Study: *Of Agency and Abstraction*

> Abstraction involves a sublimation of the material, the embodied. It could also involve what philosopher Édouard Glissant has called a 'right to opacity,' or the liberty to remain unknowable within the gaze of power...each one of us have surrendered to our mutual and inner opacities, seeking gentle alignments and blurred boundaries through the shared time and movement occasioned by the music.
>
> — liner notes, *Of Agency and Abstraction*[4]

Per Glissant, opacity consists of an alterity that exceeds existing categories of quantifiable difference. Opacity is "that which cannot be reduced."[5] It exposes the limits of colonial schemas that deny multiplicity, and functions as an aesthetic proposition as well as an ontological condition, out of which "gentle alignments" are more viable than straightforward identification. The idea of "mutual opacities," then, provides a valuable structuring principle for the celebration of multiplicity and interweaving of individual agencies that characterizes Indian-American mridangist Rajna Swaminathan's debut album, *Of Agency and Abstraction*.[6]

Swaminathan began composing at a young age, as an organic outgrowth of her upbringing in a musical family and her formal studies in mridangam, piano, and Carnatic singing. Her explorations as a composer were complemented by a robust performance schedule as a mridangist, including yearly trips to India where she would give dozens of performances each concert season. Despite, and indeed due to, this full immersion in the classical Carnatic world, Swaminathan recounts an early childhood awareness of fusion and collaborative music as viable options for herself as a performer. She describes the way her mother would organize workshops and collaborations with jazz musicians and performers of other traditions for her guru Umayalpuram K. Sivaraman: "I kind of grew up around this possibility that there was this middle space...for me [there was] an early understanding that there could be some crossover." And indeed, discussing her own early forays into composition, Swaminathan paints a picture of a child of eight or nine sitting in her bedroom with a guitar singing raga-based phrases, through which she "discovered [her] own little hybrid sound world."[7]

Swaminathan's upbringing exemplifies what I am characterizing as "hyphenation" as both an identity and a performance complex. Born and raised in the United States, but spending summers in India and socializing within the Indian diaspora community, she necessarily would have cultivated an identity based on the mutual and reciprocal influences between these two spheres; her experiences in India were shaped by her status as an American and her experiences in the U.S. were contextualized by her socialization among Indians. Similarly, her musical influences were intertwined from the outset; early Carnatic lessons were complemented by Western piano and guitar, so that her formative musical experiences, which commingled to form a single musical sensibility, cannot be reduced to a combination of multiple isolated traditions but are characterized by dialogue and interaction. As I have previously noted, this framing might seem to be in direct contrast with established notions of bi-musicality; and indeed, my interpretation of Swaminathan's music as well as my own experience as a student and practitioner of multiple musical traditions would suggest that the experience described by bi-musicality ought not to be understood in terms of code-switching between disparate forms but instead in terms of an ongoing and often instantaneous translation process that results in a commingling of multiple forms of embodied knowledge.

Swaminathan's more recent ensemble project, RAJAS, centers on mutuality and collaborative exploration of the confluences between multiple approaches to improvisation, in particular traversing the resonances between Indian music, jazz, and "creative music" (a term for original music preferred by some as an alternative to "jazz," which is understood as a racialized category). On Swaminathan's Bandcamp page, the ensemble is described as follows: "RAJAS has brought together a network of like-minded improvisers from multiple/overlapping traditions to experiment with new horizons of relation through hybrid forms, textures, and sensibilities." The original compositions featured on the album are qualified by reference to a "deeply collaborative process" and "the unique ways in which each musician carried these forms," concluding with a promise of dynamism: "These pieces will continue to evolve as we keep learning how to align and coexist with one another…"

We might begin with the obvious. The composition of Swaminathan's ensemble is highly unorthodox. Jazz musicians Miles Okazaki, Stephan Crump, and María Grand on guitar, bass, and saxophone respectively are joined by Swaminathan herself on the mridangam and her sister Anjna Swaminathan on the violin, as well as Ganavya Doraiswami providing vocals in the style of *abhang* (a form of Marathi devotional poetry that has recently begun to be included in the Carnatic repertoire). The latter three performers have a substantial background in Carnatic music, while Okazaki, Crump, and Grand have all performed in genre-blending ensemble projects but can be most readily categorized as jazz musicians. It is important to note that although Swaminathan's page explicitly describes the project using the word "hybrid," she has since disavowed that label. In our 2020 interview, she described a "process of unravelling" and her growing disillusionment with the boundaries around existing genres, citing Carnatic music's historic entanglements with colonial modernity to suggest that most musical genres are themselves hybrids. Echoing Paul Gilroy's resistance to binary distinctions between hybridity and purity, Swaminathan states: "It's not like this is hybrid and that's pure, but everything comes out of these meetings and encounters." She discusses reviews of her album in which listeners describe the work as a mixture of Carnatic music and jazz, and suggests that she does not necessarily find this description accurate. For one thing, Carnatic performance is largely structured around an inherited set of compositions, so that the mere act of composing original music represents a monumental leap within the genre. Swaminathan also describes her album's complex relationship with raga, describing the presence of individual ragas as "fleeting," so that to characterize the music as Carnatic seems reductive of both her compositions and the Carnatic genre. Ultimately, of reviewers who would ascribe to her the Carnatic-jazz genre label, she suggests:

> I feel like they're not getting this huge leap that was made…it feels like they're seeing it as just existing elements being drawn together, whereas I feel like there's so much in the process of creating this music that's about just completely creating something new that couldn't exist in either of those scenes.

Indeed, of the 12 tracks on the album, perhaps only the first, "Offering," can be said to be written "in" a single raga from start to finish. The composition is based on the raga Gavati, although given Swaminathan's stance on the role of raga in her music it might be more appropriate to describe the piece's mode as D Mixolydian with selective omissions and idiosyncrasies. (It is worth noting that Gavati is originally a Hindustani raga that was introduced into the Carnatic repertoire around the mid-twentieth century, lending further weight to Swaminathan's assertion that Carnatic music is itself a product of "meetings and encounters.") This distinction between raga and mode raises an interesting question regarding the appropriate terminology to describe raga-based musics that draw on the vocabulary of the Carnatic tradition without fully embodying its ethos. Swaminathan describes the ragas deployed in her music as points of reference rather

Figure 5.1 Comparison of Gavati Raga and D Mixolydian Mode

than structuring principles, a framing that demands a certain delicacy in whether/how we deploy Carnatic terminology when performing, analyzing, or indeed teaching Indo-jazz.

The sparsest engagement with raga might consist of treating a raga as a "scale" or a "mode" in the Western sense; an improviser or composer in this scenario would restrict themselves to using only the notes and sequences prescribed by the *arohanam* and *avarohanam*, the ascending and descending sequences of notes that outline the permitted tones within a given raga. Fuller engagement with a raga involves attention to characteristic *gamakka*, often loosely glossed as "ornaments"; *sancari*, or typical phrases; the weight and functions attached to specific *swara*, or notes within the scale; as well as the performance history of that raga, including the phrases that have become canonized over time and the body of compositions used as raw material for improvisation. T. Viswanathan writes: "[A raga] is at once a storehouse of remembered melodic history and a body of melodic potential to be drawn upon and realized in performance."[8] In the case of "Offering," individual musicians perform disparate relationships to the grounding principle of raga, while the piece as a whole espouses a respect for and attention to all components of raga performance without making the same demands of individual players.

From the preponderance of unison phrases and tight harmonies as well as the close synchronicity between melodic and rhythmic components, we can infer that "Offering" is largely through-composed, unlike many of the other tracks on the album. As such, Swaminathan's hand in the melodic structure is clear. Her Carnatic training becomes particularly audible in her explorations of rhythmic density, as frequent sequences of phrases are played first in triple and then duple meter, expanding and contracting the pulse without altering the tempo. As such, I see value in reading the structure of "Offering" as loosely referencing the structure of a Carnatic concert performance. The narrative arc of the opening melody played by bass and guitar evokes the traditional structure of an *alapana*, carefully introducing new pitches one at a time, beginning with a limited range that gradually expands, and centering around specific *sancari* that evoke the raga. Also like an *alapana*, the introduction unfolds in almost a didactic fashion, as Okazaki and Crump play the melody with minimal ornamentation and strong rhythmic accents, establishing the scale as well as the syncopated rhythmic structures within the 12-beat cycle. As we move further into the piece, the movements *ma pa ni* (G-A-C) and *ma pa ga ma ri* (G-A-F#-G-E)[9] are repeated and emphasized, demonstrating a commitment to highlighting the raga's most salient characteristics beyond treating it as merely a collection of notes. When Anjna Swaminathan and María Grand pick up the melody at 0:20, our experience of and engagement with the raga is further intensified by Anjna's use of *gamakka;* and yet this emerges slyly, with the first measure of the melody played in almost perfect unison until a subtle glide from *sa* to *ma* differentiates Anjna's style from Grand's. It is not until the pair's second iteration of the melody that the raga is fully realized in the Carnatic style, by which point the listener has had the opportunity to progress from understanding the raga as a series of notes to a collection of phrases to a more nuanced construct in which each note receives a particular treatment in particular contexts.

Rather than seeing Crump and Okazaki's introductory phrase as a superficial treatment of Gavati, then, we may interpret the beginning of "Offering" as a kind of functional *alapana*, a literal introduction to the raga that engages a varied audience by not merely introducing Gavati, but by introducing raga as a melody-structuring principle. Discussion of the composer's intentions may be somewhat unfashionable nowadays, but the pedagogical ethos that I hear in Swaminathan's work suggests a particular relationship with her audience that becomes all the more nuanced when contextualized in terms of her positioning as an Indian-American artist playing a traditional Carnatic instrument alongside non-Indian jazz musicians in an ensemble that primarily performs within the United States. Swaminathan does not teach her ensemble to play Carnatic music, but her music teaches an uninitiated audience how to listen Carnatically, and offers seasoned Carnatic listeners the chance to engage with jazz and creative music on terms that resonate with their own internalized artistic frameworks.

At the frequent moments where Swaminathan's ensemble comes together to play a composed line in rhythmic unison, individual musical languages are allowed to gently maintain their opacity and autonomy while effecting a reciprocal influence on one another and on the collective product. There is no attempt to fully synthesize the style of Carnatically-trained violinist Anjna Swaminathan with her jazz musician counterparts. *Gamakka* are left almost entirely to Anjna, for instance in the repeated movements from *pa* to *ni* characterized by a fluid glide through *sa* and a rearticulation of the *ni*. This may, of course, be a question of the affordances of particular instruments; the guitar and saxophone in their natural state are better suited to playing discrete pitches than emphasizing the fluid movements from one pitch to the next, and indeed bassist Crump comes the closest to approximating certain *gammaka* via slurs and slides, but ultimately the more intricate and expressly Carnatic ornaments are left to Anjna. Various conventions of Carnatic performance are exhibited by Anjna's playing style on this piece: repeated notes are emphasized via a pulsing that touches lightly on the note below the intended pitch; certain notes are given emphasis by approaching them fluidly from the previous note in a gesture more delicate than a slide or portamento. Insofar as certain stylistic elements can be approximated, however, it is noteworthy that the saxophonist is not asked to — or chooses not to — imitate the Carnatic approach, but is allowed to remain within her own native idiom. Rather than a more straightforward heterophony, a common feature of Carnatic ensemble performance characterized by slightly staggered timing and individual nuance around *gamakka*, Swaminathan's ensemble utilizes tight rhythmic and melodic synchronicity played in contrasting yet complementary idioms. In effect, beyond the Swaminathan sisters, the playing on this track cannot be characterized as Carnatic. In a series of improvised interludes beginning at 1:02, saxophonist Grand plays the phrases *ri sa ni* (E-D-C), *sa ni da* (D-C-B), and *ni pa ma* (C-A-G), all forbidden in this raga but technically included within the corresponding mode. In his percussive duet with Swaminathan beginning at 1:45, guitarist Okazaki hews slightly closer to the acceptable melodic patterns within Gavati, albeit by exploring an admittedly limited melodic range in favor of rhythmically complex counterpoint; his discrete and staccato playing style, however, can hardly be said to be a Carnatic exploration of the raga, lacking any *gamakka* or vocal fluidity. At the same time, the interplay between guitar and mridangam throughout the piece indicates a kind of mutuality and an interplay in which neither instrument seems to steer the conversation or determine the accepted vocabulary for the interaction; instead, both express a shared idea through separate idioms. Elliott Powell notes a similar dialogism in the use of tabla on Miles Davis's album *On The Corner* when he writes: "this is not call and response, but rather a different form of musical dialogue that…approximates collective, interlocked, mutually constitutive, and simultaneously sonic conversations."[10]

As such, there is a sense of total cohesion that characterizes this composition and the album as a whole. Rather than feeling disjointed, the stylistic differences when Anjna, Grand, Okazaki, and Crump play in unison function as complements, with Grand's straight-tone pitches providing a base for Anjna's more fluid interpretations of individual notes and the spaces between them. The term heteroglossia, coined by Mikhail Bakhtin, feels appropriate as one way we might describe the ethos of this piece; this is not a case of disparate languages, but a single-language musical text expressed via multiple overlapping and intersecting dialects. It would be a mistake, too, to assign ethnic or national markers to each player's accordant performance style. Rather, these individual styles are themselves hyphenated products of multiple influences. For instance, on "Vigil," the third track on the album, violinist Anjna moves fluidly between distinctly Carnatic phrases and more angular improvisations and slides that have no place in a Carnatic *alapana*, enacting sequences and intervallic leaps that intentionally unsettle the tonic. Likewise, a duet between voice and bass on "Ripple Effect" does not attempt to replicate the heterophonic accompaniment endemic to Carnatic vocal music; and yet Crump's dialogic responses to Doraiswamy's vocalizations clearly draw from the source material of her melodies, in some way effectuating the close relationship between voice and accompaniment that characterizes the Carnatic style as well as the distinctly vocal character of Carnatic instrumental music.

Insofar as the term "hybrid" presupposes pure or static entities that are unproblematically combined, the word is insufficient to contain the nuances of Swaminathan's music. Individual musicians' techniques, individual compositions, and the album as a whole are characterized by an approach that comfortably inhabits a space of multiplicity; it is neither a jazz album nor a Carnatic album, but at all points both and neither. When asked if she sees her music as having any particular racial or ethnic character, Swaminathan responds: "I think of it as composed of the people that make it." She acknowledges her work's indebtedness to Black music and improvised music, but attempts to move away from "jazz" insofar as jazz is understood as a white capitalist label to contain the music created by Black artists. Ultimately, however, she rejects the notion that her music is tied to any distinct ethnicity. "I think there's always this question of like how it's seen versus how it feels inside of the music. And of course people who are going to see it see it often, you know, as South Asian in some way, or Indian, or Indian classical. But I don't feel that it has those things attached to it. Especially the more that I go deeper into like, envisioning what the way forward is, I don't see it necessarily being tied to South Asian identity per se. I think it's also, like, just about me. It's like, it feels autobiographical, it's about my explorations, which can be personal and not necessarily attached to any particular identity."

Despite this insistence that her work need not express a particular ethnicity or identity, my own experience of engaging with Swaminathan's work comprises a shock of recognition described in Josh Kun's notion of audiotopia.[11] There is something audible in Swaminathan's composition style and in the harmonious coming together of her ensemble's performers that keenly reflects the diasporic experience of applying internalized knowledge to a novel context. Without disregarding her claim that her work is not necessarily Indian, we may note the way Swaminathan's music is shaped by a Carnatic sensibility, and indeed by an Indian-American diasporic sensibility—a productive act of constant translation and recontextualization that allows for the creation of something entirely new.

Insofar as the hyphen implies a certain irreconcilability, a holding apart even as it bridges a divide, we might return to Glissant on opacity: "I thus am able to conceive of the opacity of the other for me, without reproach for my opacity for him. To feel in solidarity with him or to build with him or to like what he does, it is not necessary for me to grasp him. It is not necessary to try to become the other (to become other) nor to 'make' him in my image."[12] The hyphen in Indian-American or Indo-jazz does not imply perfect transparency or even perfect understanding. Instead, this music is born of a place of mutuality, of individual and collective agencies that reside comfortably in between, and that are most generative when they draw on productive tensions and difference.

Fusion and Translation: Lessons for the Classroom

In this case study, I have attempted to demonstrate a mode of analysis that engages the "how" as well as the "what" of cross-cultural influence. When we bring crossover music, and especially Indo-jazz, into the classroom, rather than asking something along the lines of "what elements of Indian music can we hear in this artist's work?" it is essential to analyze the quality of this engagement with non-Western influences: "*How* does the artist deploy Indian aesthetic structures? What is the artist's relationship to melody, harmony, rhythm, form — and what aesthetic values are demonstrated by those relationships?" Rather than merely asking which raga or ragas are drawn upon in a given piece, we might ask how raga is deployed as a melody-structuring principle, or how individual players differ in their treatment of raga. Simply put, appropriation is not a binary concept—performers differ in the degree of their engagement with a given tradition, as well as in the additional artistic traditions they bring to bear on these collaborations. Music that can and should be analyzed in this way includes the landmark fusion experiments of the 1960s and 1970s, such as the music of the cross-cultural ensemble Shakti, as well as more contemporary explorations such as the work of Vijay Iyer and Rudresh Mahanthappa, whose personal and artistic trajectories more closely match the process of "hyphenation" I have described here; beyond the Indian diaspora, however, this mode of questioning is useful for any music that espouses an ideology of mixture, such as the music of the Caribbean, historically a rich site of syncretism and idiosyncratic development, or even the global hip hop community, distinctive in its deployment of Black American aesthetics to express local political values and subcultures of belonging.

"Fusion" as a depreciated or even derogatory term implies a certain superficiality in an artist or a composition's treatment of diverse genres. My desire to recuperate this term stems from the simple premise—commonsense among diaspora subjects—that it is indeed possible to engage with multiple cultures and genres with a certain degree of depth, and to put these in conversation in a manner that does not force any to conform to the whims or aesthetic values of the others but rather stages a generative dialogue that allows us to meaningfully engage with the productive differences and potential convergences between musics and cultures. It is, of course, part of our duty and our challenge as instructors to identify cross-cultural collaborations that merit this depth of analysis versus those that are better characterized as Orientalist or appropriative samplings of the music of the Other, a problem that I engage in more detail in the following section. At the same time, even artists and musics that minimally engage another genre are better examined in terms of the "how" than the "what," the degree of engagement with the Other becoming part of the classroom conversation rather than a reason to dismiss a project wholesale. What do Indian elements in music afford a Western performer, and vice versa? What challenges do Indian aesthetic frameworks present to an outsider? I have previously referred to the process of translation that informs diasporic cultural production. When I speak of translation in this way, I am thinking most directly with Derrida, who writes:

> The event of a translation, the performance of all translations, is not that they succeed. A translation never succeeds in the pure and absolute sense of the term. Rather, a translation succeeds in promising success, in promising reconciliation. There are translations that don't even manage to promise, but a good translation is one that enacts the performative called the promise with the result that through the translation one sees the coming shape of a possible reconciliation among languages.[13]

This framing has been used in the context of music by Deborah Kapchan, who theorizes the "promise of sonic translation" based on the premise that music can translate across linguistic and cultural divides.[14] Translation as a hermeneutic enables a more generous analysis of cross-genre performance, with Derrida's framework allowing us to search for resonances rather than emphasizing supposed deficits in a given performer's interpretation of a music that is not their own. Translation allows us to listen for process. Any description of music, whether in words, notation, or physical gesture, involves translation across communicative mediums. These translations may be understood as performative insofar as they actively enact the utopian potentiality of reconciliation while also bringing particular identities and value systems into being. What aesthetic or cultural values are preserved in a given music's translation into a new aesthetic and cultural context? How far can a raga be abstracted before it loses its essence? All music, but especially diaspora music, is the product of crossings and interactions between cultures and forms. The nature of these crossings provides fertile ground for new and compelling modes of analysis.

"What Is This Thing Called Indo-jazz?" Intercultural Collaboration and the Politics of Appropriation

We cannot discuss fusion as a category, particularly jazz fusion, without raising the question of appropriation. The history of jazz and of Black culture more broadly is rife with tales of suppression and subjugation followed by institutionalization and mainstream adoption or, in more polemic terms, cultural theft. Meanwhile, Indian music and Eastern culture more generally have often been subjected to a certain fetishization and exoticization that is the subject of Edward Said's 1978 treatise *Orientalism* and that has not subsided even as the Asian presence in the West has grown in terms of both population and influence. All of these things are true. And yet, I have to ask: must every instance of intercultural borrowing and influence be a case of either assimilation or appropriation? When we teach diaspora musics, what assumptions about identity and belonging guide the discussion of musical influences and trajectories? When we move past binaristic modes of thinking about race and ethnicity, the political implications of particular crossings come to bear on our discussions of intercultural as well as intracultural collaborations that put deeply rooted musics and traditions in conversation.

A careful disclaimer feels necessary at this point. I am not denying the existence of appropriation or its power to do harm, even in the context of interminority collaborations. Furthermore, turning specifically to the musics and communities I engage in my research, I do not intend to obfuscate the very real differences between the South Asian immigrant experience and the Black experience in the United States. South Asians have typically benefited from a much higher degree of structural and institutional privilege, particularly following the Immigration and Naturalization Act of 1965, which favored so-called "skilled laborers." I am simply suggesting that when we discuss the music of groups with shared histories of migration, assimilation, culture loss, and cultural theft in the context of colonial encounter, there are alternate and potentially more productive frameworks available to us as we consider the degree and direction of engagement across cultures whose power, influence, and affordances vis-a-vis one another go beyond Black and white. One way to approach this conversation in the classroom would be to begin with explicit and violent examples of appropriation, such as blackface minstrelsy, and to slowly progress toward more nuanced examples such as global hip hop, providing students with language and frameworks to discuss cross-racial performance before challenging them to unsettle those very frameworks.

The use value of appropriation as a conceptual framework in the context of interminority borrowings and collaborations has been brought into question by various contemporary scholars including Nitasha Sharma, Elliott Powell, and T. Roberts. Powell suggests that John and Alice Coltrane's deep-seated commitment to Indian spirituality calls for a fundamentally different mode of analysis than, say, John McLaughlin's jazz fusion experiments or the Orientalism of Madonna and the Beatles. Scholarship that emphasizes Western appropriation of Eastern influences, Powell writes,

> obfuscates the particularities of cross-cultural musical making practices between racially marginalized musicians, shores up whiteness and the West through the privileging and (re)centering of a white-nonwhite binary, and makes whiteness and white Western modes of engagement the origin of such intercultural musical innovation.[15]

Neither appropriation nor assimilation fully provide for the nuances of interminority interactions in the diasporic context. Discourses of assimilation undermine the extent to which hyphenated Americans can fully lay claim to an American cultural identity, as well as reproducing a center-periphery model in which the periphery is doomed to imitate or replicate the cultural products of the center. Meanwhile, as a frame that privileges whiteness, appropriation is perhaps an unproductive starting point for theorizing the collaborative interactions between Black and South Asian musicians. I should note here that none of the musicians in the ensemble analyzed earlier are Black, although Swaminathan has certainly collaborated with Black artists on other projects and acknowledges her work's indebtedness to Black music. When brown artists play Black music and vice versa, what alternative frameworks emerge? Classroom discussions of appropriation must necessarily take into account the way this very concept is grounded in colonialism and white supremacy. Interminority relationships, contextualized as they are by hegemonic white supremacy and anti-Blackness, require comparative investigation of the global histories of minority groups. Vijay Prashad's 2001 work *The Karma of Brown Folk* is one example of a text that situates a particular minority identity in the context of American race relations, typically understood in Black and white terms; these discussions are vital for any instructor hoping to engage the nuances of diaspora identity formation.

In this vein, Nitasha Sharma proposes a model of appropriation-as-identification, advocating for a global race consciousness that, in the context of her research, allows young South Asians in the U.S. to negotiate their own racial invisibility by identifying with Blackness and their communities' overlapping legacies of colonialism, imperialism, displacement, racism, and labor exploitation, "developing newly racialized identities that express a political consciousness of interminority solidarity."[16] Meanwhile, T. Roberts identifies multiple modes of cross-racial performance in a passage that is worth quoting at length:

> Motivated by curiosity, desire, and revulsion, minstrelsy is about defining the self while performing the Other … The temporary

crossing of racial lines serves to distance the performer from the performed—presumed to be of a different racial category—and keeps the performer's identity intact. Passing, however, involves a provisional disavowal of the self and capitalizes on the paradoxical rigidity and permeability of racial categories in order to forge a new social identity ... Finally, cross-racial "appropriation as identification" (Sharma 2010) posits retention of the self while drawing performative connections to the Other. The Other provides gestures, sounds, or techniques that allow the performer to express an *alternate or more complete version of themselves than previously available*. In each of these approaches, *self-definition is paramount and the Other serves as a model or point of contrast*.

(emphasis mine)[17]

Roberts is primarily interested in performances that blur or transcend these categorical demarcations, as am I. In these cases, the Other no longer serves simply as a point of contrast, but as a formative interlocutor in the artist or composer's sense of community as well as self. Part of the project of analyzing cross-racial or genre-blending performances involves the— again, unfashionable—task of discussing the motivations behind particular collaborations, and moreover the effect of these collaborations at the level of the ensemble as well as the individual. Hyphenated music-making blurs the boundaries between self and Other and between diaspora and nation. Moving beyond binaristic discourses of appropriation and assimilation is an important step in taking this music and these artists on their own terms.

Conclusions: Teaching Diaspora Music

The very existence of this edited volume affirms that questions of crossover and exchange are being taken seriously in the music classroom, with few claiming that fusion is in any way undeserving of or irrelevant to analysis and even fewer claiming to have "solved" the problem of appropriation. At the same time, the concept of appropriation is so very present and politically fraught in mainstream media that it seems to have lost some of its academic potential for nuance and interrogation. In this chapter, I have attempted to model a kind of analysis that focuses on the dialogue between genres and the reciprocal interactions that inform genre-blending musical explorations. I have resisted value judgments as I explore the way musicians of disparate backgrounds and trainings engage with cultural forms over which they have varying degrees of ownership and command. Instead, I have treated these differences as productive grounds for analysis and examined the ways they ultimately enrich the hyphenated product.

What might this mode of analysis look like in the classroom? The concept of hyphenation is worth some careful attention as students begin to consider the different valences of existing terms like fusion, crossover, and appropriation. Students might be asked to write a paragraph describing their own musical influences or, perhaps more interestingly and productively, to put together a playlist that illustrates their own personal soundscape. While such a project has particular resonances for diasporic or international students, it is unlikely that any student's final product will be entirely homogeneous, which will lead to a useful conversation about how these disparate influences interact to shape an artistic identity, whether as a composer, performer, or consumer. As for the language available to describe this multiplicity, at various points during this chapter I have belabored the metaphor of music as language, using frameworks including translation, heteroglossia, and, implicitly, bilingualism, to describe the process by which musicians from disparate traditions communicate artistic ideas and play in tandem. Derrida and Bakhtin are certainly useful interlocutors, but for the purposes of an introductory discussion in a music classroom a more productive starting point might be Deborah Kapchan, who explicitly deploys translation theory in relation to musical performance as she explores the transmission of sacred and devotional feelings at international music festivals, espousing a belief in the "ultimate translatability of aural (as opposed to textual) codes."[18] My point is not to impose complex linguistic analytical methods on students of music, but simply to provide a productive metaphor for understanding how musical meaning—"meaning" in the loosest and most poetic sense of the term—changes with shifting contexts.

My analysis here is predicated on my own knowledge of and lifelong studies in Indian classical music, but this deep familiarity with constituent elements is not a prerequisite for engaging with hyphenated music. When an artistic tradition is taken out of its native context, we are afforded a unique opportunity to examine the core values that define that particular tradition. For instance, hip hop as a subculture looks dramatically different from country to country and region to region, and yet is still readily identifiable by a unifying set of political and aesthetic values, including an emphasis on wordplay, opulence, and the subaltern. What does Korean or Indian or Native American hip hop have to teach us about Black American hip hop and hip hop more broadly? Or, put another way—what makes all of these things hip hop? Listening to crossover music alongside more traditional examples of a particular musical form is one way of encouraging this conversation. For example, I might present Swaminathan's track alongside a more traditional *alapana* in the raga Gavati, and encourage students to compare and contrast the two renditions. In a more advanced music classroom where students have a basic knowledge of Western music notation, transcription exercises can be used to put different musicians' approaches within a single track in conversation. While the role of transcription and Western notation when applied to non-Western musics, and especially oral traditions, warrants a chapter of its own, I find immense value in transcription as an exercise specifically because its deficits and limitations often make vividly apparent the melodic and rhythmic qualities of the music in question, and force students to find creative ways of expressing these qualities using language with which they are already familiar. In the case of the musical example explored here, a careful transcription would make apparent the differences in Anjna Swaminathan's and María Grand's performance styles, and specifically the artistic choices that lend Anjna's rendition a distinctly Carnatic flavor. Transcription as a performance in and of itself affords us a great deal as scholars in terms of exploring the musical qualities that define non-Western musics.

It is worth noting again that the problem of cultural appropriation is far from resolved in any context, let alone the academy. The works I have cited here represent some of the more contemporary and progressive voices in this conversation—primarily scholars of color and specifically Black scholars who acknowledge the ways in which discussions of race and culture necessitate historical and sociopolitical grounding as diasporic artists and artists of color draw on every resource available to them to carve out a space of their own. I hope we can encourage students to approach these discussions of minority musics with a spirit of generosity and an understanding of the ways a white-centric or Eurocentric frame cannot encompass the nuances of interminority borrowings and collaborations, even and especially on a global scale.

While a certain agnosticism toward genre is intrinsic for many contemporary musicians, particularly in the age of globalization and given the extended reach of many previously insular musical forms, we as musicologists have yet to develop a corresponding dynamism in our approaches to boundary-crossing musics. This chapter represents one of the first steps in my journey toward developing more nuanced modes of analysis and new frameworks for conversation in the context of cross-cultural collaboration and diasporic artistic production. Hybridity and fusion—or perhaps more productively, "hyphenation"—can often result in deeply meaningful cultural products that merit careful analysis as autonomous entities rather than mere byproducts of assimilation or appropriation. The everyday work of diasporic identity formation involves the synthesis of multiple cultural forms; our job as scholars and educators is to enter into this dialogue with open minds, and to treat diasporic music on its own terms. I hope these suggestions prove useful for any instructors and students hoping to engage these musics, but perhaps more importantly, I hope they provide the opportunity to feel seen for artists and scholars of the diaspora and of the hyphen, whose journey I celebrate as my own.

Notes

1 Weiss, "Listening to the World but Hearing Ourselves," 506–525.
2 Gopinath, *Impossible Desires*.
3 Niranjana, *Mobilizing India*; Ramnarine, "Musical Performance in the Diaspora: Introduction," 1–17.
4 Swaminathan, "Of Agency and Abstraction."
5 Glissant, *Poetics of Relation* (1990), 191.
6 Swaminathan, "Of Agency and Abstraction."
7 Rajna Swaminathan. Interview with author. May 4, 2020.
8 Viswanathan and Allen, *Music of South India*, 42
9 While a detailed explanation of sargam is beyond the scope of this chapter, in general, the Carnatic syllables of Sa-Ri-Ga-Ma-Pa-Da-Ni can be roughly mapped onto the Western solfège scale of Do-Re-Mi-Fa-Sol-La-Ti.
10 Powell, *Sounds from the Other Side*, 52
11 Kun, *Audiotopia*.
12 Glissant, 193.
13 Derrida qtd. Kapchan, "The Promise of Sonic Translation," 467–483.
14 Kapchan, 469.
15 Powell, 3.
16 Sharma, *Hip Hop Desis*, 3.
17 Roberts, *Resounding Afro-Asia*, 60.
18 Kapchan, 467.

References

Glissant, Edouard. *Poetics of Relation (1990)*. Translated by Betsy Wing. Ann Arbor: University of Michigan Press, 1997.
Gopinath, Gayathri. *Impossible Desires: Queer Diasporas and South Asian Public Cultures*. Durham: Duke University Press, 2005.
Kapchan, Deborah A. "The Promise of Sonic Translation: Performing the Festive Sacred in Morocco." *American Anthropologist* 110, no. 4 (2008): 467–83.
Kun, Josh. *Audiotopia: Music, Race, and America*. Berkeley: University of California Press, 2005.
Niranjana, Tejaswini. *Mobilizing India: Women, Migration and Music between India and Trinidad*. Durham: Duke University Press, 2006.
Powell, Elliott. *Sounds from the Other Side: Afro-South Asian Collaborations in Black Popular Music*. Minneapolis: University of Minnesota Press, 2020.
Prashad, Vijay. *The Karma of Brown Folk*. Minneapolis: University of Minnesota Press, 2000.
Ramnarine, Tina K. "Musical Performance in the Diaspora: Introduction." *Ethnomusicology Forum* 16, no. 1 (2007): 1–17.
Roberts, T. *Resounding Afro-Asia: Interracial Music and the Politics of Collaboration*. Oxford: Oxford University Press, 2016.
Said, Edward. *Orientalism*. New York: Vintage Books, 1979.
Sharma, Nitasha. *Hip Hop Desis: South Asian Americans, Blackness, and a Global Race Consciousness*. Durham: Duke University Press, 2010.
Swaminathan, Rajna. "Of Agency and Abstraction." *Bandcamp*. April 26, 2019. Accessed August 19, 2022. https://rajnaswaminathan.bandcamp.com/album/of-agency-and-abstraction.

Viswanathan, T., and Matthew Harp Allen. *Music of South India: The Karnatak Concert Tradition and Beyond*. New York: Oxford University Press, 2004.

Weiss, Sarah. "Listening to the World But Hearing Ourselves: Hybridity and Perceptions of Authenticity in World Music." *Ethnomusicology* 58, no. 3 (2014): 506–25.

6 African-Focused Approaches to Teaching African Popular Music in Western Classrooms

Alaba Ilesanmi

African popular musicians often engage in "crossover," "exchange," and "appropriation," while infusing intercontinental, intercultural, and intracultural materials to varying degrees. Thus, when listening to African popular music (*popular music in Africa* is a better term that captures the heterogeneity of genres and approaches), one may recognize certain *allusions*, e.g., the use of specific "non-African" instrumentation or particular musical nuances that call foreign genres to mind. Central to this phenomenon of allusive listening in African popular music is the quest to trace origin, whether prompted by the inherent allusive nature of African popular music or by our biases regarding what African music, broadly defined, should sound like. We engage in allusive listening to make sense of what we hear and ground our listening experiences and practices within our musical purview, shaped by our musical and cultural exposure, articulations, and vocabulary. This chapter addresses this allusive listening practice, its pedagogical implications, and potentials for engendering a rich and robust approach to teaching African popular music in the Western music classroom, using Fela Kuti's life and music as a case study.

When engaging and gauging my students' prior knowledge of African musics at the beginning of the "Music in World Cultures" class I taught during the 2021–22 academic year, I found that some of their comments highlighted perspectives that situate African music as a wholly rhythmic phenomenon[1] and cast African popular music as a "diluted" form, influenced by Western musics. Other scholars and educators have similarly documented such perspectives. In "Listening to the World but Hearing Ourselves: Hybridity and Perceptions of Authenticity in World Music," ethnomusicologist Sarah Weiss shares that when she played South African *mbube* (a multipart male *a cappella* style) in a "World Music" course she taught at Yale in 2010, "some students … vigorously insisted mbube is not authentic South African music because it bears traces of Western harmony and choral style brought to South Africa by Christian missionaries."[2] Likewise, Jean Ngoya Kidula, in her essay, "Stereotype, Myths, and Realities Regarding African Music in the African and American Academy,"

DOI: 10.4324/9781003415954-9

describes an encounter in which she asked students to list "stereotypes that are constructed, informed, and maintained by prevalent historical and mediated worldviews." One student's comment is particularly striking: "Africans had no classical or popular music until Westerners introduced it."[3] These stories from the classroom underscore the fact that we most often think of African popular music as a hybrid form, suggesting colonialist and imperialist views.

In my encounters with the discussions of African popular music and, by extension, the ways it is taught, I have found that we often encourage listening for origins, which I call "origin listening." I use the term "origin listening" to highlight listening practices that identify and trace the origins of tangible and intangible musical material and/or resources, e.g., the origin of the instruments used. This involves having students engage with various concepts that highlight musical "borrowing," such as syncretism and hybridity. While characterized by an "intense allusive quality,"[4] we need to consider the process of *musical indigenization* and *reinterpretation*; that is, the ways in which African musicians embody "foreign" influences and actively negotiate, redefine, and/or transform them.

Origin listening may reveal our biases and assumptions about what African music *should* sound like. Many listeners have an implicit expectation that they will encounter percussive music, which locks African music in a misconceived past. It fails to acknowledge that musical styles are "organisms" and that they change, evolve, and mutate in an organic process.[5] In the end, we need to recognize tradition "as a process of creative transformation whose most remarkable feature is the continuity it nurtures and sustains."[6]

The harm of origin listening is that we are likely to attribute Euro-American influences to music made by Africans. However, origin listening can also be a valuable pedagogical tool if employed with great care, and in this chapter, I will outline an approach to origin listening that can reveal the postcolonial realities of African music-making and ownership. We must educate our students to recognize the acts and arts of enjoying African popular music without undermining African musicians' ingenuity. Likewise, we must teach them to engage with African popular music artists as active agents who negotiate multiplicities of local and foreign musical materials, and who invest all available musical resources (tangible and intangible) in their work—not to conform but to nurture their sonic and musical sensibilities.

What are the implications of pedagogy informed by origin-centric approaches? Is the search for origin actually a search for "authenticity"? Can any culture claim not to have been influenced by another culture? As it pertains to African music, the search for origins and authenticity, as well as the idea that Africa holds our "primitive" heritage, only creates stereotypical understandings and teachings of Africa (and "Africanisms") that lock entire cultures in the past. In teaching African popular music in today's global context, we must re-shape our concepts of "crossover" and "appropriation" as regards today's pan-African musicians, and understand how the concept of indigenization challenges the inherent power interplay in ideas like "crossover," "exchange," and "appropriation."

In this chapter, drawing from my experience teaching a "Music in World Cultures" class and directing a pan-African popular music ensemble at a research institution, I propose an African indigenization-focused pedagogy. This pedagogical approach places musicians and their culture at the center of interest, embraces indigeneity, emphasizes ingenuity, and engages with African musicians as active agents and channels of artistic transformation.

Common Approaches to Teaching African Popular Music

In teaching African music, it is typical to focus on a few topics or cultures—tracing similar themes and ideas—that may provide "single stories" and thereby constitute entry points into learning about broader African cultures and traditions. Time constraints are a significant barrier. Since it is impossible to cover everything, the instructor engages in selective teaching (attempting to use the part to teach the whole); but it is essential that instructors remind students that what is being covered in their course is limited and that the foundational survey they provide is but a gateway to understanding the various African musicultural phenomena.

Additionally, instructors are challenged regarding what to teach and how to teach it, due to the African continent's musical diversity and complexity. In teaching African popular music, instructors might use what is familiar to extend students' knowledge of what they perceive as unfamiliar. Pedagogically, to use students' prior knowledge is not only reliable but appetizing. Instructors might emphasize musical allusions that students will have already identified by comparing the African musician to a (Euro-American) musician with whom the students are familiar. For example, to lecture on the late Nigerian musician and Afrobeat pioneer, Fela Kuti, the instructor might refer to Fela's music as funk, citing James Brown as his influencer; or the instructor may refer to the instrumentation as akin to big band instrumentation. Comparisons or couplings like this are not new. In a *New York Times* article, Larry Rohter describes Afrobeat as "the inviting and highly danceable mixture of West African rhythms with jazz, soul, funk and psychedelic rock influences."[7]

Though pedagogically cogent, using the familiar to teach the unfamiliar might undermine African voices and negotiations if not handled carefully. While claims of external influence are valid, a wholly allusive listening practice and non-culturally grounded discussion risk missing internal negotiations and contemporary perspectives. Since the students' prior knowledge might be grounded in stereotypical understanding and essentialized information, it is crucial to take advantage of opportunities to engage students with critical questioning and exploration of key topics and domains. Passing up these opportunities is negligent—a mere reenactment of a conclusively "one-sided story" void of local voices.[8]

Toward a Pedagogy Built on "Origin Listening"

"Origin listening" can potentially provide opportunities to enlighten students on African postcolonial thoughts and realities, as well as concepts of musical ownership and indigenization. It allows the instructor to re-present the cultures and the musicians in the way they desire. Thus, I do not suggest we desist from tracing origin altogether; rather, I push for a holistic approach to origin listening and allusive hearing, enabling culturally grounded understanding. In fact, seeking origins is vital in African musical and historical discourses to engender critical conversation, engage the past as it shapes the present, and trace out indigenous-grounded epistemologies and ontologies. There are three goals of a holistic approach to teaching African music: 1) a pedagogical emphasis on and appreciation for African approaches to musical indigenization (as integral to African processes of tradition) in lieu of outmoded origin-centric pedagogy; 2) the use of equity-centered epistemological approaches in pedagogy, in lieu of outmoded approaches based on stereotype and essentialism; and 3) an engagement with modern/contemporary African musical artists instead of/in addition to and (perhaps most importantly) in conversation with their ostensibly "traditional" counterparts, with students encouraged to understand the music in the context of tradition as a process of creative transformation, as well as in terms of tradition's inextricability from political and social forces.[9]

In the "Music in World Cultures" course I taught during the 2021–22 school year, I used "origin listening" to challenge long-held biases and assumptions and reground students' understanding of African popular music as an original African art form. To achieve this, I queried the presence of the "non-African" instruments they were hearing. I asked: why do Africans use orchestral and jazz instruments? How do they deploy those instruments and ground them to express indigenous musical sensibilities? I used these queries to build an understanding that musical instruments are outputs for creative musical imagination on which musicians maintain their indigenous musical artistry. Equally, I use them to underpin discourses on music ownership.

I tailored my lectures to focus on the *who* (Africans), the *what* (musical resources, to include external influences), and the *how* (individual or collective creativity and reinterpretation). While tracing the *who* and the *how* are essential, a broadly encompassing *what* is ultimately imperative.

For example, as we trace *what* the influences are, we must also trace *what* factors facilitated them. In this light, I ground my lectures in local cultural and historical contexts. For example, in highlighting the use of Western instruments, I discuss the colonization of Africa, the Western extraction of its resources, and the African negotiation thereof. In addition to embracing a holistic historical approach, one must acknowledge the role of human actors. Christopher Waterman writes: "Syncretism is fundamentally grounded in human actors' interpretations of similarity and difference, and in their attempts to make sense of a changing world in terms of past experience."[10] We acquire an in-depth understanding of musical syncretism when we factor in the actors' roles and negotiations.

Ultimately, to teach African popular music equitably, we cannot highlight musical "borrowing" and avoid discussing indigenization. Herskovits asserts that no "element of culture is ever taken over without some degree of reinterpretation, however free the borrowing."[11] We indeed cannot talk about reinterpretation without focusing on individuals. African musicians not only negotiate various levels of encounters and interactions but also reinterpret them. Instructors must ask: how do African musicians navigate and negotiate fluid boundaries and the complicated cultural influx and interactions happening within and across the African continent and expanding out into its diaspora? It is imperative that students understand how African musicians assimilate outside influences, retain local sensibilities, and compartmentalize and reinterpret these various musical multiplicities.

Dialogic Encounters and Pluralistic Existence in African Popular Music

Several levels of influence permeate African popular music; however, we often concentrate on the inter-continental interactions between Africa and the West while disregarding other levels of interaction among African peoples and cultures. No culture is static or fixed, and African cultures and traditions are no exception. African cultures are not homogeneous (even within one culture), nor are they completely heterogeneous. For example, African nations share a common experience with colonialism, but its lasting effects and the degree to which it suppressed local culture vary at the most integral level; colonial experience and postcolonial realities in the Democratic Republic of Congo are not the same as, say, in Ghana, although both were colonized. To use another example, there is a shared tradition and history among the Yorùbá peoples of present-day Nigeria and the Republic of Benin; however, variations in ideas and cultural phenomena are numerous. More specifically, although there is a shared understanding of the Yorùbá language, members of both cultures now speak different variations of that language. These inherent antinomies in African homogeneity and heterogeneity are inscribed through cultural borrowing and displacement and the resulting transformations effected by those processes.

To understand African music's transformations, diversities, and complexities, then, we must engage with all types of African *dialogic encounters* and *interactions*, which I categorize into three levels: intercontinental, intercultural, and intracultural. Regarding African music, Gerhard Kubik explores a similar idea,[12] which I fuse with anthropologist Arjun Appadurai's concept of fluid boundaries.[13] Culture is an organic phenomenon that mutates over time, and it is sometimes impossible to make sense of the mutation—especially now, when boundaries are blurred and increasingly fluid. I emphasize these interactions to explicate possible ways in which these different levels of interactions cause cultural changes and explore how individual musicians engage with and negotiate such encounters.

Intercontinental interactions concern the cultural traffic that happens in and out of the African continent and the ensuing influences on both African and non-African cultures. Africa has been a site for and the enabler of global "interactive system[s]."[14] These systems, or flows, are by no means new, as historians and sociologists contend, especially in terms of trans-local processes[15] and the world's economic systems of capitalism.[16] Global development has depended on webs of interaction for centuries, and the African continent has been the site of many "congeries of large-scale interactions" since the 1800s.[17]

The term *intercultural interaction* refers to the internal interactions among African cultures. Intercultural interactions in Africa thrived prior to contact with any other continent and continued after that contact. Early accounts suggest that transactions among African peoples occurred through trade by barter (the exchanging of goods and services for other goods and services). Such interactions also took place in the context of intercultural marriages and, in some cases, immigration, caused by long-distance travels (e.g., nomadic lifestyle) or war.[18] The complexity of Africa's diversity lies in the fact that there are diverse sub-cultures within a single culture (e.g., the Yorùbá culture) that is simultaneously homogeneous and heterogeneous. The dialectics of homogeneity and heterogeneity that characterize cultures, kingdoms, clans, and individuals cannot be overlooked; they are responsible for the multiplicity of African ideas. The ensuing musical and cultural diversities and complexities across the African continent call for an understanding of intercultural and intracultural influences within African communities.

Intracultural interaction refers to the more immediate and intimate level of interaction among people of the same culture. At this level, musicians adapt existing canons, (re)interpret and negotiate available "foreign" materials (including musical instruments), and combine and innovate to form new styles and genres. Appadurai contends that

> as forces from various metropolises are brought into new societies they tend to become indigenized in one or another way: this is true of music and housing styles as much as it is true of science and terrorism, spectacles and constitutions.[19]

When foreign influences are assimilated, they yield new musical possibilities through reinterpretation, recombination, and permutation of all existing materials.

The significance of this interaction is that it occurs on a localized level. Karin Barber's book *African Popular Culture* explores street culture in major African metropolises.[20] Street culture, for Barber, is the quotidian experience in both rural and urban cities. At the same time, it is *intercultural* interaction, due to its shared commonality among African nations, kingdoms, and clans; it is ubiquitous, audible, and visible. In line with Barber's exploration, I posit that both *intercultural* and *intracultural* interactions are sites of cultural production, imagination, and expression, which, in turn, privilege the generation of creative content; social and cultural norms and changes are negotiated within these interactions.

Individual musicians function within these interactions as agents and channels of artistic transformation. As a result of the various dialogic encounters between African cultures and the ensuing explorations and transformations that result from such contacts, musicians engage and negotiate the ideas of musical compartmentalization and "pluralistic coexistence"[21]—the ways in which individuals absorb different influences and yet are able to separate (or even combine) them. Writing about musical compartmentalization and pluralistic coexistence, Margaret Kartomi states:

> Members of a bi- or multi-ethnic society may absorb during childhood the musical styles of their own as well as of another ethnic group with which they have lived in close contact, keeping each music separately compartmentalized in their minds. For example, some people living near the border of Central and West Java can sing in both Central and West Javanese musical styles, much as a child living in a bilingual situation can learn to speak two languages well.[22]

At the *intracultural* level, individuals or groups make sense of influences from intercontinental and intercultural interactions. As the global cannot exist without the local, intercontinental influences and effects cannot take hold without intracultural interventions. Thus, in teaching African popular music, we must project contributions of local interventions onto African popular music and its global recognition.

Teaching African Popular Music in a Global Context: Fusing Indigenization, Pluralistic Coexistence, and Musical Compartmentalization with "Origin Listening"

To teach African popular music equitably, we must be judicious. Additionally, it requires the grounding of intercontinental interactions within inter- and intracultural interactions and negotiations, ensuring that we equitably use what is familiar to teach the unfamiliar. How do we ensure that Euro-American perspectives do not consume African musical manifestations? How do we propel genuine curiosity in students to guide them to proper culturally grounded understanding? The who/what/how approach to analyzing African popular music helps to tease out wholly encompassing perspectives on African popular music and postcolonial realities. I use Fela Kuti as a case study to explore this.

Fela Anikulapo-Kuti (1938–1997), popularly known as Fela, was a legendary composer, innovative arranger, no-nonsense bandleader, and pan-Africanist who was the father of the genre known as Afrobeat. He was an astute human rights activist, dissident political force, and iconoclast who used his music as a weapon against injustice. In the spirit of *decolonization*, he denounced his English last name, Ransome-Kuti, and changed it to Anikulapo-Kuti.

What follows are suggestions for bringing ideas regarding origin listening, pluralistic coexistence, and musical compartmentalization and indigenization to bear in teaching Fela's music. These various domains and understandings guide an accurate and culturally grounded approach to teaching African popular music and yield local perspectives.

The *Who*

The quest to use what is familiar to describe *who* Fela is (to those unfamiliar with him) forces us to focus on Fela's intercontinental positioning. Fela's biographer, Michael Veal, in the introduction to his biography on Fela, writes: "On stage, Fela combines the autocratic bandleading style and dancing agility of James Brown, the mystical inclinations of Sun Ra, the polemicism of Malcolm X, and the harsh, insightful satire of Richard Pryor."[23] To a reader who is first encountering Fela, this is alluring, and the suggestion of mysticism might draw them into the book. An instructor might use a similar approach to describe the essence of Fela and to call upon the students' prior knowledge of these persons (James Brown et al.) to build an understanding of Fela—and this is a good approach. However, while Veal used his entire monograph to tease out the personhood of Fela, his ingenuity, and the intracultural forces that shaped him, an instructor in a survey class might not get the opportunity to do the same if their approach is not fundamentally situated in highlighting African perspectives and inter- and intracultural yearnings.

The instructor should also address the impacts of intracultural forces and experiences that shaped the musician. Not doing so might revert to discourses that focus only on the "familiar." We must prioritize indigenous African perspectives to move the focus to the local persons that influenced the musician. For example, the instructor could focus on who Fela's parents were and what their lives tell us about who Fela became. An exploration of his parents reveals them as his primary influencers, musically and ideologically, and is relevant to understanding Fela's artistry. His father, Reverend I.O. Ransome-Kuti, was the principal of the Abeokuta Grammar School,[24] and Fela began his early music studies under his father's tutelage there. Stephanie Shonekan positions Fela's mother, Funmilayo Ransome Kuti (FRK), a nationalist and women's rights activist, as his primary ideological influencer. She sowed the seeds that shaped him as a *politically*-minded musician; when Fela was nine years old, for example, his mother led the Abeokuta market women in a 1947 protest in western Nigeria.[25] Afrobeat moves beyond artistic terrains. As a phenomenon, it is both ideologically and politically driven. The benefit of an exploration into the lives of Fela's parents, as an example of intra-cultural manifestations, would yield more locally focused discourse and expose students to the socio-cultural, economic, and political conditions of Nigeria during his and his parents' lives.

The *What*

Often, as "origin listening" practice suggests, we are prone to focus on Euro-American manifestations. We must, instead, ground listening in inter- and intracultural bearings. As we used Fela's family (the *who*) to consider his influences, we now turn to the *what* of the music itself. For example, to describe Afrobeat as an "inviting and highly danceable mixture of West African rhythms with jazz, soul, funk and psychedelic rock influences" is not wrong,[26] but it may trap the instructor into explaining such allusions, rather than building an informed understanding of the musical indigenization processes that birthed Afrobeat. Likewise, the focus on a partial *what* (i.e., foreign nuances in Afrobeat) undermines the learning opportunity for students to fully understand Fela's musical trajectory.

Conversely, a fully conceived *what* discussion about Fela would reveal that Afrobeat is enshrined in highlife music (a Ghanaian and Nigerian popular music genre) and Yorùbá popular and traditional musical aesthetics. On Fela's journey to realizing Afrobeat, he played with the Cool Cats, Victor Olaiya's (aka. the Evil Genius) highlife band, prior to studying at the Trinity College of Music, London (1958–1962); he later formed his own band, the Highlife Rakers, later Koola Lobitos. Fela engaged in intense musical experiments and exploration with his Koola Lobitos band, fusing highlife and jazz to create *highlife-jazz* music. These explorations and experiments later culminated in the new Afrobeat aesthetics in 1969, while Fela was on a ten-month stay in Los Angeles, with "My Lady's Frustration" being the first Afrobeat composition.[27] We lose local perspectives such as these when we fail to engage with all the levels of influences: inter- and intracultural, and intercontinental.

The *How*

Fela incorporated inter- and intracultural influences to develop his own style of music. The question is, *how*? An instructor should tease out ideas of indigenization—that is, *musical Africanization*. To undertake discussions of assimilation without stating the process of refinement (the *how*) is to position African musicians as perpetual copiers. While cultural borrowing is a human phenomenon, African musicians are adept at transforming all available musical materials. They are able to adopt and cultivate foreign musical instruments, for example, and then conform them to local parlance and musical sensibilities. These are acts of activism and cultural reclamation. Even in the face of the overt use of jazz or big band instruments, the nuances of Afrobeat are overwhelmingly enshrined in Yorùbá and West African musical traditions. For example, in the introduction to "Why Black Man Dey Suffer," Fela pointed out that the song's rhythm is "used in some particular kind of shrines" in his hometown in Abeokuta. Accordingly, Fela used the instruments to articulate the indigenous ideas he envisioned for the piece. Kartomi writes:

> The process of intercultural musical synthesis, as opposed to the borrowing of single discrete elements (such as a musical instrument), is not a matter of the addition of single elements of one culture to another. It is a matter of setting into motion an essentially creative process, that is, the transformation of complexes of interacting musical and extramusical ideas.[28]

Such transformations are brought about by individuals, who are cultural agents who adapt, interpret, negotiate, and combine the different levels of dialogic encounter, individual imagining, creativity, and exploration. These factors vary within each culture, since the personal experiences of individuals also vary. But the individuals interact, and a conglomerate is formed through dialogic webs that foster understanding within a culture and between cultures.

Prioritizing the *How*: African Indigeneity and Ingenuity

What can students steeped in Western musical tradition glean from fulsome knowledge of Afrobeat and Fela's ingenuity? Leading students to explore the *how* reveals inter- and intracultural interactions and influences that showcase Fela's process of indigenization. Such a focus helps students engage with the unfamiliar, expands their musical vocabulary, and pushes them toward appreciating African music aesthetics on their own terms. The takeaways here are multiple and magnificent. Students miss this kind of knowledge and perspective when led on a learning path that emphasizes only intercontinental influences. What follows is an attempt to tease out the intra- and intercultural manifestations of Afrobeat.

The harmonic sensibilities of Afrobeat are grounded in Yorùbá musical traditions and, more broadly, West African harmonic imaginations. Fela's conscious rejection of Westernization pushed him to reject "tonal harmony as a colonizing force" in his music.[29] The overarching harmony of Fela's Afrobeat is usually modal, which is not exclusively African; but most (if not all) West African musical traditions can be represented using the European modal system.[30] Fela utilized the Dorian mode in most of his compositions—a mode that is widely used among Yorùbá people. The important difference here, though, is that Fela's creative use of modal harmony allowed him to deviate from the norms of European functional harmony, most notably the tonic-subdominant-dominant (I–IV–V) relationship. This enabled him to express an African harmonic imagination with unending expressive possibilities. Fela's typical harmonic sensibilities are exemplified in his composition "Water No Get Enemy," in which Fela uses the Dorian mode to create a sense of bitonality, as though two tonal centers are at play. Fela uses an ambiguous Dorian/Aeolian tonal center in most of his compositions, resulting in a sense of auditory illusion. Fela's harmonic language might be interpreted as his direct response to modernism, following the influence of the Black Arts Movement (which sought to establish Black aesthetics). But Fela's harmonic imagination is ultimately rooted in Yorùbá musical idioms and traditions.

Afrobeat's melodic nuances define its aesthetics, and, by extension, these nuances are Fela's means of *Yorubalizing*, *Africanizing*, and *indigenizing* his music. First, there is an intensified level of tonality in West African languages. Second, most West African drums, like the *dùndún* (Yorùbá talking drum), serve as speech surrogates and replicate the language's tonal inflection. West African languages, thus, "serve as a gateway to the appreciation of sung or word-based melody."[31] This sense of the importance of tonality is invested in every Yorùbá child who speaks the Yorùbá language, for tonality dictates the meaning of any word by means of tonal inflections (patterns of pitch), such that a given word may have several meanings. For example, in the Yorùbá language, there are generally three levels of inflection: low, mid, and high. The word "ewa" means different things, depending on the appended mark of tonal inflections: èwà, pronounced as mid-low, means "beauty"; ewá, pronounced as mid-high, means "come"; and èwà, pronounced as low-low, means "beans." Thus, melodic contours are often shaped or influenced by language.

Similar tonal inflections in most West African languages dictate the ways in which drums are used to imitate language, i.e., the drums literally speak. Thus, the Yorùbá language's tonality dictates the shape and contour of the melody if one is to maintain the meaning of the sung words.[32] This indicates a heightened level of musicality in the Yorùbá language.

Additionally, the pentatonic scale lies at the heart of the "Africanness" inherent in Afrobeat melodies. According to Kofi Agawu, it is the most essential scale from which Fela drew.[33] He would also, from time to time, use it for musical interludes in his compositions, such as "Shuffering and Shmilling." Highlighting Fela's fascination with the pentatonic scale and the keyboard, Agawu writes:

> Most interesting is the fact that the pentatonic is also deeply associated with African traditional music, and although Fela most likely got his pentatonic from the keyboard, its ancient qualities may have reinforced his fascination with it. The meeting of an old African pitch construct and a nearly identical construct available on an instrument brought by the Europeans to Africa is a striking coincidence. For Fela, the pentatonic represents a kind of double authenticity.[34]

Finally, the voice is central to Afrobeat's overarching aesthetics. Fela's political bent and pan-African messages aimed to liberate Africans from colonial shackles. His primary audience was the proletariat and the masses. He reached them using a more accessible language: the localized lingua franca, Pidgin English. Although Afrobeat comes with some elitism in its production and performance, Fela made sure that it transcended socioeconomic barriers as he crafted intellectually dense lyrics in Pidgin English to reach and appeal to the masses. Pidgin English is a form of indigenized African expression of the English language. Fela further combined it with Yorùbá indigenization of some English words, usually by adding extra syllables. For example, in the song "Shuffering and Shmilling," the word "pope" becomes *popu*, and the word "imam" becomes *imamu*. Fela's singing combined pitched and speech-like singing, similar to techniques employed in Yorùbá chanting and spoken practices such as *oríkì* (praise-epithets), *ìjálá* (hunters' songs), and *ewì* (poems). They usually come in the form of poetry, special greetings, and praise-epithets.

The approach outlined here will help students to move beyond hearing the semblances of jazz, soul, funk, or psychedelic rock, and to experience the culturally specific elements of Fela's sound. These include a modally grounded bitonal harmony, immersed in Yorùbá harmonic sensibilities and moving back and forth between the Dorian mode and the Aeolian mode of its dominant to create a harmonic foundation for a pentatonic-based melody shaped by the tonality of the Yorùbá language, and seamless transitions between singing and speech patterns, with the lyrics in localized lingua franca, Pidgin and Yorùbálized English.

Ultimately, as instructors, we must focus on the musicians and their culture to ensure that intercontinental interactions do not overshadow the inter- and intracultural manifestations, bearing in mind the power imbalance that often causes us to gloss over these dimensions. Additionally, the instructor must be dedicated to researching the local, in order to adequately facilitate a robust and culturally situated discourse; commit to emphasizing the local; and celebrate local victories and self-actualization. Finally, by focusing on the musicians and their culture, we will unravel their lived experiences and realities, their socio-economic and cultural negotiations, and their role in advancing cultural transformation and contributing to sustenance of the global, at the individual and collective level respectively.

Conclusion

Building on the ideas of equity-centered epistemological approaches in pedagogy, instructors must engage in equitable teaching. As such, continued reflexivity and self-questioning are essential; instructors must engage in continued (re)assessment and ask if they are adequately and equitably instructing the students, properly representing the culture(s) and musicians, and using due diligence to debunk existing cultural and musical stereotypes. The following questions are useful: am I committed to representing the musician and their culture appropriately? Am I committed to doing the work/research needed, instead of glossing over the topic and using what is readily available and understood to explain a complicated process? Am I presenting new ways to understand and interpret materials?

A survey music course offers several opportunities to train and ground students as global citizens. Students come into the classroom with preconceived and formulaic ideas, often rooted in essentialized and stereotypical portrayals, and they can easily recognize musical allusions. Thus, by our actions and inactions, we can either reinforce certain hegemonic misrepresentations, or we can provide an opportunity for cultural equitability, and, in line with the ultimate purpose of learning, nurture critical thinkers.

Whether or not we acknowledge it, the humanities classroom is political, not apolitical. When cultural equitability is lacking, culture-survey classes become sites of cultural contest: a contest between the immediate and the distanced, the local and the foreign, *us* and *them*. The instructor is a facilitator of knowledge, one who serves as an intermediary between the culture and the students, the immediate and the distanced. Simply put, the instructor is a social actor, a cultural influencer, and a political agent. The instructor decides what to teach, why it is crucial, and how to teach it; thus, the sheer act of teaching is itself a political one. Conversely, the act of adopting cultural equitability in the classroom, debunking myths and stereotypes, is a form of cultural activism—one that is needed to teach African popular music in the 21st century.

Notes

1 Kofi Agawu has addressed the fetishization of "African rhythm" in his essay, "The Invention of African Rhythm," and monograph, *Representing African Music*. Kofi Agawu, "The Invention of 'African Rhythm,'" *Journal of the American Musicological Society* 48, no. 3 (1995): 380–95; Kofi Agawu, *Representing African Music: Postcolonial Notes, Queries, Positions*.
2 Sarah Weiss, "Listening to the World but Hearing Ourselves: Hybridity and Perceptions of Authenticity in World Music," 508.
3 Jean Ngoya Kidula, "Stereotypes, Myths, and Realities Regarding African Music in the African and American Academy," in *Teaching Africa: A Guide for the 21st-Century Classroom*, 144.
4 Kofi Agawu, *Representing African Music: Postcolonial Notes, Queries, Positions*, 146.
5 Huib Schippers, "Applied Ethnomusicology and Intangible Cultural Heritage: Understanding 'Ecosystems of Music' as a Tool for Sustainability," in *Oxford Handbook of Applied Ethnomusicology*, 136.
6 Michael Bakan, *World Music: Traditions and Transformations*, xx.
7 Larry Rohter, "Guarding a Legacy from Nigeria to Broadway," *The New York Times*, July 11, 2010.
8 Chimamanda Ngozi Adichie, "The Danger of a Single Story." TED. 18:34. October 7, 2009, accessed March 22, 2021.
9 Michael Bakan, *World Music: Traditions and Transformations*.
10 Christopher Waterman, *Juju: A Social History and Ethnography of an African Popular Music*, 9.
11 Melville J. Herskovits, "Problem, Method and Theory in Afro American Studies," in *The New World Negro*, 351.
12 Gerhard Kubik, "Intra-African Streams of Influence," in *Africa: The Garland Encyclopedia of World Music*.
13 Arjun Appadurai, *Modernity at Large*.
14 Arjun Appadurai, *Modernity at Large: Cultural Dimensions of Globalization*, 27.
15 Marshall Hodgson, *The Venture of Islam, Conscience and History in a World Civilization*.
16 Lila Abu-Lughod, *Before European Hegemony: The World System A.D. 1250–1350*.
17 Arjun Appadurai, *Modernity at Large*, 27.
18 Gerhard Kubik, "Intra-African Streams of Influence."
19 Appadurai, *Modernity at Large*, 32.
20 Karin Barber, *A History of African Popular Culture (New Approaches to African History)*.
21 Margaret Kartomi, "The Process and Results of Musical Culture Contact: A Discussion of Terminology and Concepts," 237.
22 Kartomi, "The Process and Results of Musical Culture Contact," 237.

23 Michael Veal, *Fela: The Life and Times of an African Musical Icon*, 4.
24 See Carlos Moore, *Fela: This Bitch of a Life*.
25 Stephanie Shonekan, "Fela's Foundation: Examining the Revolutionary Songs of Funmilayo Ransome-Kuti and the Abeokuta Market Women's Movement in 1940s Western Nigeria," *Black Music Research Journal*.
26 Larry Rohter, "Guarding a Legacy from Nigeria to Broadway," *The New York Times*, July 11, 2010.
27 See the section "Afrobeat Aesthetics, Ideology, and Style" of the author's entry on Fela Kuti: "Fela Anikulapo-Kuti," in *Oxford Bibliographies in Music*, Oxford University Press, 2021.
28 Margaret Kartomi, "The Process and Results of Musical Culture Contact; A Discussion of Terminology and Concepts."
29 Kofi Agawu, "Tonality as a Colonizing Force in Africa," in *Audible Empire*, Ronald Radano and Tejumola Olaniyan.
30 I use the terms "modes" and "modal," though commonly used in Western musical discourse, as an act of cultural reclamation. I use them in the same manner that we use the term "music" in African musical discourse; though most African languages do not have a specific word for it, the concept is not foreign to them.
31 Kofi Agawu, *The African Imagination in Music*, 200.
32 See Bode Omojola, *Yorùbá Music in the Twentieth Century: Identity, Agency, and Performance Practice*, for an in-depth analysis of the tonal qualities of the Yorùbá language.
33 Kofi Agawu, *The African Imagination in Music*, 231.
34 Ibid.

References

Adichie, Chimamanda Ngozi. "The Danger of a Single Story." TED. 18:34. October 7, 2009. Accessed March 22, 2021. https://www.ted.com/talks/chimamanda_ngozi_adichie_the_danger_of_a_single_story?language=en.

Agawu, Kofi. *Representing African Music: Postcolonial Notes, Queries, Positions*. New York: Routledge, 2003.

———. *The African Imagination in Music*. New York: Oxford University Press, 2016.

———. "The Invention of 'African Rhythm.'" *Journal of the American Musicological Society* 48, no. 3 (1995): 380–95.

———. "Tonality as a Colonizing Force in Africa." In *Audible Empire*, edited by Ronald Radano and Tejumola Olaniyan, 334–56. Durham: Duke University Press, 2016.

Appadurai, Arjun, *Modernity at Large: Cultural Dimension of Globalization*. Minneapolis: University of Minnesota Press, 1996.

Bakan, Michael. *World Music: Traditions and Transformations*, 3rd edn. New York: McGraw-Hill Education, 2019.

Barber, Karin. *A History of African Popular Culture (New Approaches to African History)*. Cambridge: Cambridge University Press, 2018.

Herskovits, Melville J. "Problem, Method and Theory in Afro American Studies." *Phylon* 7, no. 4 (1946): 337–54. .

Kartomi, Margaret J. "The Processes and Results of Musical Culture Contact: A Discussion of Terminology and Concepts." *Ethnomusicology* 25, no. 2 (1981): 227–49.

Kidula, Jean Ngoya. "Stereotypes, Myths, and Realities Regarding African Music in the African and American Academy." In *Teaching Africa: A Guide for the 21st Century Classroom*, edited by Brandon D. Lundy and Solomon Negash, 140–55. Bloomington: Indiana University Press, 2013.

Kubik, Gerhard. "Inter-African Streams of Influence." In *Africa: The Garland Encyclopedia of World Music*, edited by Ruth Stone, 293–324. New York: Garland, 1998.

Moore, Carlos. *Fela: This Bitch of a Life*. London: Allison and Busby, 1982.

Omojola, Bode. *Yorùbá Music in the Twentieth Century: Identity, Agency, and Performance Practice*. New York: University of Rochester Press, 2012.

Rohter, Larry. "Guarding a Legacy from Nigeria to Broadway." *The New York Times*, July 11, 2010. https://www.nytimes.com/2010/07/12/arts/music/12femi.html.

Schippers, Huib. "Applied Ethnomusicology and Intangible Cultural Heritage: Understanding 'Ecosystems of Music' as a Tool for Sustainability." In *Oxford Handbook of Applied Ethnomusicology*, edited by Svanibor Pettan and Jeff Todd Titan. New York: Oxford University Press, 2015.

Shonekan, Stephanie. "Fela's Foundation: Examining the Revolutionary Songs of Funmilayo Ransome-Kuti and the Abeokuta Market Women's Movement in 1940s Western Nigeria." *Black Music Research Journal* 29, no. 1 (2009): 127–44.

Veal, Michael. *Fela: The Life and Times of an African Musical Icon*. Philadelphia: Temple University Press, 2000.

Waterman, Christopher. *Juju: A Social History and Ethnography of an African Popular Music*. Chicago: University of Chicago Press, 1990.

Weiss, Sarah. "Listening to the World but Hearing Ourselves: Hybridity and Perceptions of Authenticity in World Music." *Ethnomusicology* 58, no. 3 (2014): 506–25.

7 Por ti seré
Jarocho Fusion and Revivalism in "La Bamba"

Gregory Reish

"La Bamba" in the Pedagogical Canon

Ritchie Valens's surprise hit, "La Bamba" (1958), has long occupied a special place in the canon, historiography, and pedagogy of early rock 'n' roll and, more broadly, American popular music. "La Bamba" is indeed a remarkable record, sung in Spanish and adapted from a well-known traditional song that originated in the gulf-coast Mexican state of Veracruz.[1] Released as the B-side of a 45-r.p.m. single on Hollywood-based Del-Fi Records, "La Bamba" brought a reimagined interpretation of traditional, regional Mexican music to youthful radio audiences in the U.S. and helped to catapult Valens to fame just months before his tragic death at age 17. Almost 30 years later, his rock 'n' roll adaptation of "La Bamba" once again shot up the charts in a cover by Los Lobos,[2] who also performed the song in the Ritchie Valens biopic *La Bamba* (1987), directed by Luis Perez with Lou Diamond Phillips in the starring role.[3] The scene exhibits remarkable parallels to the way in which "La Bamba" is usually presented in textbooks and classrooms—that is, as a vehicle of transference from "authentic" Mexican to mainstream American pop music. Los Lobos perform the song on screen with the instruments and stylistic trappings of a Veracruzan group, even though the scene takes place in a Tijuana brothel, far from Veracruz. In the scene, Valens immediately recognizes the song when he hears it ("La Bamba" would have been familiar to almost any Mexican American of that era), and the excitement felt by this California-born teenager encountering "La Bamba" in Mexico inspires him to play along with the band and obviously gets his creative juices flowing. The film portrays this fictionalized account as a pivotal moment of artistic inspiration and cultural transference from Mexico to the U.S., and from the folk to the popular realm.

Because of its unusual origins, cultural-stylistic fusion, and lasting popularity, Valens's "La Bamba" has proven useful in undergraduate rock history and popular music survey courses, confirmed by its frequent appearance in apposite textbooks and their accompanying playlists. An

DOI: 10.4324/9781003415954-10

examination of these books reveals the extent to which the pedagogy of American popular music has relied on this particular recording to highlight Latin American cultural influences on rock and pop music (in most narratives picked up again in the 1960s by Santana). Its inclusion rightly complicates the simplistic narrative in which rock 'n' roll emerged from a confluence of Black and white musical styles—or an appropriation of Black music by white performers and record producers. Katherine Charlton, for example, points out that Valens's Spanish-language hit was "based on a traditional Mexican dance song," and that it "has remained popular on 'oldies' radio stations, attesting to the lasting appeal of upbeat Mexican rhythms."[4] Reebee Garofalo and Steve Waksman assert that because of the record's combination of R&B and Mexican stylistic elements, "its influence on popular music has been incalculable," that it laid the foundation for "the rock/Mexican fusions of Los Lobos in the 1970s and beyond," and that "Valens drew on his Chicano heritage to add another cultural source to the musical brew that was rock 'n' roll."[5] If rock 'n' roll is to be understood as a blended music, these authors ask us not to overlook the Latin American contribution to that mix.

In their ubiquitous textbook, *American Popular Music*, Larry Starr and Christopher Waterman devote considerable space to Ritchie Valens and his "La Bamba," offering students ample details about Valens's life and an analytically descriptive listening guide for the song. Here the authors go beyond merely alluding to the Mexican folk source of "La Bamba," naming the *son jarocho* genre and positing it as a product of the "Afro-Mexican culture" (i.e., the *mestizo*, or mixed, culture) of Veracruz.[6] They rightly point out that Veracruzan son jarocho is itself a fusion, one that "reflects a blend of Spanish, African, and Native American elements."[7] Thus the fusion that created rock 'n' roll drew on another noteworthy fusion that occurred in a folk tradition south of the border. Digging deeper into the stylistic nuts and bolts of Valens's performance, however, Starr and Waterman steer their readers away from the essential style traits of Veracruzan son jarocho, pointing instead to the "simpler and sparer" texture of Valens's performance, its structural repetitiveness, its lack of instrumental and vocal improvisation, and its use of a woodblock timbre "reminiscent of the Cuban claves used in Latin dance music ... to play a rhythm derived from the then-popular *cha-cha-chá*."[8]

From this analysis emerges a sense that the Veracruzan folk song "La Bamba"—more accurately categorized as a *son*[9]—served Valens as source material, an inspiration and outline for his rock 'n' roll arrangement, but not necessarily as a model for its most cogent stylistic features. The framing of Starr and Waterman's listening guide, which introduces pertinent information about the Mexican son jarocho, implicitly encourages us to make a comparison, to seek out a recorded performance of a Veracruzan "La Bamba" to illuminate how Valens transformed the song. Indeed, I have always done precisely this in my own American music survey courses, capitalizing on the students' likely familiarity with Valens's "La Bamba" to demonstrate that well-known pop hits sometimes have surprising pedigrees. What I wanted students to hear when comparing Valens's recording of the song with one that I presented as representative of the Veracruzan style were, in reality, just surface features: obvious similarities in the melody, lyrics, repeated I–IV–V harmonic progression, and arpeggiated ostinato accompaniment. Letting students hear a harp-driven performance by one of the commercially recorded son jarocho artists of the mid-twentieth century, such as Andrés Huesca or Conjunto Medellín de Lino Chávez, felt gratifying both for me as instructor and for them as students, inasmuch as the connections to Valens's rendition are easy to perceive. Such an exercise, either together in class or as part of some directed assignment, reinforces the idea that rock and pop music have never been the exclusive province of Black and white artists, and that folk music, even from less familiar cultures, can find its way into mainstream American pop culture through a process of absorption and reinterpretation—if not outright appropriation.

The pitfalls of such an approach, which have come increasingly into focus as our disciplinary perspectives have evolved since I began teaching in the 1990s, are threefold. First, such a simple and quick comparison between Valens's recording of "La Bamba" and a more "authentic" one by musicians from Veracruz sidesteps promising opportunities for more educative modes of listening. Students readily hear that they are in fact the same song, and thus become convinced of the historical narrative that their teachers and textbooks advance. Students feel a sense of auditory accomplishment, but one that is, in reality, rather perfunctory. To their credit, Starr and Waterman invite students to pay attention to features of difference as much as similarity, but the deeper meanings of such stylistic transformation might well go unnoticed when the primary pedagogical goal is to help students appreciate the multiculturalism of early rock 'n' roll. Second, in presenting a Mexican version of "La Bamba" for students to hear as a model for the rock 'n' roll version, we reinforce problematic notions of authenticity. The Mexican version, whichever one the instructor happens to choose, stands as a paradigm of cultural purity, the real deal (as it were), but functions pedagogically only as a point of reference, entirely in the service of helping students to appreciate the novelty and brilliance of turning it into a rock 'n' roll song. The brilliance of son jarocho itself stays out of view, as the students' attention remains focused on the canonic rock 'n' roll song that lies beyond the jarocho tradition. But authenticity in son jarocho is not at all clear cut; as I shall discuss in more detail below, the history of son jarocho involves the complicated and shifting interaction of cultural, political, and economic forces, and an ongoing struggle over the genre's various modes of authenticity. To take one particular Veracruzan recording of "La Bamba" as the authentic foil against which Valens's version can be compared is to ignore the complexity and creative mutability of the Veracruzan genre, as well as the strong likelihood that Valens knew the song from some non-Veracruzan source, such as a mariachi rendition.

This brings us to the third, and related, pitfall, which is treating folk music as static source material for commercial and "high art" idioms, as a culturally and musically monolithic entity from which inventive popular, jazz, or classical musicians can draw to stimulate their own creativity and innovation. Music majors and others who engage with Western art music in their course of study will undoubtedly confront this issue in the context of nineteenth and twentieth century musical nationalism, modernism, and other music-historical phenomena. The issue of musicians using folk traditions as a font of raw material also arises in jazz studies, although perhaps with less force. In popular music studies, questions about the uses and appropriation of folk music surface in discussions of the origins of the "roots music" industry in the 1920s, and in special cases such as Ritchie Valens's "La Bamba." These historical moments offer opportunities for instructors to introduce these difficult questions as they relate to commercialization, identity, imperialism, and other socio-cultural forces. One of the central problems for instructors and students to confront is that in such situations the value of a folk tradition might be recognized only in its usefulness to artists working in other idioms.

Complicating Notions of Transference and "Authenticity"

Here it can prove fruitful to upset the narrow linear model of folk-to-popular transference by comparing Valens's "La Bamba" to adaptations in other popular styles. His early rock 'n' roll interpretation was hardly the first and certainly not the last to come from outside of the jarocho tradition. In the 1940s the song became popular with both Latin and non-Latin dance orchestras in Mexico and the United States, which students can hear in a recording like that of Marga Llergo and Rafael Mendez with the All Star Pan-American Orchestra (1945). Beginning in the same decade, Mexican *trios románticos*, including the seminal group Los Panchos, took up "La Bamba" as an up-tempo showpiece for displaying their virtuosity on nylon string guitars, in contrast to their core repertoire of more sultry boleros. By the 1950s "La Bamba" was becoming a standard in the mariachi repertoire as well, as evinced in the recording by Mariachi Vargas de Tecalitlán and numerous others.

Among the many "La Bamba" covers that postdate Ritchie Valens's hit, several clearly owe their stylistic conception to his rock 'n' roll approach. Recordings such as those by Trini Lopez (1963), Dusty Springfield (1965), and Neil Diamond (1966) reveal the direct influence of Valens's recording outside the narrow trajectory that leads from him to

Los Lobos. But students might find later versions that are less obviously indebted to Valens more profitable for thinking critically about matters of stylistic interpretation. Jazz vibraphonist Cal Tjader included a funky, strictly instrumental, adaptation of "La Bamba" on his 1968 album *Solar Heat*, alongside his interpretation of Bobbie Gentry's provocative country hit "Ode to Billie Joe," and a number of Brazilian pieces. Iconic Tejano music star Selena recorded "La Bamba" on her eponymous major-label debut album in 1989, while Mexican-American artist Lila Downs puts Veracruzan instrumental timbres into new settings with her 2004 recording of the song. Los Angeles-based eclectic rock band Ozomatli reimagined "La Bamba" with a reggae groove in their 2017 collaboration with Slightly Stoopid. The Chicano group Las Cafeteras, who met while taking son jarocho classes at a community center in east Los Angeles,[10] transformed the song into an anthem of social activism with their "La Bamba Rebelde" (2012). According to José Navarro, Las Cafeteras uses son jarocho generally and "La Bamba" specifically "to produce counternarratives to nativist, anti-immigrant racist discourses and generate an oppositional political message to dominant discourses of criminality and other exclusions in the United States."[11] Because of the wide range of musical styles and cultural contexts surrounding these and the dozens of other readily available "La Bamba" covers, directed listening activities comparing any of them to Valens's version open up new pathways to understanding his 1958 hit as much more than a simple transference of Mexican folk tradition to early rock 'n' roll.

Another approach to contextualizing "La Bamba," one that has less to do with Ritchie Valens and more to do with the song's status as a global signifier of Latin American culture and identity writ large, is to consider its use in the folk revival. "La Bamba" was taken up by a number of prominent folk revivalists, particularly those in the commercial mainstream such as Harry Belafonte, who performed it at Carnegie Hall in 1960, and Jose Feliciano, who performed the song at the Newport Folk Festival in 1964.[12] In this context, "La Bamba" served as a representative example of Latin American folk culture in the revival's concerted effort to explore and present an ecumenical cross-section of the world's folk music in commercially accessible treatments for mainstream audiences. Already a familiar song to these listeners because of Valens's success, the commercial "folk" interpretations of "La Bamba" cast it in a new and exalted light, rescuing it from the shallowness of rock 'n' roll dance music and giving it a privileged place as a marker of Latin American—but not necessarily Veracruzan or even Mexican—cultural contributions.[13]

The notion of rescuing a musical style—and with it, an entire culture—is central to the revivalist impulse, and can be a highly effective way for students to understand a song, like "La Bamba," that has been subject to countless reimaginings. In their introduction to *The Oxford Handbook of Music Revival*, editors Caroline Bithell and Juniper Hill define musical revivalism as "an effort to perform and promote music that is valued as old or historical and is usually perceived to be threatened or moribund."[14] Music majors typically encounter this phenomenon under the rubric of "historical performance practice," and engagement can have eye-opening effects on their approaches to the performance of Western art music. In popular music courses, the topic of revivalism seems most likely to appear in coverage of the U.S. folk revival, chiefly because of its importance to the understanding of rock music history. It would be impossible for students to comprehend the influence of Bob Dylan, the rise of folk rock, and the emergence of the singer-songwriter phenomenon without delving into the folk revival. In my own teaching, I have found the subject to be rich and rewarding for students, helping them to contextualize rapid shifts in the American popular music industry in the 1950s and 60s, to connect popular music trends to the Civil Rights movement and other social activism of the era, to understand and appreciate the transformation from 1950s rock 'n' roll to late 1960s rock music in all of its breadth, and, perhaps most importantly, to grapple with difficult questions about power, class, race, and representation in U.S. society.

Thoughtful study of the folk revival can also lead students to more precise and more meaningful engagements with matters of audible musical style, both in the case of revivalists who sought to recreate earlier, rural styles (e.g., The New Lost City Ramblers), and those who sought to transform those styles into entertainment for the mainstream American market (e.g., The Kingston Trio). In his study of the folk revival, Ronald Cohen explores the ongoing tensions between "traditional" and "commercial" styles within the folk revival of the 1960s, and underscores efforts by promoters such as Alan Lomax toward "transforming traditional music into modern styles and sounds."[15] From this perspective, the study of the U.S. folk revival, or any other manifestation of the revivalist impulse, can encourage students to consider matters of style—be they recreations or transformations—and the motivations behind them. And while Ritchie Valens's "La Bamba" might not have arisen from such an impulse, covers by roughly contemporaneous artists associated with the folk revival often did.

As an alternative to examining "La Bamba" as a token of Latin Americanism in early rock 'n' roll, or as fodder for commercial pop, rock, folk, and jazz artists working outside the son jarocho tradition, I would suggest that a more rewarding pedagogical approach is to consider the song's history and evolution within its original cultural context. When we place the song inside the continuum of Veracruzan culture, we find that, far from being a static source of material or point of reference, "La Bamba" stands at the center of perennially contested meanings and ever-changing stylistic reinterpretations by Veracruzan musicians who maintain and challenge the tradition from within. We find that son jarocho is itself a style born of cultural admixture, one that already went through a folk-to-commercial process of transformation long before Ritchie Valens entered Gold Star Studios in the summer of 1958. We find also that son jarocho experienced its own revival—one that might be thought of as ongoing to this day—and that the jarocho revival led somewhat ironically to a new willingness on the part of Veracruzan musicians to explore stylistic fusions between son jarocho and a range of other idioms.

Yolanda Broyles-González has argued compellingly that son jarocho's *mestizo* character is a function of its core Indigeneity—that the genre's resilience and ability to absorb and transform outside influences reflects the very qualities that have allowed Indigenous culture to survive in the face of colonial and other potentially destructive forces. She "regard[s] Son Jarocho as an Indigenous cultural practice, while recognizing that it has incorporated and modified elements from various cultures."[16] As an Indigenous form of expressive art, son jarocho is built on conceptual and philosophical foundations in nature and the life cycle. She also critiques the race-centered mindset and terminology—including mestizo—that have framed most discussions of son jarocho both historically and contemporarily. To understand this process by which non-Indigenous, colonialist influences have been absorbed and reinterpreted for centuries in Veracruz, let us turn to an outline of its historical development.

The Commercialization and Revival of Son Jarocho

Son jarocho is a regional musical and dance idiom that originated and is still strongly associated with the Southern part of the Mexican gulf state of Veracruz and closely neighboring areas. The central part of this region, often called the "Sotavento" (Leeward), was the heart of the sugar cane agricultural industry during the era of colonial New Spain, from the sixteenth to the early nineteenth century. To sustain this industry at the lowest cost, the port city of Veracruz (just to the north of the Sotavento) served as the leading Mexican intake point for Spanish trade in enslaved Africans. As a result, the European-Indigenous cultural and ethnic mixture that obtains elsewhere in Mexico has added a significant African component in this part of Veracruz.[17] Much of this trade occurred by way of Havana and other parts of the Caribbean, making the port and Southern region of Veracruz a key part of what Antonio García de León calls the "Great Caribbean," a cultural region and economic zone that encompassed the Caribbean, the Gulf of Mexico, and Atlantic areas of northeastern South America.[18]

This tripartite Indigenous-Iberian-African mestizo culture and its connection to the Great Caribbean are central to Veracruzan identity and manifest in the music, poetry, dance, and surrounding practices of son jarocho. Steven Loza describes son jarocho as a "stylistic amalgam of influences derived from the Spanish colonizers of Mexico, from Africans taken to New Spain as slaves, and from the Indigenous population of the southeastern region of Mexico."[19] Rafael Figueroa Hernández echoes this core assessment in his monographic overview of the genre, calling it "a product of Indigenous, Hispanic and African transculturation in Mexico, [which] has been kept alive thanks to a long tradition that keeps it united and recognizable among all other genres of son in Mexico and other parts of the Americas."[20] There is evidence that elements of son jarocho poetry, music, and dance date from the colonial period; its earliest archival documentation seems to be a 1766 edict of the Inquisition banning the performance of a particular son, "El Chuchumbé," for what the Church considered its lascivious nature.[21] Despite such efforts to suppress its practice among the mestizo population of the Sotavento, son jarocho continued to flourish as a community-based folk music and dance tradition through the Mexican imperial and revolutionary periods.

In the early twentieth century, son jarocho was one of several Mexican regional folk styles that underwent a process of commercialization and mobilization in connection with developments in the Mexican media and entertainment industries, as well as in politics. Like *trova* and *boleros* from the Yucatán, and *son jalisciense* (mariachi) from Guadalajara and its environs, Veracruzan son jarocho came to Mexico City with formerly rural musicians seeking to professionalize their art for a larger audience. According to Francisco González:

> By the late 1920s, Mexican regional music had begun to draw national attention through the radio, sound recording, and film industries based in Mexico City. The Mexican film industry, still in its infancy, found that films featuring regional music were profitable. The first commercially successful Son Jarocho recording artists, such as Lorenzo Barcelata and Andrés Huesca, emerged during this time.[22]

Commercialization of the genre in mass entertainment media produced changes in musical style, with a new emphasis on tight vocal arrangements and precise instrumental virtuosity in place of the spontaneity and improvisation (including poetic improvisation) that characterized the rural folk tradition.

Son jarocho entered the political sphere during the presidency of Miguel Alemán, from 1946 to 1952. A former governor of Veracruz, Alemán was the first civilian president of Mexico in the twentieth century.[23] Along with his projects to industrialize Mexico and bring its commercial infrastructure up to first-world standards of the era, Alemán also sought to promote a sense of political cohesion across Mexico through a unified national identity. Alemán had used "La Bamba" during his presidential campaign as a type of theme song, and in office he continued to use it in his project of fostering a national feeling of *Mexicanidad* (Mexicanness). In the period immediately following Alemán's presidency, son jarocho generally and "La Bamba" specifically were adopted by Mexican musicians in other idioms, becoming central features of lavish *ballet folklórico* stage productions and marketing tools of the Veracruzan tourist industry.

In the late 1970s, decades of son jarocho commercialization and mobilization produced a backlash fed by the revivalist impulse. With the son jarocho revival, commonly known to members of the jarocho community as "el Renacimiento" (the Rebirth) or "el Movimiento" (the Movement), groups of mostly younger musicians inspired by revivalist movements in the U.S. and elsewhere, as well as by left-wing anti-commercial political theory, launched a project to revive rural son jarocho—to return it to what they posited as its authentic, pre-commercial style. Leaders of the jarocho revival concentrated their initial efforts on two fronts: first, archival research to uncover *sones* that had fallen out of practice, which included poring over phonographic fieldwork from the previous two decades; and second, forming new performance groups that learned directly from and even collaborated with elder musicians whom the revivalists felt had preserved pre-commercial styles and repertory. Groups in this initial wave of revivalists included Grupo Siquisirí, Los Parientes de Playa Vicente, Grupo Zacamandú, and Zazhil, but the most prominent and enduring group was undoubtedly Grupo Mono Blanco, led by Gilberto Gutiérrez. Unlike revivals in other parts of the world, the Movimiento jarocho came from within the culture: Gutiérrez and most of the others involved in these early efforts were Veracruzanos, chiefly from the rural areas of the Sotavento.

The commercialization of son jarocho in the film and recording industries of the 1940s, bolstered by Alemán's employment of "La Bamba" as a campaign song and signifier of a unified Mexicanidad, led to the revival's reception as a noble effort to return the genre to its rural folk roots, an ideal of authenticity that seems to accept the music's colonialist origins as legitimately Veracruzan or, in Broyles-González's view, Indigenous. The young revivalists understood how to make use of institutional support from the state and from universities, obtaining grants and establishing cultural centers to advance the project. Alejandro Nieto Miranda has summarized the revivalists' advantageous ability to move between political and cultural spaces:

> The groups of young enthusiasts who sought to rescue [rural] son jarocho from extinction had the characteristics of being able to

transit between rural Sotavento and urban centres with ease. Most of them were born in the Sotavento, had intermittently moved to large cities to study or work, and had strong links with groups of people in Mexico City, Veracruz, Xalapa, and Minatitlán, and later on in San Francisco and Los Angeles, California. This capacity to move among different circles allowed them to direct economic resources provided by governmental institutions ... for projects aimed at promoting the popular culture of Sotavento.[24]

By the early 1990s, the son jarocho revival had begun spreading into urban centers throughout Mexico and into the United States. In 1992, Gilberto Gutiérrez obtained a Rockefeller-Bancomer-Conaculta grant to come to California for the purpose of promoting his concept of a community-based son jarocho to Chicano communities in the United States, wisely recognizing the importance of gaining such support for his broader project. He wound up staying in California for three years, spreading the seeds of a revitalized jarocho culture in the Mexican diaspora, bringing son jarocho to broader audiences, reformulating Grupo Mono Blanco, and building both institutional and musical partnerships.[25] Interactions with Chicano and other Latin American musicians presented opportunities for fusions with other styles—an ironic response to the earlier phase of commercialization that the revivalists considered a corruption of the genre.

The seminal moment in the creation of a new and progressive-minded jarocho fusion came with the release of the album *El Mundo Se Va A Acabar* in 1997 by Grupo Mono Blanco, in collaboration with a loose collective of Latin American, African, and other world musicians calling themselves Stone Lips.[26] In the album notes for this groundbreaking release, Eugene Rodríguez justifies the musico-cultural fusion as a reflection of the history of Veracruz, "a historically important port of entry to Mexico [that] has seen wave upon wave of cultural infusions from all over the world."[27] He describes commonalities among the idioms that the musicians immediately recognized and that descend from the mestizo and colonialist history of the Sotavento: "West African drummers immediately identified the rhythms of the son jarocho as West African, [while] East Indian musicians, Afro-Cuban *soneros*, as well as flamenco musicians of Southern Spain immediately identified with the rhythms, verse structures and dances of the son jarocho."[28] Rodríguez also emphasizes the commercial appeal of cross-cultural fusions for bringing son jarocho to broader audiences and thus ensuring its sustainability.

The jarocho fusion pioneered by the very group of revivalists that had spearheaded a return to "purer" rural folk styles twenty years earlier "encouraged the creativity of new generations that would have the means to develop it without limitations," according to César Castro, a younger-generation musician born in Veracruz who now leads the group Cambalache in Los Angeles.[29] Indeed, since the late 1990s, the jarocho fusion phenomenon has produced an explosion of creativity that has taken the music in countless conceptual directions. Groups such as Son de Madera, Los Cojolites, Chéjere, Los Aguas Aguas, Ampersan, La Manta, and Patricio Hidalgo y el Afrojarocho have explored fusions with jazz, rock, salsa, reggae, hip-hop, cumbia, and numerous other world idioms, sometimes with remarkable commercial success. It is noteworthy that most of these groups have roots in Veracruz and considerable experience with the kind of staunchly traditional son jarocho promoted by Grupo Mono Blanco and the other early revivalists.

Jarocho Fusion in the Classroom

Rehearsing some of this fascinating history with students through lectures, discussions, reading and listening assignments, or other activities—none of which require the instructor to have expertise in Mexican music—can help them to hear deep layers of meaning in a jarocho fusion treatment of "La Bamba," such as that by Sonex (also called Los Sonex), another leading fusion group based in Xalapa, Veracruz, whose members come from deep within the tradition. Their 2007 interpretation of the song, a track from the group's eponymous debut album, will strike twenty-first century students as immediately intriguing and at least partially accessible. Students will likely have heard the Ritchie Valens version of "La Bamba" or some later cover of it, but from the outset their ears will hear something different from Sonex, something contemporary, something that alludes to a range of familiar and unfamiliar sounds while seemingly bypassing the 1958 rock 'n' roll version entirely.

Son jarocho scholar Randall Kohl has analyzed aspects of the structure and musical surface features of Sonex's "La Bamba" in some detail, summarizing its eclecticism in this way:

> [T]here is a great deal of influence of other musical genres, for example hip-hop, through the inclusion of scratching, produced by the percussive sound of the needle scratching on a vinyl record. We also hear sampling, which consists of electronically recording sounds or lyrics playable through a synthesizer, as well as other electronic effects executed in the recording studio. The instrumentation is aligned with a rock band, with an electric bass playing funk-influenced lines, and drums playing marching rhythms. All of this, plus the open vocal harmonies, contribute to the production of a mix of modern styles.[30]

Kohl goes on to describe how certain traditional elements are maintained in the performance, such as the opening melodic *declaración* (used in a traditional setting to indicate to other musicians which son is commencing) played by the *requinto* (a plucked string instrument and traditional lead of son jarocho). He also outlines a "structural arrangement [that] follows the traditional versification," a crucial component of the traditional son jarocho style that mid-twentieth century commercial jarocho musicians had largely abandoned, and which the revivalists recovered, as well as a "type of *hook*" that appears in the final three verses of the performance.[31]

To Kohl's analysis, we might add certain lyrical features of Sonex's "La Bamba" that enrich and complicate its connection to the genre's Veracruzan heritage. Traditional son jarocho of the type advocated by the revivalists features lyrical and poetic improvisation, a highly valued skill exhibited during community-based performances. While Sonex's carefully produced and arranged studio recording of "La Bamba" evinces no lyrical improvisatory characteristics, the group's recomposition of the song's standard lyrical content reinforces their acceptance of it as an authentic inheritance of the revival. Their version includes subtle, but I think deliberate, allusions to the titles of other common sones embraced by the revival, such as "La Morena," "La Candela," and "La Iguana," and indirectly to "La Guacamaya," with its telltale references to flying ("volando"). By incorporating lyrical allusions to sones that are central to the revival but did not undergo the same kind of commercial transference to other cultures that "La Bamba" did, Sonex position "La Bamba" at the core of the traditional son jarocho repertory. They reclaim it as an authentic inheritance from the revivalists, who have now given the fusionists their approval to take the music in new directions.

"Is this more authentic than a version by Ritchie Valens or Los Lobos?," we might ask our students. It's a group from Veracruz, after all, whose leaders grew up steeped in the son jarocho tradition, despite its liberal stylistic eclecticism. Considering the implications of this information, the students might wonder how something that comes from within the tradition can draw so explicitly on many non-Mexican idioms. How can it come from a movement that prized rural authenticity but take so many stylistic liberties? What does it mean for this group of Veracruzan musicians to blend their beloved "La Bamba" with rock, funk, and hip-hop, while seemingly avoiding any reference to the rock and pop versions that Ritchie Valens spawned? Whose song is this and what does it become in such a postmodern cross-cultural fusion? The answers to these questions should not be simple for us or for our students. As the words of "La Bamba" repeat in hook-like fashion, the singer will be whatever we want him to be. "I am not a sailor," he repeats, but "for you I will be" ("Yo no soy marinero, por ti seré").

Notes

1 The etymology and meaning of the song's title word have been much discussed in the literature, traced to possible origins in Africa, Spain, and Cuba. For a useful summary of this research, see Kohl, *Ecos de "La Bamba,"* 170–175.

2 Steven Loza points out that the Los Lobos cover of Valens's arrangement "held the number one position on U.S. pop music charts for three weeks in 1987, and eventually sold over three million copies, achieving the status of a triple platinum single. The song reached the number one position on pop charts in at least 26 other countries as well." Loza, "From Veracruz to Los Angeles," 191.
3 It is not known where and when Valens first heard "La Bamba" or exactly how he developed the idea to transform it into a rock 'n' roll song. See Mendheim, *Ritchie Valens*, 61–64.
4 Charlton, *Rock Music Styles*, 75.
5 Garofalo and Waksman, *Rockin' Out*, 73.
6 The term "mestizo" is central to ongoing debates about Mexican identity and carries powerful connotations about legacies of colonialism, slavery, power, and representation. Its use here is meant to invoke those complexities.
7 Starr and Waterman, *American Popular Music*, 281.
8 Starr and Waterman, *American Popular Music*, 282.
9 In Mexican music, *son* indicates a network of regional folk traditions that share certain musical, poetic, and dance characteristics. The best known are son jarocho, son huasteco, and son jalisciense (the latter being the historical precursor to mariachi music). Generally, *son* is distinguished from the *canción, corrido, bolero, pirekua*, and other song types.
10 Garcia, Andres. "Las Cafeteras Tells Compelling Chicano Stories Through Music."
11 Navarro, "'La Bamba Rebelde,'" 434.
12 Both of these performances were issued soon after the concerts on commercial live albums: *Belafonte Returns to Carnegie Hall* (1960) and *The Newport Folk Festival 1964: Evening Concerts, Vol. 1* (1965).
13 It is worth noting that Feliciano is not of Mexican heritage but a Puerto Rican artist, although this probably mattered little to Newport audiences in the 1960s.
14 Bithell and Hill, "An Introduction to Music Revival as Concept, Cultural Process, and Medium of Change," 3.
15 Cohen, *Rainbow Quest*, 38.
16 Broyles-González, "Son Jarocho's Indigenous Expressivity across Geographies," 53–130.
17 There exists abundant literature on the Afro-Mexican history of Veracruz. See, for instance, Carroll, *Blacks in Colonial* Veracruz; García de León, *Tierra adentro, mar en fuera*; Malfavon, "Kin of the Leeward Port: Afro-Mexicans in Veracruz."
18 García de León, *El mar de los deseos*, 19–54.
19 Loza, "From Veracruz to Los Angeles," 179.
20 Figueroa Hernández, *Son jarocho: Guía histórico-musical*, 9. "Un producto de la transculturación cultural indígena, hispana y africana en México, el son jarocho se ha logrado mantener vivo gracis a una larga tradición que lo mantiene unido y reconocible entre todas los démas géneros del son en México y en otras partes de América." All translations mine.
21 Sheehy, "The Son Jarocho," 23.
22 González, "Musical Reflections on Mario Barradas and Son Jarocho," 43.
23 Gauss, *Made in Mexico*, 169–204.
24 Miranda Nieto, *Musical Mobilities*, 29.
25 García Díaz, *El renacimiento del son jarocho*, 215–220.
26 The personnel includes Gilberto Gutiérrez, Octavio Vega, Andrés Vega (all of Grupo Mono Blanco), David Hidalgo (of Los Lobos), Eugene Rodriguez (founder of Los Cenzontles), Shira Kammen (a bowed string player known

for her work in Medieval and Baroque European music), John Santos (a San Francisco-based Afro-Latin percussionist), César Cancino (a pianist who worked with Joan Baez and others), and Babou Sagna (a Senegalese djembe player).
27 Rodríguez, liner notes for *El Mundo se va a acabar*, 14.
28 Rodríguez, liner notes for *El Mundo se va a acabar*, 13.
29 Quoted in García Díaz, *El renacimiento del son jarocho*, 344. The band's name, Cambalache, means *exchange*. "[E]sta grabación incentivó la creatividad de nuevas generaciones que tendrían lod medios para desarrollarla sin limitacitones."
30 Kohl, *Declaraciones del son*, 57–58. "[H]ay mucha influencia de otros géneros musicales, por ejemplo de hip-hop, a través de la inclusión de *scratching*, producido por el sonido percusivo de la aguja que raspa sobre un disco de vinilo. También, se oye *sampling*, que consiste en grabar sonidos o letra electrónicamente para poder tocarlos a través de un sintetizador, además de otros efectos electrónicos ejecutados dentro del estudio de grabación. La instrumentación está alineada con una banda de rock, con un bajo eléctrico que toca líneas influenciadas por el funk, y una batería que reproduce ritmos de marcha. Todo esto, más las armonías abiertas vocales contribuyen a la producción de una mezcla de estilos modernos."
31 Kohl, *Declaraciones del son*, 58–59. "El arreglo formal sigue la tradicional estrófica." "un tipo de *hook*."

References

Belafonte, Harry. *Belafonte Returns to Carnegie Hall*. Recorded May 1960. RCA Victor LOC-6007, 1960. LP.

Bithell, Caroline, and Hill Juniper. "An Introduction to Music Revival as Concept, Cultural Process, and Medium of Change." In *The Oxford Handbook of Music Revival*, edited by Caroline Bithell and Juniper Hill, 3–42. New York: Oxford University Press, 2014.

Broyles-González, Yolanda. "Son Jarocho's Indigenous Expressivity across Geographies." In *Mario Barradas and Son Jarocho: The Journey of a Mexican Regional Music*, edited by Yolanda Broyles-González, Rafael Figueroa Hernández, and Francisco González, 53–130. Austin: University of Texas Press, 2022.

Carroll, Patrick James. *Blacks in Colonial Veracruz: Race, Ethnicity, and Regional Development*, 2nd edn. Austin: University of Texas Press, 2001.

Charlton, Katherine. *Rock Music Styles: A History*, 5th edn. New York: McGraw-Hill, 2008.

Cohen, Ronald D. *Rainbow Quest: The Folk Music Revival and American Society, 1940–1970*. Amherst and Boston: University of Massachusetts Press, 2002.

Figueroa Hernández, Rafael. *Son jarocho: Guía histórico-musical*. Xalapa, Veracruz: Conaculta, 2007.

Garcia, Andres. "Las Cafeteras Tells Compelling Chicano Stories Through Music." *UWIRE Text*, November 4, 2013. Accessed March 12, 2023. https://link.gale.com/apps/doc/A347948452/AONE?u=tel_oweb&sid=bookmark-AONE&xid=fc23fc03.

García de León, Antonio. *El mar de los deseos: El Caribe afroandaluz, historia y contrapunto*. Mexico City: Fondo de Cultura Económica, 2016.

García de León, Antonio. *Tierra adentro, mar en fuera: El Puerto de Veracruz y su litoral a sotavento, 1519–1821*. Mexico City: Fondo de Cultura Económica, 2011.

García Díaz, Bernardo. *El renacimiento del son jarocho y El Grupo Mono Blanco (1977–2000)*. Xalapa, Veracruz: Universidad Veracruzana, 2022.

Garofalo, Reebee, and Steve Waksman. *Rockin' Out: Popular Music in the U.S.A*, Updated 6th edn. New York: Pearson, 2017.

Gauss, Susan M. *Made in Mexico: Regions, Nation, and the State in the Rise of Mexican Industrialism, 1920s–1940s*. University Park: Pennsylvania State University Press, 2010.

González, Francisco. "Musical Reflections on Mario Barradas and Son Jarocho." In *Mario Barradas and Son Jarocho: The Journey of a Mexican Regional Music*, edited by Yolanda Broyles-González, Rafael Figueroa Hernández, and Francisco González, 41–51. Austin: University of Texas Press, 2022.

Kohl S., Randall Ch. *Declaraciones del son: El requinto jarocho en la creación del conocimiento sociomusical*. Xalapa, Veracruz: Gobierno del Estado de Veracruz, 2013.

Kohl S., Randall Ch. *Ecos de "La Bamba": Una historia etnomusicológica sobre el son jarocho de Veracruz, 1949–1959*. Xalapa, Veracruz: Instituto Veracruzano de Cultura, Colección Atarazanas, 2007.

Loza, Steven. "From Veracruz to Los Angeles: The Reinterpretation of the Son Jarocho." *Latin American Music Review* 13, no. 2 (Fall/Winter 1992): 179–94.

Malfavon, Alan Alexander. "Kin of the Leeward Port: Afro-Mexicans in Veracruz in the Making of State Formation, Contested Spaces, and Regional Development, 1770–1830." PhD diss., University of California at Riverside, 2021. ProQuest Dissertations & Theses Global.

Mendheim, Beverly. *Ritchie Valens: The First Latino Rocker*. Tempe: Bilingual Press, 1987.

Miranda Nieto, Alejandro. *Musical Mobilities: Son Jarocho and the Circulation of Tradition across Mexico and the United States*. London and New York: Routledge, 2018.

Navarro, José. "'La Bamba Rebelde': Chicana/o nationalism, transnational culture, and postnationalist politics." *Latino Studies* 14 (2016): 431–57.

Rodríguez, Eugene. "Liner notes for Grupo Mono Blanco y Stone Lips." *El Mundo se va a acabar*. Fonca/Urtext UL 3004, 1997. Compact disc.

Sheehy, Daniel Edward. "The Son Jarocho: The History, Style, and Repertory of a Changing Mexican Musical Tradition." PhD diss., University of California at Los Angeles, 1979.

Starr, Larry, and Christopher Waterman. *American Popular Music: From Minstrelsy to MP3*, 5th edn. New York: Oxford University Press, 2018.

Various Artists. *The Newport Folk Festival 1964: Evening Concerts, Vol. 1*. Recorded July 1964. Vanguard VSD-79184, 1965. LP.

Part III
Training Global Musicians

8 From Brazilian Worship Houses to a U.S. College

Recontextualizations of Afro-Brazilian Religious Music and Movement

Marc M. Gidal

As musicologists rigorously contextualize music, they might also consider recontextualizations. In Kay Kaufman Shelemay's framework for studying any music tradition by approaching its "sound, setting, and significance," diverse settings (contexts) can influence a tradition's sounds and significances (functions, interpretations, values, and aesthetics).[1] Ethnomusicologists have repeatedly shown that the circulation of music, musicians, and instruments associated with religious ceremonies, for example, affects the purposes and meanings of music for practitioners and audiences.[2] Deborah Kapchan asks, "what travels?" when Gnawan musicians for spirit-mediumship ceremonies perform beyond Morocco in European music festivals and collaborate with American jazz musicians. She offers:

> In the appropriation of sound and meaning it is not surprising that signs are emptied of some of their associations and infused with others. What is noteworthy is which meanings are repressed and which are taken up as metonyms of cultural identity.[3]

Recontextualized music can provide entertainment, inspire musical borrowings, foster intercultural education, and inform identities; it can reveal effects of mobility, migration, and cross-cultural encounters. The prefix "re" implies a previous setting and therefore begs comparison; however, the prior site should not be presumed original, static, or lacking its own history of change and hybridity. In short, the term "recontextualization" reminds scholars to observe ongoing processes of circulation, application, transformation, and interpretation.

By explaining recontextualizations of Afro-Brazilian religious music as a topic for collegiate teaching, this chapter addresses several questions: how did religious music with several Western-African roots develop in the Americas, specifically in multiracial Brazil with its Portuguese-speaking Catholic majority? What happens when the music and dance of semi-private religious rituals are presented in public, secular settings for entertainment, social activism, or education? How do audiences, including undergraduate

DOI: 10.4324/9781003415954-12

students in the U.S., respond to unfamiliar religious music and dance from Brazil? And how can music instructors teach about musical cultures in diverse situations, including collegiate ensembles and musicology courses?[4]

With instructors and undergraduate students in mind, this chapter's three goals are to introduce Afro-Brazilian religious music and movement in contrasting recontextualizations; to compare divergent goals, practices, and responses to the traditions; and to provide primary sources for instruction. The first setting is a worship house in southernmost Brazil, where I conducted ethnomusicological research. I summarize the worldviews, ritual goals and structure, music (chanting with drums and percussion), and congregational circumambulatory dance-like movements. Already a recontextualization responding to cultural contact, this tradition, called *Batuque*, is derived from Western Africa but practiced in a heterogeneous Brazilian milieu, in which it is a southern adaptation from northeastern Brazil. These practices are briefly compared to those of *Candomblé*, the best-known Afro-Brazilian religion. The second set of recontextualizations are from a public liberal arts college in the U.S. where I teach musicology. I helped to bring the Afro-Brazilian folkloric performance troupe Ologundê to perform for a public audience and teach workshops about the music and movement of Candomblé. This section foregrounds the goals of multicultural education and entertainment, starting with the troupe's folkloric secularization: they use non-sacralized drums, teach music from multiple sub-traditions, and perform stylized dances rather than congregational movement. During their workshops with students, anxieties about authenticity/inauthenticity and comfort/discomfort provoked intercultural reflection. I then explain how my colleague who directs the college's Brazilian Percussion Ensemble includes rhythms of Candomblé recontextualized via Carnival parading groups that have striven for social justice. I also raise issues common among collegiate world-music ensembles. Finally, I briefly share how I teach Afro-Brazilian religious music within music history and ethnomusicology courses through scalable lessons that use this chapter's materials. The sections individually and collectively provide lessons in musical recontextualization.

Recontextualization in Worship Houses in Brazil

The first recontextualizations are ceremonies in worship houses of different traditions of Afro-Brazilian religion: first a detailed example from southern Brazil and then brief comparisons to Candomblé in northeastern Brazil. Video Example 1, which I filmed with permission and posted on YouTube, serves to introduce the ceremony, ritual music, and congregational movements typical of the religion known as Batuque, *Nação* (Nation), or *Africanismo*.[5] (Watch Video Example 1 here: https://youtu.be/pdbXSuUBmOs.) Elsewhere in Brazil, *batuque* refers to Afro-Brazilian circle dance, while in this case it metonymically refers to the religion that includes a ritualized circle dance. "Nation" also refers to sub-traditions (i.e., subgroups, branches, denominations) within each Afro-Brazilian religion that are associated with different African regional/ethnic heritages; the music can vary by nation as well as by religion. Batuque is directly related to Afro-Brazilian religions based in northeastern Brazil: Candomblé, *Tambor da Mina*, and *Xangô* (also the name of a divinity). These are similar to Afro-Caribbean religions such as Cuban *La Regla de Ocha*, widely known as *Santería*. These derived from West and Western-Central African religions, developing in the majority Catholic and Portuguese/Hispanic Americas. The cross-cultural result—an example of syncretism—was the aligning of divinities from African religions with Jesus, Mary, and the Saints of Catholicism. Another development, visible in the video example, concerns multiracial communities of devotees: the religion is African-derived, yet the practitioners have diverse ancestries.

The common spiritual goals of these Afro-Latin-American religions are for devotees to communicate with gods, called *orixás*, *voduns*, or *inkises* (using Brazilian spellings) in different African languages, who are associated with natural realms and human characteristics. In addition to praising them, devotees request help from deities in exchange for devotion—a point of commonality with folk Catholicism. A third type of communication can happen during ceremonies when the divinities "manifest," as they say, in trained spirit mediums; the mediums with manifested deities may also bestow blessings and private advice upon congregants in order to assist them with personal problems. To facilitate such supernatural communications, congregational music and dance help contact the gods, coordinate praise, and create an ambiance conducive for manifestations. As with other religions, ceremonies also provide opportunities for teaching the religion, fostering sociability, expressing identity, celebrating life-cycle events, and so on.

The video-recorded ceremony occurred during an annual celebration to commemorate the divinity Ogum in the worship house (*terreiro*) of the religious leader Mãe Turca de Ogum (Mother Turca of Ogum). It took place on November 17, 2007 in Porto Alegre, the state capital of Rio Grande do Sul, which borders Uruguay and Argentina. The annual event marks Mãe Turca's first ritual connection with Ogum, who is her primary deity. The several-day feast includes a semi-public ceremony to 12 divinities in Batuque that lasts six-plus hours in the middle of the night and early morning. Although the chants call and praise the deities in individualized sections lasting around half an hour each, any of them may manifest in a devotee associated with that deity at any time.

Mãe Turca practices a common combination of nations, *Jêje-Ijexá*, in which Ogum is the second *orixá* (as this nation refers to the gods) to be praised. Leaders sing a series of chants constituting around 50 statements, 2–12 words long, sung repetitively in call-response with congregants. The musical leader (*alabê*) is usually a singer who has reached a credentialed level in the religion, though the religious leader may also lead singing. Men and women can serve as *alabês* in Batuque, though other Afro-Brazilian religions permit only men. The musical leader performs two types of praise chants: first are unaccompanied spoken salutations to each deity using their names, honorifics, and unique greetings, recited in free rhythm; second are metered responsorial sung chants with percussion accompaniment. The *alabê* at Mãe Turca's ceremony, Pai Cleber "Teixeiro" de Oxalá, only led the sung chants, whereas my teacher, the *alabê* Pai Antonio Carlos de Xangô Machado, performs both, as can be heard on his commercial recordings available online.[6]

The Video Guide and the approximating music transcription in Figure 8.1 highlight moments in the video and explain singing, drumming, and movements in a ceremonial setting. Detailed are two chants at the

Figure 8.1 Four chants to Ogum from the ceremony excerpted in Video Example 1.

beginning and two chants near the end, which accompany different dance steps. The musicians repeat each chant numerous times with variations in the calls and drumming. In Figure 8.1, the singing reveals pentatonic melodies and rhythms common in Brazil, the latter deriving from combinations of eighth and sixteenth notes, off-beat accenting, and beat anticipations. The singing lacks the consistency of commercial recordings, with out-of-tune moments and temporary modulations.[7] For instance, Cleber starts in A major but the assistant *alabê* Jorge inexplicably modulates to C-sharp major in the second chant's response, although they return to A major by the last of the chants transcribed.

Video Guide

Sung-prayers to Ogum during a Batuque celebration at the worship house of Mãe Turca de Ogum in Porto Alegre, Rio Grande do Sul, Brazil, on Nov 17, 2007. Filmed by author with permission.[8]

Timecode	Lyrics	Translations and notes
0:00	**Recited greeting:** Call: *Bata kori Ogunhê!* Response: *Ogunhê!*	"Praise Ogum!" Recited greeting to the *orixá*. Other *alabês* will recite a list of names and salutations to each divinity.
0:13	**Chant 1:** Call: *Oni-oni-oni-ra,*	Onira is a name of Ogum. The first sung chant begins in free rhythm.
0:17	*Onira do adiô [ariô], adiô lau kerê ô.*	"Ogum requests his sword and asks Bará to clean and sharpen it."
0:21	Response: *O[gum] ariô, ariô umquerê ô.*	Drummers play the rhythm *aré* (see Figure 2). Dance: Congregants move counterclockwise around the salon with a dance step to the right side (feet: RLRL) and to the left side (feet: LRLR) while hand-gesturing to mimic Ogum's sword. Four repetitions of the chant.
0:56	**Chant 2:** Call: *Iyé Áma jocole d'Ogum-ô.*	"Ogum presents his sword to all the *orixás* and asks permission to go to war." One repetition.
0:59	Response: *Erumalé, ama jocole d'Ogum-ô orumalé.*	
1:34		Nine more chants.
8:12	**Chant 12:** Call: *Ogum adeiba.*	"Ogum arrives tired and thirsty from war, Oiá shows him the drink."
8:13	Response: *Adefa iogum farerê.*	Six repetitions.

Timecode	Lyrics	Translations and notes
8:42	**Chant 13:** Call 1: *[On]ira ba foiba.* Call 2: *Ogum amo foiba.*	"Ogum returns from the war and celebrates the victory with his wife and his friend Bará, with drinking." This is the second call of this chant. The two calls alternate.
8:44	Response: *Amoro iogum fererê.*	Dance: During this chant, congregants mimic drinking with a bottle over their mouths as they pause while moving side to side. For subsequent chants, they resume the prior dance and hand gesture. Ten repetitions.
9:29		They repeat the previous chant, "*Ogum adeiba / Adefa iogum farerê*," and the section ends. After the video excerpt, the *alabê* starts a new rhythm and chants to Avagam, a different name of Ogum.

Cleber starts this section by greeting Ogum, "*Bata kori Ogunhê!*," to which congregants respond, "*Ogunhê!*" (Praise Ogum!). In free rhythm, he begins the first chant by announcing Onira, a name of Ogum, who is praised during this section. He initiates the drumming in meter while continuing the chant, "*Onira do adiô, adiô lau kerê ô*" (others say "*ariô*"). With the drumming, the congregants start moving and singing the response line, led by Jorge, "*O ariô, ariô umquerê ô*" (Machado teaches, "*Ogum ariô, ariô umquerê ô*"). The Video Guide includes the chant's meaning according to Machado's understanding: "Ogum requests his sword and asks Bará [another *orixá*] to clean and sharpen it." The transliterations are also based on Machado's unpublished teaching materials, with modifications to match what Cleber and Jorge sing in the video. Indicative of recontextualization, there exist countless variations of chant lyrics, transliterations, and interpretive meanings in Brazil, due to the fact that the original lyrics in Yoruba, Fon, Kikongo, and other African languages have been modified through centuries of oral-aural transmission among Portuguese speakers in this diasporic country.

In Batuque, the singing is accompanied by one or more double-headed barrel drums (*ilú/tambor*), beaded gourd shakers (*agé/xequerê*), and an occasionally used double-bell (*agogô*). A second type of double-headed conical drum (*inhã*) is used by specific nations in certain circumstances. Depending on the musicians and nation, one-to-two dozen drum rhythms are used to accompany medleys of chants. Some rhythms accompany multiple deities; others are specific to a chant, and thus a deity; some rhythms accompany particular moments in the ceremony; and a few rhythms are associated with nations. For instance, the video example features a percussion pattern widely known as *aré*, which is used throughout the ceremony

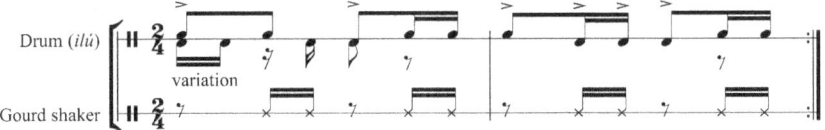

Figure 8.2 The Batuque rhythm *aré*, with a variation, as performed by Pai Cleber "Teixeira" de Oxalá in Video Example 1.

(see Figure 8.2). By contrast, a later chant to Ogum Avagam has a drum rhythm called *deiri* that accents the syllables of the opening phrase, including both the call and the response; it is only played in that part of the ceremony. Through these consistent usages, devotees develop associations between the rhythms and divinities or settings in addition to recalling personal experiences. The comingling of rhythms from different nations also illustrates recontextualization.

Ceremonies include movements for congregants and dances for mediums with manifested divinities. The video example captures the first type though not the second. While singing, the congregants move counterclockwise around the main room with simple dance steps and sometimes hand gestures that mimic the movements of a deity or the meaning of lyrics. In the video excerpt, congregants move forward while dancing side to side with their feet: to the right side (right foot, left foot, right foot, left foot) and to the left side (left foot, right foot, left foot, right foot). They also mimic Ogum's sword by chopping with one open and straight hand onto the other, in time with the beat. During a later chant in the video, which I have numbered "Chant 13" and which is understood to mean that Ogum is drinking, congregants pause in their steps on each side to mimic drinking from a bottle above their mouths while singing the response line (timecode 8:44).

Intentionally absent from this video are mediums with manifested *orixás*, which means that we cannot witness here their dance steps, hand gestures, altered bodily comportment, and facial expressions. When a devotee receives a divinity, they tend to lose a certain amount of control, noticed by others around them who then greet the deity, for example calling out, "*Ogunhê!*" (Praise Ogum!). Some congregants surround the medium and ensure they do not hurt themselves, such as by removing their glasses. Knowledgeable practitioners may guide the mediums as they make conventional bows to the religious leader, the altar alcove, the open front door, and the musicians. They are then led to the center of the room, where they methodically greet other mediums with manifested divinities, dance with gestures and characteristics of their divinity, and possibly bestow blessings upon congregants. Before the ceremony ends, any remaining manifestations are ritually released from the mediums. As is standard etiquette for Batuque worship houses, Mãe Turca gave me permission to record video until the first manifestation, and only audio thereafter, because the tradition forbids mediums to see images of themselves in this state. During other events I was allowed to video-record if far enough back that individuals were not identifiable. Nevertheless, this etiquette varies: it is easy to find online videos of mediums receiving divinities, and a Candomblé house I visited in Rio de Janeiro video-recorded the ceremony.

The Batuque practices described here, far from static, are iterations in a long dynamic history of adaptation to new settings. All Afro-Brazilian religions derive aspects of West and Western-Central African religious beliefs and practices first brought to South America during the transatlantic slave trade and shaped thereafter by subsequent migrations, travelers, merchant traders, and an ongoing multi-directional "live dialogue" in the Afro-Atlantic, as J.L. Matory has explained.[9] The traditions of Batuque's *Jêje* nation, for instance, were shaped by nineteenth-century migrations south from northeastern Brazil—the drums come from the Recife's Xangô religion—and, at the turn of the twentieth century, by a religious leader who migrated from the Bight of Benin in West Africa; Machado's grandfather was his *alabê*. The Brazilian worship communities combined elements from their various African regional and ethnic heritages. Hence, the ceremony to 12 divinities is a combination of *Ijexá* and *Jêje* nations with Yoruba and Mina Coast influences, respectively, which includes drum rhythms and divinity names from both traditions, such as the deity called both Bará and Elegua.

Candomblé

A brief comparison between the music and dance in Batuque and Candomblé will familiarize the reader with the best-known and most influential Afro-Brazilian religion, discussed in the next section.[10] Candomblé boasts far more adherents and receives more attention than Batuque, perhaps because Candomblé is from Salvador in the northeastern state of Bahia, the first colonial capital of Brazil and a former epicenter of its slave trade. Candomblé expanded to the major Brazilian cities of Rio de Janeiro and São Paulo, among other locations. Throughout the twentieth century, Candomblé has been a major topic of study for social scientists and an epicenter for Afro-Brazilian social-justice activism. Candomblé ceremonies praise more divinities than those in Batuque, and mediums wear costumes particular to the deities when they receive them. The music of Candomblé directly influenced emerging secular genres such as samba, *afoxé*, *axé* music, art music, and Brazilian-jazz fusion, as well as countless popular songs. Similar to Batuque, Candomblé also has nations with African regional/ethnic heritages and musical differences: *Nagô*, *Ketu*, *Ijexá*, *Jêje*, and *Angola*. Also similar are the gourd shakers and double-bells played with the drums. In contrast to Batuque, Candomblé uses conical single-headed wooden drums often called *atabaques*, either carved from a single trunk or of barrel construction with slats. Musicians play *atabaques* in sets of three—called *rum* (the largest), *rumpi* (medium), and *lê* (small)—and employ distributed polyrhythmic patterns that differ from rhythms in Batuque. For use in worship houses, *atabaques* are ritually consecrated and wrapped in cloth, which is not required for Batuque drums. Using the *rum*, the lead drummer plays the most complicated rhythms, interacting with mediums with manifested divinities. Depending on the Candomblé nation, drummers play with or without sticks. Similar to Batuque, Candomblé has a repertoire of drum rhythms that accompany sung chants; some are used throughout the ceremony while others are particular to certain divinities or moments. In addition to text sources cited here, an excellent resource to assist teaching the music used in Candomblé of Bahia is the 2018 documentary film *Orin: música para os Orixás* (Orin: Music for the Orixás) by Henrique Duarte, currently available on YouTube with accurate English translations in close captions.[11] The film includes footage of mediums with manifested deities, dancing characteristically and dressed in the attire of each. Less useful are the many amateur videos filmed at worship houses and posted online, for which contextual information is rarely provided.

Recontextualization of Folkloric Performance in the U.S.

At the public liberal arts college in New Jersey where I teach ethnomusicology and music history courses, we have presented and taught Afro-Brazilian religious music in several settings: a staged performance by a visiting folkloric troupe, hands-on workshops with culture bearers, a weekly rehearsing ensemble focused on Brazilian percussion, and music history and regional ethnomusicology courses. About these recontextualizations we can ask: how do performers, instructors, students, and audiences interpret the music? Do they appreciate the music and dance as spiritually communicative or through a secular aesthetic lens? To what extent are students taught a combination of the musical techniques and contextual information for interpretation? This section and the next explain a program I co-organized—the artistic residency of Jailton "Dendê" Macedo and his troupe Ologundê at Ramapo College of New Jersey—while the last two sections consider the ensemble and classroom settings.

Ologundê recontextualized the ritual music and dance of Candomblé via folkloric performance both to present an entertaining concert to the general public and to teach students during workshops. They perform staged renditions of dances to the *orixás*, the Brazilian martial-art/dance/game *capoeira*, and Bahian secular folk-dances *maculelê* and *samba de roda*. This format and repertoire have been common among Afro-Bahian folkloric dance troupes since the 1960s, in Brazil and abroad.[12] Educational institutions (K-12 and higher education), cultural centers, museums, and arts festivals hire Ologundê either to give stand-alone performances or to present within holistically minded curricula in order to achieve intercultural or multicultural learning objectives.

Macedo is an Afro-descendent musician from Salvador who specializes in performing and teaching the music of Candomblé and Brazilian popular genres. He was raised as a congregant and percussionist in an old and famous Candomblé house of the combined *Nagô-Ketu* nation called Ilê Axé Iyá Nassô Oká, also known as Casa Branca de Engenho Velho. His family also frequented a house of the Candomblé *Angola* nation, where he learned different ceremonial music. Later in life he studied music of the *Jêje* nation, making him a well-rounded expert on music of Candomblé. After moving to New York City in the year 2000, Macedo applied this expertise to establish Ologundê, meaning "the warrior has arrived" in Yoruba. He explained this decision to me:

> We put together this group because when I came here, I saw a lot of wrong things about folkloric shows. I saw a lot of fake stuff, I saw a lot of people only making money, not really educating the kids, not really educating the school, not really representing your family… I said I want this folkloric group here and we have a huge opportunity.[13]

He organizes this ensemble with his wife Leslie Malmed Macedo, a Jewish-American singer and presenter of international music who had more than a decade of professional experience primarily at The World Music Institute. As she summarized her contribution to Macedo's projects:

> He brings very high-quality understanding and performance of these traditional art forms, and then also his own creations. And what I bring is this very high level of understanding of how to administer those types of things and how to deal with a major performing art center or major presenter.[14]

I co-organized the artist residency in 2011–12 with Paula Straile-Costa, professor of Spanish, and the college's arts presenter Jane Stein. "From Candomblé to Carnival: Afro-Brazilian Music, Dance, and Culture" was the title of the year-long program, which offered learning experience to students through hands-on performance-based activities. The program included workshops about Candomblé in the fall semester and Bahian-style Carnival in the spring, all led by Macedo and assisted by dancer Janete Silva and percussionist Amarildo Costa, Straile-Costa's husband. That year, Costa and I co-founded the college's Brazilian Percussion

Ensemble (renamed Brazilian Latin Percussion Ensemble) as part of the same grant. A final concert by the entire Ologundê troupe included a dozen student performers from the Carnival workshops and Brazilian Percussion Ensemble, who joined in the second half after Ologundê presented the *orixá* dances, *capoeira*, and folkdances.

Video Example 2, an excerpt from Ologundê's performance that I filmed and posted on YouTube with the Macedos' permission, can be compared to the ceremonial settings described earlier. (Watch Video Example 2 here: https://youtu.be/Wat4jhrKJn4.) Macedo transformed the circular and participatory arrangement characteristic of religious ceremonies into a concertized presentation. The ensemble played three *atabaque* drums wrapped in white cloths to mimic their appearance in sacred contexts. The other musicians played a basket shaker (*caxixi*) and *agogô* double-bells, while all musicians had microphones to sing the call and responsorial lines in the absence of a singing congregation. As *alabês* do during ceremonies, Macedo played the largest drum (*rum*) with stick and hand, led the singing of chants, and cued musicians and dancers using drum patterns. They first called together all three dancers, who were dressed as the *orixás* Iemanjá, Xangô, and Iansã, with a sung chant transliterated as "*Avamunha la ijojo aye koizo*" (translation unavailable) and a drum rhythm variously called *avamunha/ramunha* or *avaninha/avania* (see Figure 8.3). Figure 8.4 presents an approximate transcription of the opening chant, revealing a pentatonic melody. The chant and rhythm are used in the Candomblé *Ketu* nation to initiate ceremonies, call all *orixás*, end ceremonies, and accompany mediums with manifested *orixás* and dressed as the *orixás*.[15] Then, for each *orixá*, Macedo recited a greeting and led the ensemble with three sung chants, starting with Iemanjá, the divinity of salt water, included in the video example. He led two responsorial chants with Yoruba-derived lyrics and a third chant in Portuguese:

Call: "*Eó-guó*" (translation unavailable) / Response: "*Iemanjá*"
"*Saia do mar minha sereia, saia do mar e vem brincar na areia.*"
(Come out of the sea my mermaid, come out of the sea and play in the sand.)
"*Ogolo nayé ogolo Iemanjá odé*" (translation unavailable)

Meanwhile, Silva danced characteristically as Iemanjá, dressed in white while holding a mirror, and moving with fluid undulations, like a mermaid or sea waves. She has a professional background dancing in a folkloric troupe in Bahia and teaching Brazilian dances in New York.[16] After segments dedicated to Xangô and Iansã, not in the video, the musicians repeated the initial chant with the *avamunha/avaninha* rhythm as all three danced together. Since there were no congregants on stage to complete a

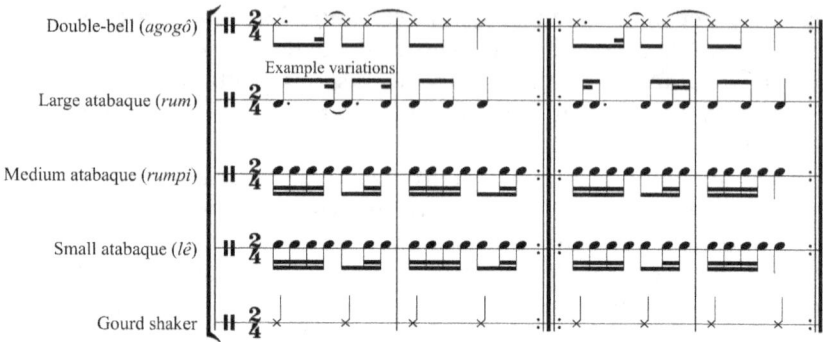

Figure 8.3 The Candomblé rhythm *avamunha/ramunha* or *avaninha/avania* as performed by Ologundê in Video Example 2.

circle, the dancers faced the audience, the musicians, and each other. They were already in costume and presumably had not received manifestations of the *orixás* as mediums would during ceremonies.

Folkloric performances that attempt to entertain, educate, and celebrate cultural diversity while removed from their prior contexts will inevitably stir up issues of authenticity, power inequality, and stereotyping; performing artists and scholars recognize and grapple with these risks and benefits.[17] In her historical study of Afro-Bahian folkloric dance troupes, Ana Paula Höfling foregrounds ongoing tensions between authentic folk arts, artistic experimentation, appropriation, and tourism—tensions that the participation of Black dancers from the culture, in combination with educational intentions, have partially mitigated.[18] The arts presenter Judith Eissenberg, who organized Ologundê's 2007 weeklong residency at Brandeis University, reflected, "I think there are two big issues… how to put something that is inherently participatory into a presentational mode… and how to put a religious ritual onto a public stage."[19] By using non-consecrated drums and excluding particularly potent rhythms, practitioners of Afro-Latin religions have successfully presented sacred music and dance in

Figure 8.4 The first Candomblé chant performed by Ologundê in Video Example 2.

secular situations.[20] In Katherine Hagedorn's words, musicians can ensure that "the religious intent of [the] performance is contained."[21] Hagedorn explored several sacred-to-secular "folkloricizations" of Afro-Cuban religious music and dance in Cuba: performances by folkloric troupes, presentations in ethnographic conferences, and ceremonies staged for tourists.[22] Juan Diego Díaz Meneses, discussing recontextualizations of Candomblé music in Bahia, observed that locals judge some situations as respectful borrowings while others as exploitative appropriations, often based on the criteria of community engagement, insider status, consent, and respect. He found, "Candomblé practitioners use an aesthetic based on their knowledge and experience of ritual embodiment when listening to Candomblé outside the religious context."[23] Macedo, while striving to present a respectful recontextualization, may have been the only one to interpret the music from a perspective of ritual embodiment at Ramapo College. Most feedback I received praised the technical abilities of the musicians and dancers, and celebrated the students' participation in the show.

Recontextualizations in Higher Education

Guest Workshops with Students

The objectives for Ologundê's workshops at Ramapo College were to teach musical skills, impart an appreciation of Afro-Brazilian culture, and increase intercultural awareness. The workshops focused on teaching students how to play the instruments and dance as the *orixás*; yet, due to time and possibly language barriers, Macedo only briefly explained the history, theology, purpose, and ritual actions to which the music and dance contribute. In these ways, like the concert, the workshops resembled folkloric performances more than religious ceremonies. Scholars have argued that recontextualizations often run this risk, foregrounding artistic technique while diminishing or even ignoring the social, economic, political, and religious dynamics of both the prior and new contexts.[24] On the other hand, Macedo and Silva adjusted their performance practices with the intention to increase accessibility both for the student participants and, visually, for the concert audience.

Although it would be difficult to determine all the ways in which students interpreted the Candomblé workshops, their responses highlighted religious differences and gender divisions. The religious content did not seem to bother the students, a vast majority of whom are Christian. I mistakenly worried that students would be uncomfortable with the polytheism of Candomblé, playing music and performing dances intended for the worship of deities, mimicking supernatural possession, or hearing about Christian syncretism and animosities toward Afro-Brazilian religions in Brazil. None of this appeared to offend anyone. In post-workshop writing assignments, many students in my courses noted differences between Candomblé and their family religions. Comparing Catholicism, students mentioned differences in theologies, moods, and dance, and similarities in the presence of praise, singing, gender-based roles, and dress codes. One student added:

> In Catholic Church it's much more solemn and reserved and the relationship is more private and personal. The music is more of a chorale style and much less upbeat. It seemed that in Candomblé, the relationship with the *orixás* is much more group-oriented and to be shared.

Another student compared receiving *orixás* to receiving the Holy Spirit in Protestantism. Students in my course "Music and Dance of the African Diaspora" recognized similarities with the Yoruba and Ewe religious music we had studied from West Africa. All these responses constituted respectful, non-judgmental cross-cultural comparisons.

A more discomforting tension emerged regarding gender divisions. Macedo had arrived to the workshop excited to teach Candomblé music and dance as it is practiced in the worship houses of Bahia, he told me. So, the first thing he did was to divide students into men and women. He taught the men the percussion parts for the *Nago-Ketu* and *Angola* nations: the rhythms are different and drummers use sticks in *Nago-Ketu* instead of their hands, as in *Angola*. Meanwhile, Silva taught the women dances of the *orixás* Ogum, Iemanjá, and Oxossí—male and female divinities. While this division of men and women reproduced Candomblé practices, it conflicted with campus requirements for equal opportunity. After the first workshop, we agreed that everyone would learn the music and the dances. In the second workshop, Macedo and Silva still grouped the students by men and women, but switched their duties half way through so that everyone could experience the instruments and the dances. Macedo seemed comfortable with this change but also preoccupied with it. He told students that this was not the traditional way and once told women who did not want to play the instruments that they were turning down a unique opportunity. Discomfort seemed to have shifted from me, the organizer, and the students to Macedo, the guest instructor. These divisions proved memorable for the students, as post-workshop evaluations revealed. "I wish women could play the instruments!" was the most critical comment in an anonymous survey from the first workshop. Almost everyone in my two music courses wrote about gender roles as a distinguishing contrast between Candomblé rituals and the workshops. Despite the potentially productive role that discomfort can lend to intercultural learning, we removed gender inequalities to increase access for students, which distorted an authentic element that the culture bearer wished to maintain in this recontextualization. Instructive here are pedagogical insights from Gage Averill, who came to embrace discomfort as a central objective for stimulating cross-cultural comparisons in a collegiate ensemble that recontextualized international music: "The dialogical approach to intercultural studies that I advocate privileges the space of the encounter rather than the mastery of the codes."[25] Although discomfort can kindle productive reflections for students, and perhaps for Macedo as he adjusts to life in the U.S., it is not his objective to cause workshop participants or audiences to feel uncomfortable. Quite the opposite: his personality puts most people at ease and encourages participation. Indeed, Macedo's welcoming demeanor likely minimized student discomfort during his residency at Ramapo, for better or worse from an educational perspective.

Although the active-learning aspects of the Candomblé workshops certainly gave students a taste of the instruments, polyrhythmic percussion grooves, and mimetic dance steps, the workshops fell far short in teaching about the worship-house contexts and histories of these cultural expressions. Dissatisfied with the degree to which we taught about Afro-Brazilian religions and history, or even about folkloric performance troupes, we contextualized the music and dance more during the spring workshops concerning Bahian Carnival. Yet, our mini-lectures and conversations with guests took away precious time from performance instruction. A more effective approach is to teach students the background during class meetings in advance of workshops, which I did in "Music and Dance of the African Diaspora." Class meetings after the workshops could be spent debriefing, reflecting, and critiquing the workshops, including a consideration of how they recontextualized ceremonial and folkloric presentation settings.

Brazilian Percussion Ensemble

Aside from one-off performances and workshops, the music of Afro-Brazilian religions appears in two regularly occurring settings at my college: the Brazilian Percussion Ensemble, which emphasizes performance training, and musicology courses, which contextualize music in society, culture, and history. Costa and I founded the ensemble the year of the workshops through the same funding grant, following upon several years during which Costa had provided intermittent workshops in *capoeira* and percussion at the college. The ensemble's status changed during its first decade from an extracurricular activity funded by a multicultural grant into a two-credit section of a generic music course with funding from the Student Activities office; it eventually became a course under its own name, recently renamed the Brazilian Latin Percussion Ensemble. Costa grew up in Salvador playing primarily secular music in the percussion sections of famous parading Carnival organizations: the *afoxé* group Filhos de

Gandhi and the *bloco afro* Olodum. The ensemble features music of these groups and surveys other Brazilian genres and, more recently, Dominican merengue. Costa teaches students to play diverse polyrhythmic grooves on percussion, though without singing or dancing.

In the ensemble, Costa teaches two polyrhythms from Candomblé, *avamunha/avaninha* and *ijexá*—the latter rhythm having been recontextualized by Carnival parading ensembles. Historically, *ijexá* was adopted from the semi-private settings of Candomblé worship houses into the hyper-public setting of Carnival parades in Salvador. When all-Black *afoxé* collectives prior to Filhos de Gandhi began to parade in Carnival in the early twentieth century, they intentionally performed Candomblé music in the public sphere for the general public as a celebration of Black pride and to protest anti-Black police brutality. This gradually transformed Bahia's Carnival from a predominantly Euro-Brazilian event into a largely Afro-Brazilian event. *Ijexá* became the signature rhythm of this social-justice activism and maintains this significance in addition to its association with Candomblé rituals. Perhaps more than any other rhythm from Candomblé, *ijexá* has been played in countless popular Brazilian songs, evoking pride in Afro-Bahian heritage.[26] Costa has the ensemble enter the stage during performances while playing *ijexá* on *agogô* double-bells, later adding drum parts on stage (see Figure 8.5). Not only is it easier to walk with bells than drums, the movement also harkens the parades and affectively establishes a calm, medium-tempo musical atmosphere before the ensemble transitions to its faster, louder, and more complex music. On stage, Costa uses conga drums instead of *atabaques* and has also incorporated samba percussion to include more students, a pragmatic element of ensemble recontextualizations.

Costa combines *avamunha/avaninha* with a similar rhythm that accompanies Ogum in Candomblé ceremonies, while explaining to students the

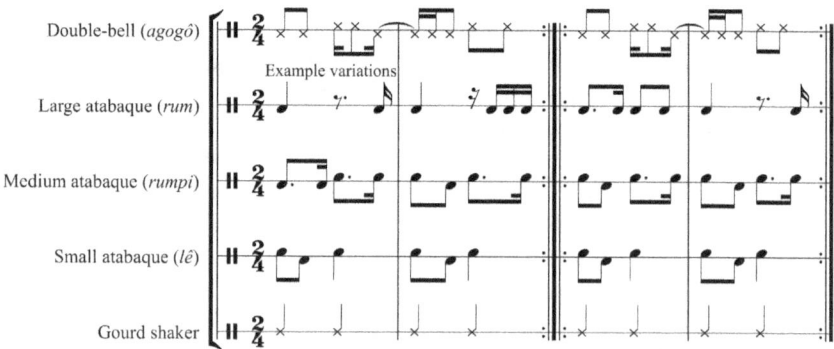

Figure 8.5 The rhythm *ijexá* as taught by Amarildo Costa of Ramapo College's Brazilian Latin Percussion Ensemble.

music's relevance to Candomblé rather than to Carnival. This rhythmic pairing is one of the ensemble's most complex pieces, played at a brisk tempo with off-beat accenting and distinctive instrument parts that are difficult to maintain without listening closely to and synchronizing with the other instruments. When the ensemble plays such complex polyrhythms, Costa must circulate to remind students of their rhythms, occasionally adding patterns associated with the large *rum* drum himself.

Student engagement has remained consistent over the ensemble's first decade, except for a hiatus during the pandemic; and students describe their experiences as musical rather than as religious, folkloric, or activist, though they learn about these settings during the course. The six-to-twelve students per semester self-report to enjoy the ensemble and have noticed their improvement playing complex rhythms within polyrhythmic textures. Some have also mentioned the ensemble's social and therapeutic benefits, and Latinx students have observed resonances with their heritages.

The performance-based workshops and collegiate ensembles offer opportunities to study the music and appreciate aspects of musical cultures that reading, lectures, discussions, and writing may not inculcate. Relevant dilemmas and solutions are discussed in the volume *Performing Ethnomusicology: Teaching and Representation in World Music Ensembles*.[27] On the one hand, performance training has its own merits. Ricardo Trimillos, paraphrasing Charles Seeger, wrote: "learning (and, by implication, teaching) through performance commands parity with, if not superiority to, the logocentric processes of conceptualization, reflection, and analysis, which he characterizes as 'armchair study.'"[28] Unlike the one-day workshops, the ensemble provides prolonged study and an ensemble director who can impart nuggets of cultural insight over the course of a semester or year. On the other hand, collegiate world music ensembles face challenges due to their recontextualizations—in this case, the inauthenticity of teaching music for Carnival and Candomblé in a secular educational setting through percussion instruction rather than gradual enculturation within an Afro-Brazilian cultural community that includes singing, movement, ritual frames, spiritual functions, or social-political activism. As Ted Solís remarked about this predicament among collegiate world-music ensembles, "In the end, whether we adhere fiercely to what we perceive as orthodoxy, or shed all pretexts to 'accurate' reproduction, we know we may be charged with either neocolonialism or irresponsible cultural squandering."[29] Additionally, this ensemble course does not emphasize contextual education. To rectify, Costa tells students about the historical, cultural, or political significances of the music, such as the roots and functions of *ijexá* and *avamunha/avaninha* in Candomblé ceremonies and *ijexá* in Carnival.[30] He supplements the performance training with an assigned reading, research assignment, and occasional guest lecture.[31] Costa cooks a Bahian dinner for students during which he describes life in Salvador and addresses contemporary social issues. This informal setting fosters relaxed conversations about students' interests in Brazil, music, food, and other topics. The ensemble has not yet formally reflected on recontextualization itself.

Musicology/Ethnomusicology Courses

Contrasting with collegiate workshops and ensembles are musicology/ethnomusicology courses that prioritize non-performance teaching methods. These courses typically include reading, listening, lectures, discussion, synthesis, writing, and examinations, though performance instruction—however superficial—can also support learning goals. My shortest lesson about Afro-Brazilian religious music appears in a music appreciation/history survey, in which it is presented as an example of a religious chant tradition along with Gregorian chant, Qur'anic recitation, Vedic chant, and the Navajo Enemy Way ceremony. I present the basics, as introduced earlier in this chapter, but without transcriptions or performance instruction. Nevertheless, the case study contrasts musically with the others, and features responsorial singing, syncopated and sometimes polyrhythmic percussion accompaniment, and topical issues of divine communication, aural/oral transmission, polytheism, and syncretism. In regional ethnomusicology courses—"Music and Dance in the African Diaspora" and "Music in Latin America"—which offer more time and narrative continuity, I can take one day to focus on Afro-Brazilian religious music. A practical source, in addition to those presented previously, is Tiago de Oliveira Pinto's article explaining four *orixás* praised in Candomblé, their characteristics, a rhythm used for their dance, and the basic movements used by congregants to circumambulate the room.[32] Prefaced as an optional, non-religious activity for educational purposes, I have the students clap the rhythms while moving around the classroom with the footsteps for each divinity; or have some students play the rhythms in a small percussion ensemble while the others dance around the room. Subsequent meetings teach the applications of Candomblé-style worship to Carnival music in Bahia and Brazilian popular music, such as the example of *ijexá*.[33] Depending on the course, related lessons might compare these case studies to West African music, Afro-Caribbean religious music, eclectic religions like Umbanda, Afro-Brazilian-jazz hybrids, and so on. Finally, the topic of recontextualization using the examples in this chapter can frame any of these lessons.

Conclusion

Consider the presence of recontextualizations in your own musical activities or the music being made on your campus. Have music or musicians come from different geographic locations? Did music associated with a certain type of activity become part of a different musical situation? Has the music or its meaning changed through any of these relocations? Have tensions or dilemmas emerged in the new contexts? This chapter described several settings with Afro-Brazilian religious music and dance: from a worship house in southern Brazil (a recontextualization itself) to Carnival parades in northeastern Brazil, and from a folkloric performance troupe on a U.S. stage to educational activities in an undergraduate college. At each site, people affirmed the religious associations and retained core musical characteristics, yet the functions and meanings of the music varied widely. In ceremonies, the music aids sociability and communion with divinities, whereas in public parades the same music has supported protests against racism and celebrations of Black pride. On college campuses, this music is used to improve student competencies with percussive polyrhythms, increase their intercultural and international awareness, and support education about Afro-Brazilian cultural history. If every musical context is potentially a recontextualization, teachers and students can utilize any musical example to explore comparable transformations.

Notes

1 Kay Kaufman Shelemay, *Soundscapes: Exploring Music in a Changing World*, 3rd ed. (New York: W.W. Norton, 2015).
2 For a survey of this literature, see Marc Gidal, "Transnationalising Brazilian Ritual Music: Quimbanda in Argentina and Charismatic Catholicism in the USA," *Civilisations* 67 (2018): 113f.
3 Deborah A. Kapchan, *Traveling Spirit Masters: Moroccan Gnawa Trance and Music in the Global Marketplace* (Middletown, Conn.: Wesleyan University Press, 2007), 2, 150.
4 Juan Diego Díaz Meneses has discussed recontextualization of Afro-Brazilian religious music in Brazilian jazz created in Salvador, Bahia. Juan Diego Díaz Meneses, "Listening with the Body: An Aesthetics of Spirit Possession Outside the Terreiro," *Ethnomusicology* 60, no. 1 (Winter 2016).
5 For more about Batuque and its music, in English, see Marc Gidal, *Spirit Song: Afro-Brazilian Religious Music and Boundaries* (New York: Oxford University Press, 2016).
6 Examples of tracks titled "Ogum" from his commercial recordings posted to YouTube.com, https://www.youtube.com/watch?v=X7WCDV-v0IA and https://www.youtube.com/watch?v=VWWv7qC2c3Q, accessed May 25, 2022.
7 In addition, Cleber strained with a sore throat, fighting a cold.
8 The musicians are *alabê* Pai Cleber "Teixeiro" de Oxalá and assistant Jorge. The texts are based on unpublished transliterations that Antonio Carlos de Xangô Machado provides his students, including me. The loose interpretive translations are from Machado's teaching manuscripts, and are based on his understanding.
9 J. Lorand Matory, "Afro-Atlantic Culture: On the Live Dialogue Between Africa and the Americas," in *Africana*, eds. Kwame Appiah and Henry Louis Gates (New York: Basic Civitas, 1999).

10 On music in Candomblé, in English, see Gerard Béhague, "Patterns of Candomblé Music Performance: An Afro-Brazilian Religious Setting," in *Performance Practice: Ethnomusicological Perspectives*, ed. Gerard Béhague (Westport, Conn.: Greenwood Press, 1984); Tiago de Oliveira Pinto, "'Making Ritual Drama': Dance, Music, and Representation in Brazilian *candomblé* and *umbanda*," *The World of Music* 33, no. 1 (1991); Clarence Bernard Henry, *Let's Make Some Noise: Axé and the African Roots of Brazilian Popular Music* (Jackson: University Press of Mississippi, 2008); Larry N. Crook, *Focus: Music of Northeast Brazil*, 2nd ed. (New York: Routledge, 2009), 63–78; Genevieve E. V. Dempsey, "Captains and Priestesses in Afro-Brazilian Congado and Candomblé," *Ethnomusicology* 63, no. 2 (2019); Juan Diego Díaz, *Africanness in Action: Essentialism and Musical Imaginations of Africa in Brazil* (New York: Oxford University Press, 2021).
11 "Orin. music for Orishas," posted to YouTube.com, https://www.youtube.com/watch?v=hL-A29ILa5Y, accessed on May 16, 2022.
12 Ana Paula Höfling, "Staging Capoeira, Samba, *Maculelê*, and *Candomblé*: Viva Bahia's Choreographies of Afro-Brazilian Folklore," in *Performing Brazil: Essays on Culture, Identity, and the Performing Arts*, eds. Severino João Medeiros Albuquerque and Kathryn Bishop-Sanchez (Madison, Wisconsin: The University of Wisconsin Press, 2015).
13 Jailton Macedo, interview by author, Oct 10, 2013.
14 Leslie Malmed Macedo, interview by author, Oct 10, 2013.
15 Béhague, "Patterns of Candomblé Music Performance," 238; Henry, *Let's Make Some Noise*, 66; Díaz, *Africanness in Action*, 272.
16 "Janete Silva," Steps on Broadway (website), https://www.stepsnyc.com/faculty/bio/Janete-Silva/, accessed May 25, 2022.
17 Terese M. Volk, *Music, Education, and Multiculturalism: Foundations and Principles* (Oxford and New York: Oxford University Press, 1998), 177; Höfling, "Staging," 99.
18 Höfling, "Staging," 99, 103, 05, 14.
19 Judith Eissenberg, email correspondence, Feb 13, 2013.
20 Katherine J. Hagedorn, *Divine Utterances: The Performance of Afro-Cuban Santería* (Washington [D.C.]: Smithsonian Institution Press, 2001), 99–101; Höfling, "Staging," 114–15.
21 Hagedorn, *Divine Utterances*, 223.
22 Hagedorn, *Divine Utterances*, 11–12, 149.
23 Díaz Meneses, "Listening with the Body," 90, 118–19n1.
24 Hagedorn, *Divine Utterances*, 127ff; Michelle Kisliuk and Kelly Gross, "What's the 'It' That We Learn to Perform? Teaching BaAka Music and Dance," in *Performing Ethnomusicology: Teaching and Representation in World Music Ensembles*, ed. Ted Solís (Berkeley: University of California Press, 2004), 252.
25 Gage Averill, "'Where's "One"?': Musical Encounters of the Ensemble Kind," in *Performing Ethnomusicology: Teaching and Representation in World Music Ensembles*, ed. Ted Solís (Berkeley: University of California Press, 2004), 101.
26 On this history, see Crook, *Focus*, 51–54, 78–90. Henry, *Let's Make Some Noise*, 64–75; Díaz, *Africanness in Action*, 113.
27 Ted Solís, "Introduction. Teaching What Cannot Be Taught: An Optimistic Overview," in *Performing Ethnomusicology: Teaching and Representation in World Music Ensembles*, ed. Ted Solís (Berkeley: University of California Press, 2004).
28 Ricardo D. Trimillos, "Subject, Object, and the Ethnomuisicology Ensemble: The Ethnomusicological 'We' and 'Them'," in *Performing Ethnomusicology:*

Teaching and Representation in World Music Ensembles, ed. Ted Solís (Berkeley: University of California Press, 2004), 24.
29 Solís, "Introduction," 14.
30 Amarildo Costa, telephone conversation, May 19, 2022.
31 Currently students research contexts of their choice rhythm from the course, whereas previously they read this article: Larry N. Crook, "Black Consciousness, *samba reggae*, and the Re-Africanization of Bahian Carnival Music in Brazil," *The World of Music* 35, no. 2 (1993).
32 Pinto, "Making Ritual Drama."
33 For examples, see Henry, *Let's Make Some Noise*, 69–81.

References

Averill, Gage. "'Where's "One"?': Musical Encounters of the Ensemble Kind." In *Performing Ethnomusicology: Teaching and Representation in World Music Ensembles*, edited by Ted Solís, 93–111. Berkeley: University of California Press, 2004.

Béhague, Gerard. "Patterns of Candomblé Music Performance: An Afro-Brazilian Religious Setting." In *Performance Practice: Ethnomusicological Perspectives*, edited by Gerard Béhague, 222–54. Westport: Greenwood Press, 1984.

Crook, Larry N. "Black Consciousness, *Samba Reggae*, and the Re-Africanization of Bahian Carnival Music in Brazil." *The World of Music* 35, no. 2 (1993): 90–108.

———. *Focus: Music of Northeast Brazil*, 2nd edn. New York: Routledge, 2009.

Dempsey, Genevieve E. V. "Captains and Priestesses in Afro-Brazilian Congado and Candomblé." *Ethnomusicology* 63, no. 2 (2019): 184–221.

Díaz, Juan Diego. *Africanness in Action: Essentialism and Musical Imaginations of Africa in Brazil*. New York: Oxford University Press, 2021.

Díaz Meneses, Juan Diego. "Listening with the Body: An Aesthetics of Spirit Possession Outside the Terreiro." *Ethnomusicology* 60, no. 1 (Winter 2016): 89–124.

Gidal, Marc. *Spirit Song: Afro-Brazilian Religious Music and Boundaries*. New York: Oxford University Press, 2016.

———. "Transnationalising Brazilian Ritual Music: Quimbanda in Argentina and Charismatic Catholicism in the USA." *Civilisations* 67 (2018): 111–128.

Hagedorn, Katherine J. *Divine Utterances: The Performance of Afro-Cuban Santería*. Washington, DC: Smithsonian Institution Press, 2001.

Henry, Clarence Bernard. *Let's Make Some Noise: Axé and the African Roots of Brazilian Popular Music*. Jackson: University Press of Mississippi, 2008.

Höfling, Ana Paula. "Staging Capoeira, Samba, *Maculelê*, and *Candomblé*: Viva Bahia's Choreographies of Afro-Brazilian Folklore." In *Performing Brazil: Essays on Culture, Identity, and the Performing Arts*, edited by Severino João Medeiros Albuquerque and Kathryn Bishop-Sanchez, 98–125. Madison: The University of Wisconsin Press, 2015.

Kapchan, Deborah A. *Traveling Spirit Masters: Moroccan Gnawa Trance and Music in the Global Marketplace*. Middletown: Wesleyan University Press, 2007.

Kisliuk, Michelle, and Kelly Gross. "What's the 'It' That We Learn to Perform? Teaching Baaka Music and Dance." In *Performing Ethnomusicology: Teaching* and *Representation in World Music Ensembles*, edited by Ted Solís, 249–60. Berkeley: University of California Press, 2004.

Matory, J. Lorand. "Afro-Atlantic Culture: On the Live Dialogue Between Africa and the Americas." In *Africana*, edited by Kwame Appiah and Henry Louis Gates, 36–44. New York: Basic Civitas, 1999.

Pinto, Tiago de Oliveira. "'Making Ritual Drama': Dance, Music, and Representation in Brazilian *Candomblé* and *Umbanda*." *The World of Music* 33, no. 1 (1991): 70–88.

Shelemay, Kay Kaufman. *Soundscapes: Exploring Music in a Changing World*, 3rd edn. New York: W.W. Norton, 2015.

Solís, Ted. "Introduction. Teaching What Cannot Be Taught: An Optimistic Overview." In *Performing Ethnomusicology: Teaching and Representation in World Music Ensembles*, edited by Ted Solís, 1–19. Berkeley: University of California Press, 2004.

Trimillos, Ricardo D. "Subject, Object, and the Ethnomuisicology Ensemble: The Ethnomusicological 'We' and 'Them'." In *Performing Ethnomusicology: Teaching and Representation in World Music Ensembles*, edited by Ted Solís, 23–52. Berkeley: University of California Press, 2004.

Volk, Terese M. *Music, Education, and Multiculturalism: Foundations and Principles*. Oxford and New York: Oxford University Press, 1998.

9 Crossing Over Popular and Classical Traditions through Musical Theater

Alex Bádue

In the fall of 2019, I was walking in downtown Chicago and saw a poster for an upcoming performance of Adam Guettel and Craig Lucas's 2005 musical *The Light in The Piazza* at the Lyric Opera, featuring soprano Renée Fleming and actor Alex Jennings. In addition to the note-to-self to purchase a ticket, the poster reminded me that the Lyric had caused some stir in previous seasons for including musicals in its programming, and I realized that an important example of crossover was happening a few blocks from the Chicago College of Performing Arts at Roosevelt University, where I was a Visiting Assistant Professor of Music History. I had been asked to teach a graduate seminar the following spring and wanted it to pertain to my main research interest, musical theater. Having engaged deeply with the scholarship on crossover between popular and classical traditions, I concluded that a seminar focusing on musical theater's presence in opera houses, along with the history behind musicians who were as comfortable in the popular music industry and Broadway as they were in the concert hall and opera house, could provide room for broader discussions on crossover practices.

I titled the seminar "Musical Theater and Opera Crossovers," and it met twice a week for 75 minutes. I had 15 master's students in music performance, five of whom were instrumentalists and ten vocalists. In that same semester I taught an undergraduate special-topics class, "Gershwin and Bernstein," in which I addressed how George Gershwin and Leonard Bernstein crossed between popular and classical traditions. This class had nine students (juniors and seniors), all of whom were instrumentalists.

The two courses confirmed that music majors often enter music programs with somewhat unrealistic ideas about the life and work of a professional performing musician, which the programs themselves might not always seek to attenuate. It does not help that many schools and conservatories in the United States operate under the assumption that musical theater is theater and not music and separate the disciplines, missing the opportunity to bridge departments. Although some of my students

DOI: 10.4324/9781003415954-13

(both undergraduates and graduates) had performed in musicals before and intended to do so again in the future, collectively they had never critically considered the fact that, if hired by an orchestra or opera house, they would have to perform a wide variety of music, spanning from pop songs and Disney soundtracks to canonical symphonies and concertos. By the end of the courses, especially in the final projects, students agreed that crossing over between popular and classical traditions was just as important to twentieth- and twenty-first-century music history as electronic music and minimalism, and they were happy to have delved into the topic and explored music beyond the orchestral and operatic repertoires.

Courses like these expand on the often-tangential references made to musical theater in Western music history textbooks and surveys, and provide students with a perspective that surpasses the mere positioning of musical theater within a twentieth- and twenty-first-century chronology. A semester-long study of musical theater allows students to focus on several aspects, including: performance practices for both vocalists and instrumentalists; the roles played by composers, lyricists, book writers, directors, choreographers, orchestrators, producers, and performers in the development of the musical as a genre; recent developments in musical theater aesthetics and form; and the acquisition of a wider repertoire. The emphasis on crossover is key to demonstrating the relevance of these topics to music majors and helping them to achieve competence. Students are often already interested in musicals; many grew up listening to them, attending performances, and singing or playing the repertoire.[1] It is very likely that music majors will perform in musical theater as actor-singers, pit orchestra instrumentalists, rehearsal pianists, or music directors/conductors. They can only benefit from musical theater joining the many other forms of Western music that they study in music history special-topics courses and seminars. In this chapter, I draw on my experience teaching those two courses to show how the music history and musicological classroom can address popular/classical music crossovers. I discuss selected pedagogical practices from those courses and evaluate their impact on the students' interests, activities as musicians, and career goals, demonstrating that the music history classroom cannot ignore popular/classical crossover.

Class Content and Pedagogical Goals

In both courses, I sought to historicize the line that conventionally divides popular and classical traditions, and to explore the musical characteristics of works that blur that line. We studied how different composers active in the United States in the twentieth and early twenty-first centuries saw musical theater as a fertile space in which to fuse popular music with jazz, opera, and concert music. Hybridization was the main point, and categorization of genres remained open to interpretation and was less important than understanding the selected composers' aesthetic, artistic, and commercial agendas. I also clarified that most of the composers that we studied did not use the term crossover, which has been applied in retrospect.

The courses' goals differed in important ways. The "Musical Theater and Opera Crossovers" seminar spanned from the 1940s to the early 2000s, although we also discussed the hybridity of operettas (especially Gilbert and Sullivan) and the Gershwin brothers and DuBose Heyward's *Porgy and Bess* (1935). In the first three weeks of the course, we covered the economic and social concerns that led American opera houses to add musicals to their repertoires and Broadway composers to venture into operatic composition. We then turned to the study of eight works: *Street Scene* (1947), *The Golden Apple* (1954), *Candide* (1956), *West Side Story* (1957), *Sweeney Todd* (1979), *Passion* (1994), *Marie Christine* (1999), and *The Light in the Piazza* (2005). Some of the musicals have been filmed and are commercially available, and students watched full productions. We had to rely solely on original cast recordings of those that are not available on video. In either case, I provided scores (either full orchestral, when available, or piano-vocal of selected songs), and students had access to the videos, scores, and selected readings before class (I discuss the assignments below). The seminar included the study (and comparison) of vocal preparation and orchestration for musicals versus that for opera.

"Gershwin and Bernstein" surveyed these composers' careers, together spanning from the 1910s to the 1980s. As an undergraduate course, it included readings and lectures on these composers' biographies and compositional styles. We studied their musical theater works in addition to several of their concert pieces, and crossover was just one aspect of the music that we covered in class. The selected works provided opportunities for me to draw parallels between the composers' careers and developments in both classical and popular music in the twentieth century. For example, we examined how Gershwin's *Rhapsody in Blue* (1924) can be interpreted as modern/modernist music, and how Bernstein's *Mass* (1971) incorporates rock music of the 1960s the same way that *West Side Story* (1957) responded to the mambo craze of the 1950s. Finally, this class focused on reception of the works more than did the graduate seminar.

Pedagogical Practices

The readings I selected for the graduate seminar unpack ideological and cultural changes that contextualize the trend of opera houses programming musicals.[2] The journalistic articles in particular address this, in tandem with the differences between musical theater and opera. Anthony Tommasini argues that the best crossover works conform to the practices of one tradition. He writes, "it's fine to pull in other styles and influences as long [as] you stay rooted in what you, and your art form, do best."[3]

Fred Plotkin, in the wake of *Porgy and Bess* winning the Tony Award for Best Revival of a Musical in 2012 (a production famous for making changes to the work), promotes the hybridization of musical theater and opera, not the upholding of differences, contending that crossover artists and works bring "awareness of the aesthetic differences between the forms and the ability to make them real on the stage."[4] These perspectives helped students to draw important connections. All of the vocalists in the class had training in opera, while several liked to attend and sing in musicals; some of the instrumentalists had experience in a musical theater pit. Students had considered the differences between musical theater and opera, and whether or not those differences mattered, but the seminar was the first time they were provided a space in an academic setting to engage in informed discussion.

This blend of journalism and academic research shed light on the commercial and economic reasons behind American opera houses including musicals in their seasons. In "What's New for Opera Houses? 'Cats'?," Jaime Weinman discusses what motivated the Lyric Opera of Chicago, the Vancouver opera, Glimmerglass Opera, and Théâtre du Châtelet (in Paris) to include, respectively, *Show Boat*, *West Side Story*, *Annie Get Your Gun*, and *A Little Night Music* in their seasons.[5] Weinman reveals that opera house directors did not intend for musicals to replace operas but rather sought to add options for their subscribers. In "The Changing Face of Opera in America," Justin John Moniz offers further insights based on interviews that the author conducted with the directors of five American opera companies: the Utah Festival Opera and Musical Theatre, the Charlottesville Opera, Tri-Cities Opera (in Binghamton, NY), the Houston Grand Opera, and the Glimmerglass Festival. Moniz demonstrates that goals other than revenue improvement motivated crossover programming, which in turn invites the students to further problematize the fine line between musical theater and opera. For example, for the director of Charlottesville opera, since some musicals of the 1940s were written for opera singers with no amplification, the company provides the audience "a true operatic experience" by staging these works.[6] Some students had auditioned for and even performed with some of the opera companies mentioned in these readings, but they were not familiar with the process of selecting repertoire. All students mentioned that these were opera companies that they would likely audition for in the near future. The readings, therefore, informed the students about practices in the music industry that they would not otherwise have encountered until they were actively auditioning in opera houses and orchestras.

Readings on vocal training for both musical theater and opera performers, and on the necessity for a singer to be trained in both, are essential for the study of musical theater and crossover music. This is an opportunity to bring the students' pre-existing interests into the discussion. Several of the vocalists in the seminar mentioned that they were introduced to singing in high school musicals, and several (including instrumentalists) had grown up listening to musicals, although they were trained exclusively in the classical tradition. The readings on vocal training introduced techniques to tackle a repertoire that they liked, knew, and were happy to perform, but that was not part of their academic curriculum. The vocalists also interrogated gaps in the scholarship. Based on their own experiences as singers and the performances analyzed in class (discussed below), they claimed that the differences between singing opera and musical theater (and crossing over from one to the other) were greater than indicated in the selected texts. Thus, they found themselves in a position to make a meaningful contribution to the scholarly discourse.

Readings that introduce the creators' own words and agendas reveal the extent to which the blurring of the line between musical theater and opera (and classical and popular traditions) was intentional, and why such activity became prevalent in American culture at different times between the 1940s and the early 2000s. The first work we studied was Langston Hughes, Elmer Rice, and Kurt Weill's *Street Scene*, a tragic story of a housewife who has an affair with the milk collector and is caught in his arms by her murderous husband. Weill had for years strived to establish an American genre of opera. He articulated his vision in the essay "Two Dreams Come True," in which he concludes that such a genre would have to be born on Broadway, since "[Broadway] represents the living theater in this country."[7] American opera would mingle traditional operatic features with those more common to the Broadway stage. *Street Scene* fulfills this goal, as it contains musical numbers that range from jitterbug and the blues to full-blown operatic arias.

Written by John Latouche and with music by Jerome Moross, *The Golden Apple* adapted and transferred Homer's epic poems *Iliad* and *Odyssey* to the United States in the early twentieth century (the action takes place between 1900 and 1910 in the fictional town of Angel's Roost in Washington State). Moross and Latouche structured the work without spoken dialogue and in the published libretto drew parallels between musical comedy and opera. According to Latouche, the musical flow

> develops out of musical comedy, consisting of what can be called a series of interlocking production numbers. The sung dialogue, instead of the artificial recitative of opera, is rendered in short songs whose separate melodies become part of the major production number.[8]

Moross, who also composed music for Broadway revues, ballets, film scores, and a symphony, writes that the "starting point had always been musical comedy rather than the operatic theater … [T]he limitations the popular stage imposed on its writers and composers and the hothouse atmosphere in which so much modern opera was being produced were equally restrictive."[9]

The writings of Stephen Sondheim and Michael John LaChiusa, musical theater composers whose works are often labeled as opera (and performed in opera houses), provide thought-provoking perspectives on crossover musical theater at the turn of the twenty-first century, mainly because both refute the use of the term opera to categorize their works. Sondheim and James Lapine's *Passion* is a musical about a young soldier, Giorgio, who is obsessively pursued by Fosca, the cousin of a superior officer in 1863 Italy. Sondheim's introduction to *Passion* in his book, *Look, I Made a Hat*, contextualizes the viewing of the musical for the students. He denies that the work is operatic but concedes that the two forms share some musical structures. For him, opera composers

> seem to have little sense of theater. They spend as much time having their characters sing about trivialities as about matters of emotional importance, and they too often resort to recitative to carry the plot along—for my money a tedious and arid solution to a problem easily solved by dialogue.[10]

Concerning the score of *Passion*, Sondheim writes (using operatic terminology), "the 'songs' in *Passion* lie somewhere between aria and recitative, with an occasional recognizable song form thrown in."[11] For LaChiusa, musical theater is representative of the United States' "mongrel" culture, whereas opera is "what Europeans used to write."[12] After *Marie Christine*—a modern take on the Greek play *Medea*—opened on Broadway, many critics referred to it as an opera, including Terry Teachout in his article "A Musical That's Really an Opera," which questioned LaChiusa's reasons for preferring the term musical.[13] In support of Teachout's perspective was the fact that the main female roles were played by Audra McDonald and Sherry Boone—two actress-singers with classical training and active as crossover performers. LaChiusa defends his arguments in the essay "Genre Confusion," in which he expands on the differences between musicals and opera based on social class issues and audience expectation in the United States.[14] Thus, learning about the creators' intentions provided new insights into theater music in the United States between the 1940s and the 2010s. These writings (from Weill to LaChiusa) show that crossover between musical theater and opera had been both desired and questioned in that time span, revealing the reason for what LaChiusa calls "genre confusion."[15]

The students in "Gershwin and Bernstein" also read selected primary sources, including essays by the composers and reviews of *Porgy and Bess*, *Fancy Free*, *On the Town*, *West Side Story*, and *Mass*, although they primarily engaged with secondary literature concerning the ways in which the two composers combined popular music, jazz, and concert music. Readings on compositional process and musical analysis underscore the aspects that characterize these works as crossover pieces (see reading examples listed in Appendix A), while selected articles and book chapters provide the perspective of the musicologist conducting research on Gershwin's and Bernstein's music. They invite students to consider the task of the researcher analyzing and writing about such eclectic compositional styles, and students gain understanding of a crossover that occurs in musicology itself, since Gershwin and Bernstein scholars write about Broadway musicals, opera, symphonies, concertos, Tin Pan Alley, and jazz. These readings accompanied the study of instrumental pieces exemplifying the use of elements from popular music in concert works, including Gershwin's *Rhapsody in Blue*, Concerto in F, *An American in Paris*, and "I Got Rhythm" Variations; and Bernstein's *Symphonic Dances from West Side Story*.

It is crucial to introduce and discuss the purposeful social elevation of certain musical styles during the twentieth century. This occurred when composers, performers, and critics argued that jazz should move beyond its racialized origins and be accepted in the concert hall, and that musical comedies should have the structure of opera. The racism inherent in this rhetoric, especially regarding the elevation of jazz, is not missed by the students, and selected readings contextualize this and initiate class discussion.[16] Larry Stempel's discussion of "Opera on Broadway" describes the "boundary-setting process" that separates musicals and opera and argues that, for classically trained composers, opera on Broadway was a chance "to expand their reach and reinvigorate their work," while for songwriters with Broadway roots, opera was "the ultimate challenge," the chance to expand their craft and legacy.[17] David Savran's analysis of the rhetoric concerning the stratification of both American theater and jazz in the 1920s,[18] and Adorno's essay "On Popular Music," in which he critiques "serious" music, popular music, and mass culture in the 1940s,[19] help cement the elevation of music and invite students to consider its social context critically.

In "Gershwin and Bernstein," discussion was inspired by Carol Oja's book *Bernstein Meets Broadway*, which considers the creation of the musical *On the Town* (1944). In one chapter, Oja details the casting of the musical and how the creative team "selected people with backgrounds that were ... broad-ranging, including a significant number who straddled high and low realms of performance."[20] In another, Oja discusses the musical numbers and writes that in the song "Carried Away," sung by the characters Claire and Ozzy, Bernstein's music "parodies operatic tropes as a way of seeming totally out of control."[21] Students listened to the original cast recording of "Carried Away," sung by Betty Comden and Adolph Green (who wrote the book and lyrics of the musical) and explained in writing what they heard, in either the vocal or instrumental parts, that sounded operatic and therefore supported Oja's argument. In class, we discussed the actors' backgrounds (as presented in the reading), and several students expressed concern with the author's usage of the words "highbrow" and "lowbrow," which to them read as outdated and elitist. They certainly needed to understand that these were not the author's word choices, but terms that were used in mid-century music and theater criticism.[22] Thus, in both courses, readings by Stempel, Savran, Adorno, and Oja opened the students' eyes to a twentieth-century ideology and rhetoric that shaped the creative process of theatrical works in the United States and sought to elevate popular forms of music and theater to the standards of opera and "serious" music.

Assigning activities to reflect on the impact that musical theater/opera and popular/classical crossovers have on the students' own music-making and career goals can have a number of pedagogical benefits in the music history classroom. In the first two weeks of the seminar (when we were reading about the economic and marketing reasons behind the staging of musicals in opera houses), the students undertook online research into orchestral and operatic programming in the United States in recent years. As part of their homework, students consulted websites of opera houses and orchestras from all over the country and brought the results to class. Not only did this show the students how orchestras and opera companies were embracing crossover practices, but it also allowed them to discuss their own preparation for entering the music job market. It helped that the Lyric Opera of Chicago was a key participant in the trend. In addition to *The Light in the Piazza* in December 2019, the Lyric also featured a production of the musical *42nd Street* and the new opera *Blue* by Jeanine Tesori (a composer more widely known for her Broadway musicals than operas), both scheduled for spring and summer 2020.[23] Among the examples that students found of crossover orchestral programming, those that most excited their attention were live performances of film scores to accompany screenings, including *Fantasia*, *West Side Story*, *The Lord of the Rings*, and *Coco*. Students continued to bring additional examples to class on their own terms as the semester went on.

As another activity, we watched and analyzed selected performances in class. In the seminar, the examples were based on the musical under discussion in a given week, and we took two approaches. Sometimes, we watched multiple performances of the same song by different performers. Other times, we compared and contrasted different songs. We considered vocal placement, techniques, and timbre, as well as articulation, orchestration, and acting choices. Examples in the first category included Weill's

"Lonely House" (from *Street Scene*), sung by tenor Kip Wilborn and musical theater actor-singer John Riddle (who in 2018 originated the role of Hans in the Broadway production of Disney's *Frozen*); "I Am Easily Assimilated" (from *Candide*), sung by mezzo-soprano Christa Ludwig and musical theater stars Andrea Martin and Patti LuPone; two performances of Sondheim's "Green Finch and Linnet Bird" (from *Sweeney Todd*); and Bernstein's 1985 recording of *West Side Story* featuring opera singers José Carreras and Kiri Te Kanawa, which was compared to the original 1957 cast recording. Examples in the second category included Kristin Chenoweth's performance of "Glitter and Be Gay" (from *Candide*) compared to Marina Poplavskaya's rendition of Gounod's "Jewel Song" ("Ah, je ris de me voir") from *Faust*; and Kelli O'Hara's performance in "Statues and Stories" (from *The Light in the Piazza*) compared to "In uomini, in soldati" (in her Metropolitan Opera debut as Despina in Mozart's *Così fan tutte*). Some of these were videos while others were audio-only; I always provided the score.

Songs that were composed for the specific purpose of combining musical theater and opera in a single performance, often to showcase a performer's ability in both, are excellent self-contained case studies of crossover music. These include "The Girl in 14 G" by Tesori and Dick Scanlan, written for Chenoweth and in which she sings in the styles of musical theater, opera, and jazz while impersonating three different characters. We contrasted that with "They Don't Let You in the Opera (If You're a Country Star)," written by Dan Lipton and David Rossmer for O'Hara, in which she mixes country music with *bel canto coloratura*. Two additional examples satirize music-writing for musical theater. In "Alto's Lament," by Zina Goldrich and Marcy Heisler, the singer complains that she never sings the high notes or the song's main melodies and instead is restricted to repetitive pitches that fill in the harmony. The song has become associated with musical theater singer Megan Hilty, who has operatic training and shows it in performances of the song. Michael Heitzman and Ilene Reid's "Not Funny," written for Rebecca Luker, allows the musical theater singer to display operatic vocal skills as she bemoans that jokes are not funny when delivered in high tessitura.

In "Gershwin and Bernstein," I introduced the students to Bernstein and Alan Jay Lerner's "Duet for One" from *1600 Pennsylvania Avenue*, in which one singer plays two American First Ladies, one leaving the White House (Julia Grant) and the other entering it (Lucy Hayes). The music for Grant is in *parlando* style, syllabic and closer to musical theater performance practices, while Hayes is embodied in operatic melismatic passages and *bel canto*. We listened to two performances, the original by Patricia Routledge (audio available on YouTube) and a second one by Judy Kaye (accompanied by the London Sinfonietta and conductor John McGlinn).

No videos exist of either performance, and I shared with the students that Routledge transitioned from one First Lady to another by simply flipping her wig and changing vocal techniques. All of these in-class music listening and performance analyses demonstrate how musical theater composers adopt styles and techniques from opera for a variety of reasons. These textbook examples of crossover music allow students to learn how skills from one tradition can be applied in another, and give them insight into what both performers and listeners gain when they are aware of the traditions from which the composer or songwriter borrows.

As another activity, I require the students to prepare short presentations on either the music or the readings for the day. Presentations encourage students to be vocally active in class discussions and connect their musicianship skills and activities as performers with musical theater scholarship. On some days I divided the list of readings among the students so that each student was responsible for just one or two texts, and they had to present on the article or book chapter in class and teach it to their classmates—an efficient way to master any material or skill. On other days, I assigned readings to some students, while others had to prepare a presentation on the musical examples. I provided them with the piano vocal score of the musical under study, and they could choose any musical aspect that caught their attention during the viewing/listening to share with the class, with the requirement that they demonstrate why that musical passage was relevant. I implemented a rotation to ensure that all students had to undertake equal amounts of reading and listening in preparation for class. It happened that several students had performed some of the music previously (such as Gershwin's *An American in Paris*, Weill's *Street Scene*, Bernstein's *Candide* and *West Side Story*, and Sondheim's *Sweeney Todd*), and they were able to bring their own experiences and interpretations to the music discussed in class.

Final projects should extend the student-centered learning environment promoted in the classroom, invite the students to look forward, and lead them to engage in their own analyses, evaluations, and conclusions, applying newly acquired skills and knowledge. In both classes, the final project allowed students to focus on their own instrument/voice type, experiences as a performer, and career goals. In "Gershwin and Bernstein," the students explored an occurrence of crossover between popular and classical traditions pertaining to a composer, performer, album, or piece of their choice (see prompt for the assignment in Appendix B). They had to focus on the music itself, including analysis and an account of specific characteristics, in order to establish how certain musical works cross over from one tradition to another. The assignment also required them to do a little bit of research to demonstrate the reasons behind the crossover, exploring social, economic, cultural, aesthetic, and/or historical circumstances that led the musician of their choice to borrow from one style or another, just as we had witnessed in Gershwin's and Bernstein's careers. I provided several questions in the assignment's prompt to inspire and guide the students' research and arguments.

In the graduate seminar "Musical Theater and Opera Crossovers," the final project consisted of a reflective essay (see prompt in Appendix C). I again asked students to focus on the music, but this time they were to analyze at least three pieces that they had performed or would like to perform in the future. One piece had to fall on one end of the crossover spectrum (either classical or popular), while the other two—like the musicals and performances that we had studied in class—had to fall in the middle of the spectrum. Instead of discussing general musical characteristics, students had to explicate precise performance practices that they had learned or developed in order to perform in one tradition and determine whether or not these practices applied to (or differed from) the performance of crossover pieces. They also had to connect their selections with some of the readings that they had completed throughout the semester, applying the scholarship to their own musical interests and practices. These two assignments invited undergraduate and graduate students to engage with the topic of crossover on their own terms and think critically about the extent to which understanding crossover music is an important, if not crucial, skill to have in their professional careers.

Among the many composers and performers discussed in the final projects, some whom the students successfully demonstrated to sit in the middle of the popular–classical crossover spectrum included Jody Karin Applebaum, June Bronhill, Diahann Carroll, Anthony de Mare, Nelson Eddy, JacobTV, Yo-Yo Ma, Arturo Márquez, Bobby McFerrin, Kate Miller-Heidke, Astor Piazzolla, Paul Schoenfield, Bryn Terfel, Chris Thile, the Three Tenors, Time for Three, 2Cellos, Deborah Voigt, Well-Strung (string quartet), Yiruma, and Takashi Yoshimatsu. I created two playlists (one for each class) with all the pieces in their final projects (including the non-crossover ones) and shared the playlists on Blackboard, so students would gain insight both into what their classmates listen to and perform, and also into the diversity of genres, interests, and tastes in their music history classroom.

Results and Conclusion

The courses led students to revise audition packages so that they were better-equipped to audition in both classical and popular traditions (this was mentioned not just in class discussions but also in their final projects and course evaluations). Students shared that they were inspired to take crossover music to their lessons and vocal coachings and have conversations with their applied teachers about the pieces covered in studios and selected for recitals. A piano major from "Gershwin and Bernstein" who performed de Mare's *Liaisons* on his senior recital that semester wrote his final project on selected pieces from this album.[24] A singer from the graduate seminar asked his voice teacher to include Candide's soliloquy "It Must Be So" in his repertoire. Another one, a soprano, had started a project to revitalize Weimar-era cabaret songs and include them alongside the standard repertoire for her voice, and the seminar helped her by providing the academic foundation to continue pursuing that goal.

Several students articulated (either in class discussion or written assignments) how much popular music was fundamental to their formation as a musician. They shared current and past musical tastes as well as the music that they were exposed to in their families and the communities in which they grew up. They then contrasted that with conventional curricula in musical performance, which tend to focus exclusively on classical music. Learning in depth about crossover music convinced students that they receive a richer musical education and better preparation when a conservatory takes into account the students' own backgrounds, pre-existing interests, and musical tastes.

This alerted me to the importance of bringing the music that students listen to and are interested in to the music history and musicological classroom. Since most of my teaching is on twentieth- and twenty-first-century music, I have since included units on crossover music in my music history survey. When I get to the turn of the twenty-first century, I introduce students to the topics of postmodernism and pastiche, but I digress from the narrative by lecturing on crossover between popular and classical music and how it connects to the musical practices that we studied before in the class, and asking the students to bring their own examples. My lectures rely on pieces and musicians brought to my attention by previous students, and I update my notes as I introduce the topic to new students and learn about crossover examples in instruments and genres that are not my main focus as a musicologist. It is fascinating to explore crossover music with my students, put them in the roles of teacher or co-investigator, and open the music history classroom to music that is meaningful to them both as listeners and performers. It is rewarding to observe in class discussions, final projects, and course evaluations how much this pedagogy models music-learning for my students.

My ultimate goal is that music students engage in both classical and popular traditions and think critically about what is lost when a musician (performer, composer, conductor, researcher, or teacher) fails to understand the intricate connections between the two traditions and the borrowing processes that define crossover music. The inclusion of crossover in the music history and musicological classroom opens the door to questioning the dividing line between popular and classical, set in place by music rhetoric of the nineteenth and early twentieth centuries but debunked by our globalized and eclectic music market. The two courses discussed in this chapter continue to inspire me to expand musical theater's presence in the music history classroom and make music history a course that bridges pedagogical practices to the practical life of students, a goal for which every instructor should strive.

Notes

1. This is true not only about U.S. American students but also international students.
2. See Appendix A for a list of readings covered in the courses but not discussed in this chapter.
3. Anthony Tommasini, "Opera? Musical? Please Respect the Difference," *New York Times*, July 7, 2011.
4. Fred Plotkin, "The Blurry Line between Opera and Musical Theater," June 12, 2012, https://www.wqxr.org/story/215908-blurry-line-between-opera-and-musical-theater.
5. Jaime Weinman, "What's New for Opera Houses? 'Cats'?," *Maclean's*, November 16, 2011. The Lyric Opera of Chicago included *Oklahoma!*, *The Sound of Music*, *Carousel*, *The King and I*, *My Fair Lady*, *Jesus Christ Superstar*, and *West Side Story* in subsequent seasons between 2012 and 2019.
6. Moniz, "The Changing Face of Opera in America," 28.
7. Weill, "Two Dreams Come True," 26.
8. Moross and Latouche, *The Golden Apple*, xv–xvi.
9. Moross and Latouche, *The Golden Apple*, xix.
10. Sondheim, *Look, I Made a Hat*, 147.
11. Sondheim, *Look, I Made a Hat*, 147.
12. Michael John LaChiusa, "I Sing of America's Mongrel Culture," *New York Times*, November 14, 1999.
13. Terry Teachout, "A 'Musical' That's Really an Opera," *New York Times*, January 2, 2000.
14. Michael John LaChiusa, "Genre Confusion," *Opera News* 67, August 2002.
15. LaChiusa, "Genre Confusion."
16. See Karl Koenig, ed., *Jazz in Print (1856–1929): An Anthology of Selected Early Readings in Jazz History* (Hillsdale: Pendragon Press, 2002) for primary sources on issues of jazz and race in the early twentieth century.
17. Stempel, *Showtime*, 375–78.
18. Savran, *Highbrow/Lowdown*, 12–39.
19. Adorno, "On Popular Music," 197–209.
20. Oja, *Bernstein Meets Broadway*, 96.
21. Oja, *Bernstein Meets Broadway*, 249.
22. For more on the connections between the terms "highbrow" and "lowbrow" and issues of social class and race, see Lawrence Levine, *Highbrow/Lowbrow: The Emergence of Cultural Hierarchy in America* (Cambridge: Harvard University Press, 1988).
23. These were canceled after the Covid-19 pandemic started in March 2020, but nonetheless provided a picture of contemporary programming practices.
24. *Liaisons: Re-Imagining Sondheim from the Piano* (2015) is an album by de Mare in which each piece is inspired by a song by Stephen Sondheim and arranged by a different contemporary composer, including Michael Daugherty, Jake Heggie, and Steve Reich.

APPENDIX A

This appendix provides other texts that were assigned in both courses and are not discussed in this chapter.

Bañagale, Ryan. "'Each Man Kills the Thing He Loves': Bernstein's Formative Relationship with *Rhapsody in Blue*." *Journal of the Society for American Music* 3, Special Issue: Leonard Bernstein in Boston (2009), 47–66.

———. *Arranging Gershwin: Rhapsody in Blue and the Creation of an American Icon*. New York: Oxford University Press, 2014.

Blyton, Carey. "Sondheim's 'Sweeney Todd': The Case for the Defence." *Tempo, New Series*, no. 149 (1984), 19–26.

Horne, David. "Who Loves You Porgy? The Debates Surrounding Gershwin's Musical." In *Approaches to the American Musical*, edited by Robert Lawson-Peebles. Exeter: University of Exeter Press, 1996).

Macpherson, Ben. "A Voice and So Much More (or When Bodies Say Things That Words Cannot)." *Studies in Musical Theatre* 6, no. 1 (2012), 43–57.

McLaughlin, Robert. *Stephen Sondheim and the Reinvention of the American Musical*. Jackson: University Press of Mississippi, 2016.

Pollack, Howard. *The Ballad of John Latouche: An American Lyricist's Life and Work*. New York: Oxford University Press, 2017.

Schneider, Wayne, ed. *The Gershwin Style: New Looks at the Music of George Gershwin*. New York: Oxford University Press, 1999.

Seldes, Barry. *Leonard Bernstein: The Political Life of an American Musician*. Berkeley: University of California Press, 2009.

Simeone, Nigel. *Leonard Bernstein, West Side Story*. Burlington, VT: Ashgate, 2009.

Smith, Helen. *There's a Place for Us: The Musical Theatre Works of Leonard Bernstein*. New York: Routledge, 2011.

Sondheim, Stephen, and Mark Horowitz. *Sondheim on Music: Minor Details and Major Decisions*, 2nd edition. Lanham, MD: Scarecrow Press, 2010.

Willis-Lynam, Keyona. "The Crossover Opera Singer: Bridging the Gap Between Opera and Musical Theatre." DMA Document, Ohio State University, 2015.

Wyatt, Robert, and John Andrew Johnson, eds. *The George Gershwin Reader*. New York: Oxford University Press, 2004.

Zalman, Paige. "Operatic Borrowing in Stephen Sondheim's *Sweeney Todd*. *American Music* vol. 37, no. 1 (2019), 58–76.

APPENDIX B

Gershwin and Bernstein

Final Project

The term crossover refers to a practice in music when a composer or performer incorporates musical elements into a performance or composition that are not specific to his or her genre. Throughout this semester, we saw several examples in both Gershwin's and Bernstein's oeuvres that combine popular and classical music traditions.

Please write a 5- to 6-page, double-spaced paper in which you demonstrate an occurrence of crossover between classical and popular genres or styles. You can choose any composer, performer, album, or piece that you would like.

If you have played a piece that you believe fits the crossover framework, you may write about it and use your own interpretation and performance choices to support the point that the piece is an example of crossover. The same idea applies if you know a piece in your instrument's repertoire that can be considered a crossover. You can then use this paper to familiarize yourself more thoroughly with the piece and its style.

Content of your paper:

In the first part of your paper, you must introduce the piece, composer, performer, or album and provide some background information. You must then explain characteristics that reveal elements of both popular and classical traditions. You may consider rhythm, harmony, melody, instrumentation, etc.

In the second part, please consider the context for the crossover. Here are some questions to help you write this context. You do not have to answer all of these. Use them to generate ideas.

1. What is the reason for the crossover? (For example, with Gershwin we saw that he started out in Tin Pan Alley and aspired to be a successful composer of concert music; Bernstein started out in the world of classical music but saw the benefits of working in the popular theater.)
2. What are some influences on your piece, composer, performer, or album? The influence can come from people whom a composer or performer met in the past and who helped them in their career, other forms of art that they came in contact with, or trends of the time.
3. We saw in class how New York City played a role in the crossover pieces of Gershwin and Bernstein. Maybe the composer or performer of your piece traveled to places that inspired them?
4. Are there historical happenings that may have led to the adoption of crossover practices? You may consider social changes (such as war) or intellectual/cultural changes, such as the advancement of modernistic ideas.
5. Would you say the composer's curiosity played a part in it? Maybe in instrumentation or adoption of a different style?
6. Did audiences play a part in the crossover? Was there a desire to appeal to or reach wider audiences? Did the music market play a role in this?

7. Do you think that the piece, composer, performer, or album that you chose removes boundaries of genre classification? How? Is this beneficial to performers of this music?
8. Crossover pieces and performers can be controversial, applauded by some and despised by others. Please do not shy away from any controversy or debate that your piece, composer, performer, or album has raised.

APPENDIX C

Musical Theater and Opera Crossovers

Final Project

For the final project for this class, please write a 7- to 8-page double-spaced paper covering the points below. The main idea is that you reflect on the impact that a musical crossover has had on your own activities and career goals as a musician.

1. This semester we studied the musical theater/opera crossover, and you are more than welcome to continue that discussion in your paper. However, there are other forms of musical crossover, such as jazz and popular music, jazz and classical music, pop-opera (performers like Andrea Bocelli and Sarah Brightman), and crossover instrumental music (such as composer/performer Yanni, who writes new age music for orchestras; or the violinist and conductor André Rieu, who targets his performances of classical music to mass audiences, not necessarily those in the concert hall).

   Please first specify which type of musical crossover is relevant to your discussion. Please do not feel restricted to the examples above if you know another form of crossover. Make sure that you address the following questions. How much did you know about this crossover before this class? Had you performed pieces that fall into the crossover's spectrum before? Have the readings and pieces that we discussed in class changed your mind about musical crossover? In what ways?

2. In this section of your paper, you will discuss <u>at least three</u> pieces of your choice and your approaches to performing them. The three pieces must adhere to the following requisites. First, select <u>one</u> piece that falls strictly into one end of the crossover, the one which you have been performing more often in your career. In the context of our class, this would be an operatic aria by Mozart or Verdi; or a concerto or sonata for a given instrument. Then, select <u>at least two</u> pieces that you would

argue fall in the middle of the crossover. In the context of our class, it could be songs from *West Side Story* or *Sweeney Todd*, which we heard performed by both musical theater and opera singers. I encourage you to focus on pieces that you have performed before or know that you might perform in the future. (You may write about more than two crossover pieces, if you would like.) Please argue why these pieces adhere to the requisites above and show the stylistic features that make each of these pieces adhere to those portions of the crossover.

You may answer any of the following:

How do you learn and execute performance practices to play or sing the pieces? Are there differences in how you learn and perform them? What does one piece offer to you as a performer that the other two do not and vice-versa? If you used any of these for auditions, why would you choose one over the others?

You may also discuss pragmatic reasons why you would perform crossover pieces. Do you think or know if the current music job market expects you to navigate a music crossover? Do you think a performer in your instrument or voice can make a difference in the job market by performing styles beyond those they were trained in?

Please feel free to incorporate any topic that you would argue is relevant to explaining why or how you would perform the pieces that you selected.

3. Finally, choose <u>two</u> of the readings that we did this semester and explain how and/or why the author's ideas relate to your selections and performance choices. Please identify the text and the author and explain how the texts can help you interpret or perform the selected pieces. You can also use your pieces as counterargument to some author whose text we read and discussed this semester.

I ask that <u>at least one of the crossover pieces</u> that you select be a piece of music not included in our class. The other one (or ones) may be repertoire that we covered and discussed in class this semester. You can write about music for an instrument that is not your main focus.

References

Adorno, Theodor W. "On Popular Music." In *Cultural Theory and Popular Culture: A Reader*, edited by John Storey, 2nd edn, 197–209. Athens: The University of Georgia Press, 1998.

Koenig, Karl, ed. *Jazz in Print (1856–1929): An Anthology of Selected Early Readings in Jazz History*. Hillsdale: Pendragon Press, 2002.

Latouche, John, and Jerome Moross. *The Golden Apple: A Musical in Two Acts*. New York: Random House, 1954.

Levine, Lawrence. *Highbrow/Lowbrow: The Emergence of Cultural Hierarchy in America*. Cambridge: Harvard University Press, 1988.

Moniz, Justin John. "The Changing Face of Opera in America: Musical Theatre on the American Operatic Stage." Doctor of Music Treatise, Florida State University, 2017.

Oja, Carol J. *Bernstein Meets Broadway: Collaborative Art in a Time of War*. New York: Oxford University Press, 2014.

Savran, David. *Highbrow/Lowdown: Theater, Jazz, and the Making of the New Middle Class*. Ann Arbor: The University of Michigan Press, 2009.

Sondheim, Stephen. *Look, I Made a Hat: Collected Lyrics (1981–2011) with Attendant Comments, Amplifications, Dogmas, Harangues, Digressions, Anecdotes, and Miscellany*. New York: Alfred A. Knopf, 2011.

Stempel, Larry. *Showtime: A History of the Broadway Musical Theater*. New York: W.W. Norton, 2010.

Weill, Kurt. "Two Dreams Come True." In *Street Scene: A Sourcebook*, edited by Joanna Lee, Edward Harsh, and Kim Kowalke, 26. New York: Kurt Weill Foundation for Music, 1994.

10 The Anti-Colonial Conservatory
The Case of the University "Folk Band"

Christopher J. Smith

> *To try to find a way to situate vernacular values within the cultivated space of the conservatory can be a challenge.*[1]

The standard models of the North American university music program and its ensembles emerge from an inherited European pedagogical philosophy that emphasizes canonical works, reified linear histories, heroized individuals, and hierarchized valuations. These factors result in an exclusionist and unjust system of access, by which music programs' valuations of context, history, and meaning are in turn contaminated. As I wrote in 2006, "No one can work in this field...without coming to understand that there has long been conflict between commodification and community in the practice and the handing on of traditional music."[2] Interrogating the university music program's hierarchical structures—including those that govern ensembles—is therefore a necessary first step in dismantling such structures and decolonizing these values.[3]

At the same time, incorporating vernacular idioms and ensembles into the procedures, organization, and assessment methods of North American conservatories carries both positive benefits and particular challenges.[4] Those benefits include enhanced pedagogy, increased student engagement, and direct fulfillment of program requirements stipulated by the U.S.A.'s National Association of Schools of Music (NASM). At the same time, there is a real risk of distorting source idioms' aesthetics, values, and musical/organizational principles. The incorporation of vernacular idioms within the conservatory must not come at the cost of eroding those idioms' core priorities. Maximizing benefits and addressing challenges requires sensitivity, imagination, flexibility, and attention to detail: both nuts-and-bolts musical and pedagogical experience, and constant awareness of the potential conflicts between vernacular and conservatory values.

In response, this essay moves from analysis of the North American conservatory's historical relationship with vernacular musics; to discussion of three programs in three countries, each of which engages heavily in imaginative constructions or reconstructions of vernacular musics

DOI: 10.4324/9781003415954-14

as 21st-century conservatory topics; and then to a more extended operational discussion of practices I myself have employed as program director in one of those three. I also reference various examples of university-based community arts and engagement, including Travis Stimeling and Sophia Enriquez on West Virginia University's bluegrass programs, Juniper Hill on a range of university folk bands, and my own multi-decade experience as a leader of both campus- and community-based vernacular music learning settings.[5] I will thus progress from more analytical articulations of goals and sources to more colloquial discussion of three ensembles' procedures and results, while referencing other "imagined worlds" both within and beyond the conservatory. I will close with a reflection upon the future possibilities of thus reimagining the university folk band.

As a specialist in the cultural history and performance practices of vernacular arts—that is, participatory expressive forms that are learned, taught, and passed on by ear and stored in the memory—it is incumbent upon me to recognize that these arts' contrasted procedural, aesthetic, and functional expectations are at odds with the neoliberal university's hierarchized metrics of progress and assessment.[6] Stimeling and Enriquez describe the "compromises between the ways that musical practices are taught within their traditional contexts and the ways that academic music departments teach music," and cite the conservatory's imperatives, which frequently conflict with what I have called elsewhere "the indigenous pedagogies."[7] Like the leaders of the programs in Argentina and Finland which I cite later in this essay,

> [Stimeling and Enriquez] believe that a decolonial pedagogy…has great potential to support the creation of more just, equitable, and inclusive environments… [Such a pedagogy] invites people from different backgrounds to come together around a shared project while decentering the instructor's expertise and allowing for greater collective ownership of the work. It critiques conventional narratives and makes those critiques concrete through collaboration, dialogue, and direct action… It shifts institutional power away from faculty and administrators who might have good intentions but competing priorities and places it in the hands of the very students whose future well-being is often threatened by the neoliberal attitudes and practices in higher education.[8]

An anti-hegemonic approach to ensembles must dismantle dichotomies between "legitimate" and "illegitimate" instruments, genres, and experiential practices. To enhance inclusion for previously silenced voices, we might abandon canons altogether—or at the barest minimum, abandon the idea of "flagship" repertoires or ensembles. We would instead empower and evaluate command of processes and recast our assessment tools to more effectively value musicians' capacity to operate, creatively and collaboratively, within diverse and shifting situations.

The ethnomusicologist Juniper Hill, whose early work on the Sibelius Academy and subsequent ethnographic writings about university folk music programs in Finland, California, and Cape Town is a strong influence upon my thinking, propounds an "experiential model of musical creativity," suggesting that

> The six processes that musicians regularly experience while perceiving themselves to be engaged in a creative activity are (1) generativity, (2) agency, (3) interaction, (4) nonconformity, (5) recycling, and (6) flow. Although some cultures may place greater value on some of these than on others, all six components were reported across all the musical idioms and cultures in this study.[9]

Yet reimagining the conservatory's definition of technical virtuosity in terms of "generativity, agency, interaction, nonconformity, recycling, and flow" requires a fundamental revision of the goals, articulation, and assessment of artistic progress. It necessitates valuing a range of integrated skill-sets (both music-technical and also professional-entrepreneurial) to be inculcated in the training of instrumentalists, singers, and composers, and significantly adapting assessment tools to recognize processual expertise.

I have written elsewhere about the scope of institutional change that might be necessary in order for such anti-colonial work to operate throughout the conservatory context.[10] In this chapter, I want to talk specifically about a more pro-active, more imagination-driven, more aggressively "alternate-historical" approach to imagining ensemble work, collaboration, improvisation, and artistic identity.

Many conservatories in Europe, the UK, Ireland, and in South America, Mesoamerica, and North America, especially those sponsored by or associated with national or state governments, have invested effort in developing "folk music" ensembles and other training. While training in such programs builds both practical musicianship and pedagogical skill, by and large their focus is upon celebration and replication of culturally-specific traditions associated with national identity. That sort of identification, though it has built effective regionally-identified and conservatory-based folk music programs, is experienced by some as paradoxically limiting; as Juniper Hill puts it, "Most of my informants were sick of nationalist discourse and seemed to be more interested in presenting cultural and ethnic identities that stretch beyond national borders...and in defining themselves as an affinity-based subculture of artists."[11]

In contrast, there is the less-common case of the ensembles that engage with both vernacular musics and also new creativity (in terms of repertoire or experimental genres), new compositions, and/or syncretic and individual training. Because such organizations are necessarily much more speculative—often, because they seek to advocate not on behalf of specific nationalist repertoires or associations, but rather for a different student understanding of the relationship between "traditional" and "new" genres—they are much fewer. In the present essay, I discuss three, including the Folk Big Band (FBB) of the Sibelius Academy, a small, federally-subsidized, and highly innovative program in Helsinki; La Orquesta de Instrumentos Autóctonos y Nuevas Tecnologías, an ensemble developed by visionary creative directors at the Universidad Tres de Febrero in Argentina; and the cluster of ensembles sponsored by my own Vernacular Music Center at Texas Tech University in the U.S.A. Southwest.[12]

Helsinki: The Sibelius Academy's Folk Big Band

Heikki Laitinen (b. 1942), a composer who had written an MA thesis on "folkloristics," was appointed the founding director of the Department of Folk Music at the Sibelius Academy in 1989. With a strong remit from the Finnish government, he argued that "teaching folk music [in university contexts] can enrich music culture by encouraging musical versatility, multiple values, multi-facetedness, open-mindedness, and multilingualism."[13] Hill writes,

> Laitinen, formerly the director of Kaustinen Folk Music Institute, had a background in folklore, avant-garde art music composition, ethnomusicology, and theology—influences that can be found in his application of folklorist Albert Lord's theories, emphasis on the avant-garde, valuation of field and archival research, and deliverance of riveting sermon-like speeches on creativity and folk music's potential.[14]

During and since Laitinen's tenure, the Sibelius Academy, in the ambitious diversity of its musical training (detailed ahead), has showcased this nexus of "traditional music – new music – improvisation" creativity in the particular vehicle of its Folk Big Band (FBB), which performs both traditional material and also new works in traditional styles in a highly arranged, theatricalized, and spectacular concert style.

In a February 2014 concert performance of "Paimendisco" ("Shepherd disco," a setting by the Band's leaders and students of a traditional shepherd's song) celebrating the FBB's debut CD recording, the synthesis of a folkloric source, the Band's massed instrumentation, and the players' movements and dress—they are explicitly costumed as for a rave—combine to yield a clear and intentional sense of the spectacular.[15] Again, this is not ostensibly "folkloric" music; rather, the argument, explicit in Laitinen's statements and implicit in this concert presentation, is that there need be no philosophical contradiction between a vernacular tradition and either popular or avant-garde artistic approaches. To the traditional melody and text are added massed and combined folkloric and orchestral instruments (notably the *munniharppu,* the bowed and keyed *nyckelharpa*, and the *kantele* plucked zither which is emblematic of the core epic poem of the *Kalevala*), drum set and percussion grooves, and section choreography clearly developed and rehearsed by the performers. The tune is a traditional and "crooked" one, but the orchestration, control of section dynamics, use of house-style bass lines, and polytonal string washes all come from contemporary popular musics.[16]

The FBB in this way embodies onstage Laitinen's and the Sibelius Academy's vision for a 21st-century engagement with vernacular traditions in which "innovation" and "tradition" are perceived as co-existent and energizing. Juniper Hill emphasizes the Academy's goals with regard to such synthesis:

> To make folk music relevant to contemporary society; *to recapture the creative processes of a (reimagined) oral past*; to give folk musicians the freedom to develop folk music as an art; and to give students the artistic skills, courage, and freedom to create and perform their own personal, original (folk) music.[17]

The FBB actualizes the mandate that music students should be "conversant with basic folk music repertoire while analysing and internalising the musical logic and resources of *orchestrated folk music.*"[18] This conception, of an "orchestrated folk music" which is "conversant" with folkloric repertoire, is found in both ensembles discussed next.

Buenos Aires: La Orquesta de Instrumentos Autóctonos y Nuevas Tecnologías at Universidad Tres de Febrero

As Laitinen has done at Helsinki, Alejandro Iglesias Rossi (b. 1960), an electroacoustic composer and the founding director of La Orquesta de Instrumentos Autóctonos y Nuevas Tecnologías ("the Orchestra of Native Instruments and New Technologies," hereafter OIANT) at the Universidad Tres de Febrero in Buenos Aires, has, since 2004, charted an ensemble path that seeks to revive and re-engage with pre-Columbian Indigenous experience, instruments, and aesthetics. Like Laitinen, Rossi describes a synthesis that accommodates both 21st-century university requirements and folkloric aesthetics, and a blended vision of artistic freedom and flexibility consistent with the operating aesthetics of new music and improvisation:

> The project seeks to reverse the effect of the disciplinary compartmentalization that has been taking place in the arts since the Industrial

Revolution, when what we now call music began to separate from dance and theatre, a logic that did not exist and does not exist to this day in the Indigenous communities.[19]

Emphasizing the artificiality of the neoliberal conservatory's siloing of "classical" versus "folk" versus "new" versus "improvisational" music experiences, Rossi posits an idealized vision of Indigenous values and practices as more inclusive and less prone to such separations:

> It is very rare to find an indigenous community where they talk about music [exclusive of other arts]. In general [performance] is a ritual that involves the sound event, the physical event, dance, choreography, as a whole...*There is a colonial thought that leaves aside everything that does not fit with the hegemonic paradigm.*[20]

In espousing the idea of an anti-hegemonic aesthetic inspired by Indigenous models, Rossi has created an ensemble, a community of artists, and a multi-valent performance idiom that synthesizes not only "Instrumentos Autóctonos y Nuevas Tecnologías" but also costumes, masks, props, and movement. In a short documentary from 2004, music director Rossi, movement and theatrics director Susana Ferreres, and their collaborators discuss both the intentions and the communal creative processes which the Orquesta centers. Participants engage in pre-concert physical and mental practices, rooted in Rossi's own rather mystical version of tai chi and related meditative practices; costuming plays a significant role; and imagined and experimental responses to ethnographic source material are welcomed.[21] Commenting upon instrumental music and singing, sound effects, nature sounds, electronics, and spoken word, directors emphasize that the ensemble depends upon student musicians' sense of confidence in the directors' artistic vision. Communal realization of that vision, in performance, itself becomes part of the immersive apprenticeship.

In the context of a 2015 TEDx video presentation, their concepts are laid out in a usefully and artfully telescoped version of the orchestra's more expansive full-length concert programs.[22] On an elaborate stage set under complex theatrical lighting, Rossi and his players, all in costume, move in synchronization and with a sense of visual gravitas. Sound is integrated with movement, and the choreography of the instrumentalists itself becomes part of the performance.[23]

Throughout, there is a sense of abstraction—that is to say, in no sense is this folkloric "recreation" of "traditional performance practices." Rather, the folkloric instruments are treated as inspirations and sound sources for new compositions whose ritual intent is explicit. Dancers costumed in traditional garb and in more abstract representations of spirits and nature interact with the players; there is a strong visual focus upon Rossi as the crucial creative spirit, and the ensemble's practices reflect his leadership and both creative and physical centrality within performance.[24]

It is a strong, affecting, and spectacular mode of presentation, playing well across a recital hall's footlights and proscenium, but it also reflects the degree to which the orchestra is an invention; what North American folk musician Tim Eriksen calls an "imagined village."[25] As always in the case of university ensembles that borrow from traditional or vernacular sources, there are complex negotiations, both intentional and inadvertent, between appropriation, imitation, and inspiration. This is a delicate path to tread, because the neoliberal university itself has been a vehicle for extraction and appropriation, a process of colonialist exploitation within which performing arts programs are also culpable. Therefore, to situate an innovative, norms-challenging, genre-combining ensemble within a university setting, particularly when such an ensemble addresses vernacular idioms that may be distant to participants' experience and cultural identities, is a tricky challenge.

Texas Tech University Celtic Ensemble / "Elegant Savages Orchestra"

My own Texas Tech University ensemble is a large orchestral group of winds, brass, strings, percussion, rhythm, voices, and dancers, whose artistic mission is to explore the possibilities that a *vernacular* conception of orchestral folk music might present. Since its 2006 foundation as a small, traditionally oriented "Celtic ensemble," the group has evolved into a space for experimentation in the areas of composition, repertoire, and presentation, intended to foster imaginative collaboration, center student agency, and permit developing artists to explore beyond their Conservatory experiences, models, and hierarchies. When the ensemble was first convened around 2006, the general concept was to employ both traditional Celtic and related North European repertoires and traditional techniques for purposes of learning and arranging. Primarily, this involved focusing upon traditional instruments such as flute, fiddle, tin whistle, and chordophones (guitar/mandolin/bouzouki), and a method of passing along tunes that prioritized listening and imitating as the tune was taught by oral/aural methods. This is an effective means of transmission within a number of melody-based vernacular traditions, but it succeeds best when students possess both prior experience with learning by ear and also the time and concentration required to develop the skill set and the body of tunes.

Subsequently, as the ensemble became more popular amongst a wider community of students, attracting a more diverse range of instrument types and prior experiences, the stipulation to retain traditional methods of learning by demonstration and by ear became somewhat unsupportable.

We were able to maintain our emphasis upon highly traditional vernacular sources and familiarization with those repertoires via listening to original recordings. But it was not realistic to employ exclusively aural/oral techniques with a 52-piece ensemble preparing three programs per academic year, especially because a significant majority of the students would have very little prior experience with learning by ear.

As a lifelong vernacular musician, I remain committed to by-ear learning as the core method for acquiring interpretative and expressive subtleties uncaptured or even violated by notation. But as a teacher, I also seek to meet student musicians where they are in terms of their physical technique, prior experience, and capacities for learning in unfamiliar ways. The compromise is that, in the current orchestral version of the ensemble, the students do read from (my own) notated orchestral arrangements, but—as in the case of the jazz big band, which selectively employs notation—there is extensive supplemental instruction, direction, and coaching happening in real time, through verbal and visual means.

In rehearsal and even in concert, as they play, I conduct and give cues, using hand signals and spoken instructions, training the players to execute their notated parts but *also* to listen, respond, and react in real time. In this way, notation becomes a means of empowering students possessing less vernacular music experience, because it plays to familiar skills, and then employs or subverts those skills for expressive and interpretative purposes. At a certain point in the acquisition of a new piece, for example, the students will be instructed to turn their music stands around, and to play as much of their parts as they can recall by ear; I tell them, "It is totally OK to play a lot of wrong notes right now, but you *must keep playing*: this is how we develop the skill to play by ear." Even if we then return to the use of the notated parts for concert purposes, the experience of attempting to recall a part and play it by ear is something that most of the students find empowering and liberating.

History and Alternate History

The alter ego element of the Celtic Ensemble (the catalog title) as the "Elegant Savages Orchestra" (ESO) evolved as an alternate history frame that, while permitting the more plausible inclusion of diverse musics in an atypical ensemble configuration, also provides an inclusive back story.[26] The background for the ESO is the (invented) former Soviet Republic of "Bassanda." Drawing on the experience of state folkloric ensembles at the time of the USSR's dissolution, the ESO is imagined as a former national state orchestra that finds itself in exile after the USSR's dissolution.[27] In turn, and in order to provide fresh opportunities for historical creativity, each academic year the newly-configured ensemble, which incorporates both returning students and new recruits, is imagined at a particular historical moment.[28] Stimeling and Enriquez likewise suggest that "using storytelling as a decolonial tool allows for the mobilization of lived experiences and stories toward the project of decoloniality, reimagining the narratives of…white settler colonial history," and, though the WVU Bluegrass ensembles effectively situate their student musicians within the extractive landscapes of their region, the use of "storytelling as a decolonial tool" is equally powerful within the very different lives of the university students who discover, imagine, and then inhabit these stories.[29]

Over the years, the back story of Bassanda has grown to encompass an entire mythology, geography, history, and cosmology: a kind of multiverse. The existence of this body of material impacts not only repertoire choices and arranging procedures, and the way these are framed to the audience, but also how student musicians are themselves empowered to imagine and indeed mythologize their future artistic paths. These are not random inventions; rather, the ESO seeks to create an immersive and empowering environment within which students who may lack strong family or community traditions of vernacular performance can engage with an invented and syncretic aesthetic that honors—but avoids appropriating—Indigenous traditions.[30] Other advocates, historians, and ensemble leaders—most notably the cluster of English folk musicians called "The Imagined Village," the pop singer Janelle Monáe, and the multi-instrumentalist, singer, and teacher Tim Eriksen—have likewise developed "alternate imaginaries" as zones for teaching and learning creativity.[31] Of his invented New England village of "Pumpkintown," the site for his alter ego's *Josh Billings Voyage or, Cosmopolite on the Cotton Road*, Eriksen comments:

> When people talk about traditional music or folk songs, they often imply isolation. But even in the smallest places, travel has more to do with how music develops than isolation does. By making this sideways, half-told story, I can get at a number of things by implication, that [would] take me hours to say in complete sentences.[32]

Similarly, the pop singer Janelle Monáe's android alter ego, "Cindi Mayweather," develops over a narrative running through *Audition* (2003), *Metropolis: The Chase Suite* (2007), and *Dirty Computer* (2018); other musicians spanning from Gorillaz (new-funk) to Hank Williams and Garth Brooks (country) have similarly created alter egos.[33] Working from the opposite direction—that is, from world-building in words to music/sound, instead of from music to words—the speculative fiction author Ursula K. LeGuin's 1985 *Always Coming Home*, set in future-pastoral Northern California, was issued with an accompanying cassette that "imagine[s one] folk music of the future."[34] Regarding his own work, Tim Eriksen comments: "I realized that I could start 'lying' and get at truths."[35] In this sense, the made-up stories of Pumpkintown or Bassanda can center factual, emotional, or autobiographical truth while—precisely because they are fictionalized—simultaneously decentering the solitary author. The stories can seek the mythic and communal while avoiding individualistic egocentrism.

The invention of Bassanda encourages the exploration of alternative imaginative spaces and of syncretic (and/or invented or reinvented) music-making; as Juniper Hill puts it, in terms of the Sibelius FBB: "The pedagogical method of simulated oral composition, in its focus on re-creating the folk creative processes of an [imagined] oral culture, has led to extensive personal variation of traditional source material."[36] And, as Rossi insists in the context of OIANT: "*There are elements both traditional and new in the lives of each one of us,* there always have been, ever since the beginning of time, and there always will be until the end of the world."[37] Bassanda, like the "invented tradition" of the FBB and "elements both traditional and new in the lives of each one of us," recognizes that human imagination, especially in collaborative situations, is how new, alternate, and/or reparative possibilities can be visualized and brought into being.

Teaching "contingency"—the realization that history is not a chain of sequential inevitabilities—requires enhancing students' skills in understanding experience, context, and narrative as products of complex multi-factored situations, shifts in whose details yield contrasted consequences and events. Both historical imagination, in the lecture hall or student essay, and improvisation in performance, depend upon the capacity to engage with, and within, contingent situations. The use of role-playing games, whether paper-based or digital, is by now accepted as a means of teaching contingent history, philosophy, ethics, and social skills, for multiple clienteles and at multiple grade levels.[38] The Bassanda Universe is a similar sort of cultural/historical role-playing game, writ large: encompassing an entire (fictional) nation's history, culture, demography, geography, socio-political perceptions, and all the ways that such a nation, and its diverse peoples, might interact with the global 20th century. Centered around the Cold War-and-after adventures of the "Bassandan National Radio Orchestra" and its offshoots, it provides a platform within and through which to explore a wealth of cultural/historical factors that shaped transnational experience in that era. As pedagogy and creative catalyst, the Bassanda Universe "reverse-engineers" Bassanda's cultural and political history into the larger arcs of 19th–20th century Eastern and Western bloc dynamics. Though this former Soviet Socialist Republic's geographical location is intentionally unspecific (Eastern Europe? Central Asia?), its characters' historical, cultural, demographic, philosophical, and transnational experiences are in every case rendered consistent with wider histories.

Participants in the ensemble's alternate-history identity are explicitly invited to collaborate in the group narrative, and are free to suggest or request events, biographical details, and presentational ideas. We maintain an Imagineering Committee that is given additional influence upon aspects of staging, costume, theme, and so forth; we do this precisely in order that students may assume as much agency as they wish. The parallel Inclusivity Caucus has a separate charge, though its decisions may also impact aspects of staging, biographical detail, and back story (Bassanda is a non-heteronormalizing culture, for example). In all cases, the major requirement regarding students' narrative input is that, in order to be adopted, an idea or suggestion must (a) fit the known, real-world historical context in which that year's iteration of the band is operating, and (b) fit within the existing and expanding detail of the Bassanda multiverse, which itself must likewise fit into known real-world history.

Most student members quite enjoy the game-space of Bassanda, but don't necessarily feel the need to co-author its scripts/storylines themselves. Historical curiosity leads some to investigate independently, but for most, participation is centered on their contributions to their own fictional biographies: a participant expresses interest in a Bassanda bio, and is invited to supply family anecdotes, genealogical information, aspirations, favorite films, books, places, and dreams for the future. In turn, I construct a fictional biography that incorporates all the supplied material as either content or inspiration, while also slotting into the existing Bassanda universe. The priority in these bios is to use the student's *own* words and values to inform the fictional persona: when this is successful, students report feeling moved and empowered to see their aspirations and dreams rendered into effective narrative prose.[39]

In my observation, a student participant who encounters historical events and actors in the Bassanda bio with whom their own fictional persona is claimed to have interacted is much more inclined to investigate those same real-world events and actors. Eriksen makes a parallel observation regarding audiences' responses to his invented New England village:

> Part of the thing with Pumpkintown is that it's improvisatory and wherever I go I try to root it in that place, in that particular group of people and it's remarkable—this may be one of the things [that is] like tarot card reading or something—it's remarkable how directly relevant it becomes immediately to strange particular groups of people through one or two little details that then animate others.[40]

Our practice intends an enriched imaginative experience and a complementary means of engaging with history.

History learning in this ensemble is in that sense a byproduct of participation—albeit a welcome and rewarding one—just as a player of *Assassin's Creed Odyssey* might in passing learn quite a good bit about ancient Greece and its core literatures. For me, as the de facto designer, it is important that imagined events and individuals moving through historical moments should be factually and culturally consistent with a known historical record and interpretation. Like the Dungeon Master in *Dungeons and Dragons*, I seek competent and rigorous world-building and a consistent "canon," and to know how all the pieces fit together, in order to liberate the players (in both senses) to experience the world and build their knowledge of it through participation. This has the added advantage of building what in the world of long-form television would be called "the show bible": a centralized repository to which all writers can contribute and which they can all reference in order to ensure that new contributions fit within larger indirect narratives, or "canon."

This canonic material is contained in a large tranche of written documents, taking various formats, from news reports, personal bios, fragments of dialogs, descriptions and readings of material evidence, and so forth.[41] This has the added advantage that as a new player, event, or fictional character enters the band and universe, its back story can be reverse engineered to fit within the existing canon. This is very similar to the way that authors creating new stories within existing "IP" (Intellectual Property, like the Star Wars or Marvel Comics Universe) can reference the existing materials, finding creative satisfaction and indeed new possibilities through that reverse engineering. Students participating in the ensemble tend to encounter the alternate history frame in relatively indirect fashion: through verbal references made in rehearsal or in programming, and through the visual elements of costuming and staging that support the particular moment in the Bassanda narratives through which the band is moving. Not all students will be interested to follow up further with the vast written material, which numbers well over 300,000 words, but—as with the world building of Tolkien or Terry Pratchett—the written material laying out the world is available for those who do have interest. Over the 15 years of the ensemble's existence, I have observed that the vast majority of players are very happy to participate in the cosplay, which reminds them of gaming or science fiction conventions, while a smaller but still significant percentage will be active in pursuing Bassanda-themed prose, original games, short films, stage shows, and other creative outputs that we have generated in the ESO's history.

Taking to the Stage

Performances are constructed using the programming considerations common in rock and jazz performances: strong openers and closers, full-ensemble numbers balanced with reduced-force chamber pieces, breathing spaces after dances and before choral works, songs versus dance tunes. In all cases, players are asked to costume in a fashion that is consistent with the year's "theme" (really, the geographic and historical moment in which "this year's band" is depicted as operating), with assistance from the costumers of the Imagineering Committee, who will compile Pinterest "view books," drawing from game designers, cosplayers, and historical visual documentation. Those ESO members who also happen to be cosplayers and drag performers are often particularly useful consultants for those members with less experience—though the phenomenon of the "One Act Play" competitions in Texas public high schools, and the costumed theatricalized movement of high school marching bands and summertime drum corps, yields a surprisingly large percentage of students who are comfortable with costume and synchronized movement.

We employ pre-concert audio tracks, often based on period sound sources, and, since 2020, have collaborated with our school's digital-design faculty to build holographic, synchronized, and projection-mapped digital imagery into performances. Concert repertoire is constructed to facilitate theatricalized entrances and exits, deploying performers throughout performance spaces, employing movement vocabularies (processionals, marches, circle dances) that lend themselves to spectacular and narrative connotations. All players are encouraged to learn the steps of the traditional dances so that their rhythmic interpretations can benefit from embodied insights. Speaking of the ESO, ethnochoreologist and movement director Anne Wharton says:

> I have the opportunity to introduce musicians to movement which informs musical performance practice and facilitates physical and psychological well-being... Participating in these dance forms also exposes students to skills inherent in vernacular dance practices such as body awareness and social interaction. I can use vernacular dance as a vehicle to teach ease and efficiency of movement, heighten proprioceptive senses, and help students often isolated by long hours of studio practice find a communal space of fellowship and trust.[42]

The goal is that performers should feel sufficiently safe that they can embark on expressive adventures, including movement and improvisation, that are comparatively unavailable in more conventional band, choir, and orchestra programming. In the pre-COVID era, ESO performances always climaxed with a large-scale tutti dance piece, during which players, singers, and dancers would invite the audience to come to the stage and dance together.

Many of these techniques, and the priorities they reflect, are a product of experience in music-making beyond the university curriculum, especially rock, folk, and traditional idioms. Collapsing the boundary between audience and performers, direct address to audiences' imaginations, the integration of sound and movement, and the metaphorical modeling of social community are fundamental "vernacular values" that we derive from our sources and seek to transmute and transmit through the medium of ESO performances.

Performance occurs in a ritual space; its power and capacity to effectuate lasting changes (emotional, archetypal, imaginative, and/or intentional) amongst participants arises precisely as a result of the intensity and conviction with which performance is collectively created. In the ESO, the face-painting at the center of the pre-show ritual is the raising of aspect: the invocation of archetypes that participants seek to discover and embody for purposes of expressive power.[43] As members costume and paint, we celebrate that what is about to occur can reverberate across time and space. At an ESO show, when you encounter a player, singer, or dancer with a painted face, you are receiving a symbolic indication that you are dealing with a bigger, more charismatic, more archetypal, and more impactful version of the person behind the paint in the mundane world. Paint becomes another resource in our expressive palette as we seek to draw the audience into a magical, shared experience.

Engaging "The Vernacular" in Repertoire and Rehearsal

Practically speaking, we tend to focus upon dance tunes and monophonic songs associated with northwest Europe; that is, from the linguistically linked zones of Ireland, Scotland, Wales, Brittany, Cornwall, Galicia, and the Isle of Man, and from language groups within and on their peripheries. This is a legacy of the ensemble's origin in "Celtic musics," and of its subsequent evolution in terms of thematic organization, regional specifics, the historical moment being depicted in the fictional alter ego, and practical considerations and conclusions driven by the expansive instrumentation. For example, my own core inheritance of Irish traditional dance tunes—jigs and reels—does not typically lend itself so readily to our full instrumentation; those tunes' strings of 8th notes run the risk of being lost in the sheer density of the orchestral sound. So, for technical reasons, I am likely to select dance tunes whose rhythmic profiles are a bit more varied, more expansive, and less fast-note oriented. Various types of piping tunes, song melodies, Breton and French tunes, English hornpipes, Scandinavian tunes, and Galician tunes all tend to breathe a bit more in this respect.

However, the more "notey" traditional repertoires are not neglected: we can still accommodate those who are interested in playing hardcore traditional Irish tunes, for example, or highly specific or technically demanding repertoires, through the medium of our chamber groups. These are smaller ensembles, more focused upon the traditional instruments of flute, fiddle, tin whistle, pipes, and accompanying instruments, within which the traditional dance tunes can be learned and replicated in a less notated and more traditional process than that employed with the full orchestra. These smaller ensembles can also accommodate individual musicians' special requests for particular songs. This structure is analogous to the ensemble organization in a jazz program: in a full-scale program, like the one at Indiana where I cut my bebop teeth with David Baker, almost all players will occupy a seat in a jazz big band, but those who have interest and/or suitable skills may in addition participate in the small group combos, which focus on more specific repertoires or performance practices.

As ensemble director, I engage with the vernacular by grounding my programming choices in repertoire that can be traced to vernacular tradition bearers, myself having learned through extended, direct contact with such persons in both the U.S.A. and Ireland. If a student brings me a piece of repertoire that is rooted in a North European or related folklore tradition, but in a version that has appeared in a film or game in a more popular idiom, I will usually go back to the original source and suggest to the student that perhaps we might operate from the vernacular source instead. For example, a student might request "Siúil a Rún" or "Sí do Mhaimeo Í," encountered in a pop version from the group/album *Celtic Woman*, at which point I might suggest a return to the field recording by Elizabeth Cronin (from the early 1950s) for the first, or Altan's 1992 recording of the second, as our preferred source. This is also an effective way to nudge students' listening toward more traditional versions and repertoires.

To situate ESO repertoire in sources from within the heart of the respective vernacular traditions, we find the earliest source of a particular piece—not infrequently, a field recording—and use that source recording as inspiration for the orchestral arrangements. Within this mandate, I have gone so far as to transcribe unaccompanied wax cylinder recordings, or recordings of wild animals in nature, or spontaneously-improvised field recordings, and to orchestrate them for the full ensemble in ways that replicate the source's phrasing, intonation, timbre, and other subtle musical parameters. We have melded those source recordings with our live performances, embedding the first within the second; our arrangement of the English-language "Rufford Park Poachers," for example—a song we first heard from the revival singer Martin Carthy, but which was originally collected on wax cylinder by Percy Grainger from the singing of Joseph Taylor in 1908 (and which Grainger employed in his orchestral *Lincolnshire Posy*)—segued in concert from a pitch-shifted recording of Taylor himself to the full orchestra's instrumental arrangement.[44] Similarly, our orchestral version of Swedish *kula* came from a remarkable YouTube video by Åsa Larsson of a spontaneous outdoor *kulning* (herding call) that, over the course of 2:40 minutes, called a curious swan across a pond to her side.[45]

Part of the creative appeal of the ensemble has been the opportunity to develop and practice my own arranging skills, and to arrive at imaginative approaches to orchestral arranging procedures that are reflective of vernacular aesthetics. In other words, this is not a "classical" chamber orchestra playing arrangements of folk tunes; rather, it is a large ensemble that happens to use music notation because that medium is accessible to most (though not all) of the players, and that reimagines the orchestra *as if it were conceived and populated by vernacular players*. As arranger, my own artistic mandate is to try to find ways to exploit familiar ensemble procedures of arranging, notating, or conducting, but to do so in a fashion that fits the aesthetic of the source musics, or at the barest minimum avoids doing violence to their originating aesthetics.

There is not a direct one-to-one correspondence between the context and moment of the alter ego and the selected repertoire; instead, I allow repertoire choices to interact synergistically with that alter ego, generating new ideas. The year's persona may be "the 1936 International Brigade/Spanish Civil War *Libertarias* Band," situating the fictional Bassanda characters within the historical actors and events that brought the multinational members of the International Brigade to fight on the Republic side in 1936, for example, but only some of the pieces will be drawn from repertoires associated with that time and place; others will simply be subsumed under the fictional conceit "these are the tunes this Band in this time and place liked to play."

Thus, we do not presume that all repertoire on a given program must be entirely consistent with or operate within the alter ego's historical moment; to do so might be "historically accurate"—and thus suitable for, perhaps, a "historical-informed performance" (HIP) ensemble—but for an intentionally syncretic ensemble, it would feel excessively constrained and indeed rather arbitrary. A more fruitful way to think about repertoire is instead to exploit the alter ego's alternate-fiction persona, so as to imagine a band from 1912 or 1928 or 1936 or 1952 playing a perhaps-esoteric grab bag of repertoire precisely because they come from an imagined and anciently cosmopolitan national identity. Of his Pumpkintown ensemble, Tim Eriksen says similarly:

> It was kind of a new concept to me [to] realize that [through] this imaginary place, I wouldn't have to go to this complicated number of places in order to tell all the stories; I could tell them based in this one imaginary place. Having it be a place, rather than a genre even if it's an imaginary place, it was amazing how instantly it made it easier for people to relax and just listen.[46]

The rehearsal process is also unlike that of a conventional chamber orchestra. While the players may be mostly sightreading from notated parts, the actual practice is more like that of a jazz big band—even, perhaps, a jazz big band playing head arrangements (that is, learned by rote aural assignment rather than from notation). One of my major pedagogical goals is to encourage classical orchestral or choral musicians to learn to think more like jazz players: to make adjustments in real time, to play by ear, to receive instructions while playing, and to execute those instructions. My models for this mode of rehearsing and conducting are my own jazz big band mentors, and I believe that this kind of experience provides an especially valuable and efficacious mode of experiential learning, especially for orchestral or choral musicians otherwise lacking jazz experience.

Conclusion

Tools, images, models, visions, and practical experiences that help the young aspirant concretize a day-to-day and decade-to-decade vision of being a working artist can be deeply empowering. This is at the heart of what we teachers of arts practice do—we not only describe but also demonstrate, not only verbalize but also model, what it is to be a working artist. In the performing arts, especially, we do this by involving our students in the collaborative processes within which new art and arts experiences are born. Playing in the band, dancing in the corps, brainstorming in the improvisation sessions: we teach our students how to be artists by collaborating with them in making art.

Art is by definition a visionary experience: an artist envisions an expression—a painting, sculpture, monolog, dance, composition, improvisation—prior to its realization, and then works to bring that realization into concrete form capable of being experienced by others. All humans have visions, but artists must find ways to embody those visions sufficiently that they can be experienced and shared. It is our professional obligation to envision and then embody a community's shared sense of experiential beauty.

But in order to envision and then embody, the young artist must locate, envision, and then embody a sense of their own creative identity. All artists, whether intuitive or intellectual, need their own autobiographical myths—the conviction that their own metaphorical, emotional experiences can be the source for artistic objects and processes that speak across a community. The young artist, particularly the aspiring artist born into a society which devalues creativity, can often use some help in concretizing that empowering personal myth: a persona of sufficient metaphorical and inspirational power that it provides the courage and stamina to be an artist in the Americas for the long haul. The speculative-fiction novelist Erin Morgenstern says:

> You may tell a tale that takes up residence in someone's soul, becomes their blood and self and purpose. That tale will move them and drive them and who knows what they might do because of it, because of your words. That is your role, your gift.[47]

The creation of a liminal space in which new imaginative possibilities can emerge is a fundamental part of twentieth-century performance, particularly in multigenre and cross-disciplinary settings: these include, for example, the movement/music/dramatic works of Harry Partch in the 1960s; the multimedia happenings of John Cage and Merce Cunningham at Black Mountain College in the 1950s; Jerzy Grotowski's *Towards a Poor Theatre* (1968), which insisted upon an experimental vision of theater as a co-creation of performers and audience; and the activist street theater, inspired by *commedia dell'arte*, of the 1960s Diggers and San Francisco Mime Troupe. Analogous ritual elements, which may combine movement, speech, song, instrumental music, masks, props, costumes, and face-paint, operate within the "invented" (synthesized, syncretic) traditions of the ensembles in question.

Of course, any time that the systemic and colonialist impulses of the neoliberal university engage with vernacular traditions and intellectual value, those vernacular traditions are at risk of racist, classist, and/or gendered appropriation and symbolic violence. But I would argue that this is precisely why the "invented" universes of the Sibelius Folk Big Band, of the OIANT, of Janelle Monáe and Tim Eriksen, and of the Vernacular Music Center's ESO and the in-world "Bassanda biographies" of individual participants can be so rewarding. By recognizing the capacity of creative *metaphors*—metaphors addressing experience, history, culture, injustice, community, aesthetics, values, and ethics—to create cross-cultural learning that is sympathetic, engaged, and compassionate, such ensemble settings enable more inclusive and responsible values.

In the Bassanda universe—as I believe is equally the case in the universes of the Sibelius Academy's FBB and of Rossi's OIANT, of Eriksen's Pumpkintown and Monáe's Cindi Mayweather—participants realize that the warp and weft of performance is itself the Net of Indra: a complex web of connections across the universe whose infinite knots and joints and ligatures each, at every point of intersection, manifest the precious unique jewel that is the individual human consciousness. Every point connects to every other, every jewel reflects all the others, and, as a result, students' sharing of connection yields a group consciousness in which all human experience—the theatricalized experience, the ritual experience of moment-by-moment shared understanding—links in that moment to every other experience of beauty.

Notes

1 Smith 2021.
2 Smith 2006.
3 Land acknowledgment: I live and work on the unceded tribal homelands of the Hoosac, Mahican, Comanche, and Kiowa, and I acknowledge the historical

injustices which have led me to occupy those ancestral homes. I likewise wish to acknowledge my own positionality: I am a white cisgender, straight, male-identifying, tenured professor. I acknowledge the systemic privilege that this status provides to me and I vow to employ that privilege for purposes of justice and inclusion.
4 By "vernacular," I mean art forms whose core repertoires are learned, taught, and passed on by ear and in memory, via a process of demonstration, imitation, and critique. The locution draws upon the original linguistic connotations of the term, to wit: "We call it vernacular music because [that] word originates as a linguistic term. It refers to the languages, especially of medieval Europe, that were spoken in the street, along with the formal official church language of Latin. So Latin was the language of learning, reading, and writing of official church communications, but the vernaculars of middle English or old French or other regional dialects, those were the languages that people spoke to get business done in the streets to buy and sell, to mourn and celebrate. To…experience human emotions" (Smith interview, 2021).
5 See Smith 2006, and also Bani, et. al., 2022.
6 Hill 2009b; Smith and Caswell 2000; Smith 2006; Stimeling & Enriquez 2019.
7 Stimeling and Enriquez likewise emphasize the tripartite relationship between regional vernacular musics and social organizations, that region's history of colonial extraction, and the [neoliberal] university's own culpability in such colonialist practices (Stimeling and Enriquez 2019; see also Smith 2005).
8 Stimeling and Enriquez, 68.
9 Hill 2018; see also Hill 2012 and Hill 2009b.
10 Smith, 2022.
11 Hill 2009a, 94.
12 Videos that capture the multi-medial and "spectacular" intentions of these ensembles can be found in the following playlist: https://www.youtube.com/playlist?list=PLw6Auy2SqK8KDv5ZSYljxYTGQldlDxQ3_.
13 See Laitinen 2003.
14 Hill 2009a.
15 As with the Elegant Savages Orchestra, discussed ahead, these sorts of combinations likewise have the very appropriate and desirable pedagogical impact of permitting a wide range of players, instruments, and levels of expertise to meet and collaborate in a group performance. Ethnomusicologist Gage Averill has written on the specific pedagogical possibilities for "staging spectacle," in his "Where's 'One'? Musical Encounters of the Ensemble Kind," in *Performing Ethnomusicology: Teaching and Representation in World Music Ensembles* (University of California, 2004), 94.
16 *Paimendisco* (Levyn julkkari live). Shepherd disco (trad. arr. Iida Savolainen, Irina Cederberg, Sirkka Kosonen, Petri Prauda & FBB) CD release live recording. https://youtu.be/ORzty_b0WJY
17 Hill 2009a. Emphasis added; parenthetical insertions original.
18 No author, "University of the Arts Helsinki Sibelius Academy Bachelor of Global Music Curriculum." https://artsdocbox.com/Music/80960826-Sibelius-academy-uniarts-bachelor-of-global-music-180-cr.html Accessed July 23, 2022.
19 Alejandro Iglesias Rossi, quoted in "La Orquesta de Instrumentos Autóctonos y Nuevas Tecnologías: un proyecto único en el mundo," *Mundo UNITREF*, 01.23.2008. https://untref.edu.ar/mundountref/orquesta-instrumentos-autoctonos-nuevas-tecnologias-xirgu, Google Translate, accessed July 23, 2022. Interpolations and emphasis added. As will be mentioned ahead, OIANT's stag-

ing is reminiscent of the sung, played, and danced multi-media "new ritual" approaches of the American avant-gardist Harry Partch, who may have been an influence on Rossi's own conception.

20 Alejandro Iglesias Rossi, quoted in "La Orquesta de Instrumentos Autóctonos y Nuevas Tecnologías: un proyecto único en el mundo," *Mundo UNITREF*, 01.23.2008. https://untref.edu.ar/mundountref/orquesta-instrumentos-autoctonos-nuevas-tecnologias-xirgu, Google Translate, accessed July 23, 2022. Emphasis added.
21 https://youtu.be/CFpZeVYjuLA. Accessed July 23, 2022.
22 https://youtu.be/myhFbqnMDEc. Accessed July 26, 2022. TEDx RíodelaPlataED.
23 Although Rossi does not tend to cite outside sources, there is a strong aura of the multimedial approaches of Harry Partch's on-stage ensembles, a not-implausible connection given Rossi's own training as a new music composer.
24 https://youtu.be/myhFbqnMDEc. Accessed July 24, 2022.
25 Musician Tim Eriksen says, "All nationalism is rooted in an imaginary village, and all folk music as well. Anything that is onstage and is called folk music is from an imaginary village, a constructed place" (Eriksen 2022). It is worth noting that yet another manifestation of 21st-century, technology-friendly, multicultural "New Folk," the Martin and Eliza Carthy-fronted English supergroup "The Imagined Village," uses this locution as well.
26 Very occasionally (e.g., twice in the 12-year history of the ensemble), criticisms alleging cultural insensitivity have been leveled at the use of the intentionally-paradoxical phrase "Elegant Savages," and/or at the ESO's mindful and intentional synthesis of disparate performance genres. Both the connotations of words like "autochthonous" and "primitive," and this fusing of genres, have been anticipated in usages by Laitinen and Rossi, among others; see for example Laitinen's "Primitive Music Orchestra" [*sic*], who conceived themselves as "avant-garde traditionalists" (Austerlitz 2000). Also relevant is that in contemporary Hiberno-English dialect, a "savage" musician is "a musician of great intensity and expressive power." See Averill's "Is there a space for critical *and* sensual involvement that doesn't reproduce exoticist voyeurism?" (Averill, 94).
27 A real-world corollary is the experience of the Ensemble for Folk Songs of the Bulgarian Radio, later "The Bulgarian State Television Female Vocal Choir," founded by Filip Kutev (1903–82) in the 1950s to perform costumed choral arrangements of various regions' folkloric musics (May 2017; see also Buchanan 1995).
28 For example, various iterations have centered upon the Stalinist 1950s, the early or mid-1960s, the American Southwest in the 1880s, a parallel dystopian universe in the 1890s, New Orleans in 1912, West TX in 1928, in the wake of the COVID-19 pandemic quarantine, a 1930s Popular Front configuration blown sideways in time and space by a real-world West Texas electromagnetic dust storm, a 1936 International Brigade *Libertarias* Band, and so forth. La Orquesta de Instrumentos Autóctonos y Nuevas Tecnologías similarly employs a mythic back story which imagines an alternate "post-Columbian history" blending Indigenous values and myths with contemporary technologies and staging.
29 Stimeling and Enriquez 2019, 69.
30 Jirviluoma and Miiki-Kulmala 1992.
31 Eriksen 2016.
32 Eriksen 2012.
33 Romano 2018.

34 The LeGuin cassette, with texts by LeGuin and musical arrangements by Todd Barton, was sufficiently persuasive as a work of imagination that Barton ran into copyright challenges from the Library of Congress: "They wrote me back to say I'd filled out the forms completely wrong…They said: 'You can't copyright indigenous music, you can say you arranged it. And you can't copyright the poetry, but you can copyright your translation.' So I called them, and I said, 'Wow, OK, I think you missed the boat here.'" Barton, in Pattison 2019.
35 Eriksen 2022.
36 Hill 2009a.
37 Rossi 2003. Emphasis added.
38 See for example *Reacting to the Past* (http://reacting.barnard.edu), Jeremiah McCall's *Gaming the Past: Using Video Games to Teach Secondary History*, and others. This method of delivering historical and contextual content via contingent game-playing is a qualitatively different approach than that which delivers traditional content but tests and assesses via game-like points systems. For the latter, see for example Sheldon, 2012.
39 "Thank you. This is like a beautiful gift." – from K.O., email, 08.01.14. "This is beyond amazing." – from J.L., email, 27.04.18. "I really love it!" – from N.B., email, 09.08.19. "Thank you so much! These are amazing! I love everything about these bios!" – from A.S., email, 12.26.19.
40 Eriksen 2022.
41 See Max Brooks, *World War Z: An Oral History of the Zombie War* (Crown, 2006). Interestingly, Brooks has explicitly stated that his inspiration for *World War Z*'s "dossier of sources" format came from Studs Terkel's 1984 *The Good War: An Oral History of World War Two*, and other similar archival and journalistic collections. See also "Exclusive Interview: Max Brooks on World War Z" (20th Oct 06; https://www.eatmybrains.com/showfeature.php?id=55 Accessed 7.22.22).
42 Wharton 2021.
43 The use of the term "Aspect" to connote a performer's larger-than-life persona and expressive powers is borrowed from the SFF author Roger Zelazny, in whose novel *Lord of Light* a group of human interstellar travelers populate and rule a distant planet by using technology-assisted telepathy and telekinesis to impersonate gods of the Hindu pantheon (Roger Zelazny, *Lord of Light* (Doubleday: 1967), 8).
44 YouTube "Rufford Park Poachers – Joseph Taylor (1908)". https://youtu.be/4f6pXtZ2EEA Accessed 06.12.22.
45 YouTube "Kulning – How to Call a Wild Swan with Traditional Swedish Singing". https://youtu.be/Yy90wZbepiE Accessed 06.12.22.
46 Eriksen 2022.
47 Morgenstern 2012.

References

Universidad Nacional de Tres de Febrero. "La Orquesta de Instrumentos Autóctonos y Nuevas Tecnologías: un proyecto único en el mundo." *Mundo UNTREF*. January 28, 2018. https://untref.edu.ar/mundountref/orquesta-instrumentos-autoctonos-nuevas-tecnologias-xirgu.

Sibelius Academy. "University of the Arts Helsinki Sibelius Academy Bachelor of Global Music Curriculum." https://artsdocbox.com/Music/80960826-Sibelius-academy-uniarts-bachelor-of-global-music-180-cr.html.

Austerlitz, Paul. "Birch-Bark Horns and Jazz in the National Imagination: The Finnish Folk Music Vogue in Historical Perspective." *Ethnomusicology* 44, no. 2 (Spring–Summer 2000): 183–213.

Averill, Gage. "Where's 'One'? Musical Encounters of the Ensemble Kind." In Ted Solis, ed.*Performing Ethnomusicology: Teaching and Representation in World Music Ensembles*. 93–112, Berkeley: University of California, 2004.

Bani, Rachel, with Larissa Mulder and Heather Sparling. "Reclaiming the Commons: Scottish and Irish Gaelic Musical Traditions" [Conference Session]. Society for Ethnomusicology Annual Meetings, New Orleans, 2022. Accessed January 28, 2023. http://www.amsmusicology.org/resource/resmgr/files/2022_annual_meeting/new-orleans-final-program-gu.pdf.

Brooks, Max. "Exclusive Interview: Max Brooks on World War Z." October 20, 2006. https://www.eatmybrains.com/showfeature.php?id=55.

———. *World War Z: An Oral History of the Zombie War*. Crown, 2006.

Buchanan, Donna A. "Metaphors of Power, Metaphors of Truth: The Politics of Music Professionalism in Bulgarian Folk Orchestras." *Ethnomusicology* 39, no. 3 (Autumn 1995): 381–416.

Eriksen, Tim. "Interview." Zoom, July 2022.

———. "Interview with Tristra Newyear Yaeger." *Rock Paper Scissors, Inc* (2012).

———. "Old Folks' Singing and Utopia." *The Massachusetts Review* 57, no. 4; THE MUSIC ISSUE (Winter 2016): 773–81.

Hill, Juniper. *Becoming Creative: Insights from Musicians in a Diverse World*. New York: Oxford University Press, 2018.

———. "Improvisation, Exploration, Imagination: Techniques for Composing Music Orally." *Revue de Musicologie* 98, no. 1 (2012), 85–106.

———. "Rebellious Pedagogy, Ideological Transformation, and Creative Freedom in Finnish Contemporary Folk Music." *Ethnomusicology* 53, no. 1 (Winter 2009a), 86–114.

———. "The Influence of Conservatory Folk Music Programmes: The Sibelius Academy in Comparative Context." *Ethnomusicology Forum* 18, no. 2 (November 2009b), 207–41.

Jirviluoma, Helmi, and Airi Miiki-Kulmala. "Folk Music and Political Song Movements in Finland: Remarks on 'Symbolic Homecoming'." In *1789–1989: Musique, Histoire, Democratie III*, 691–93. Paris: Editions de la Maison des Sciences de l'Homme, 1992.

Laitinen, Heikki. 2003. "Mita on paikallisuus" [What Is Localness]. In *Iski Sieluihin Salama: kir joituksia musiikista* [*Lightning Hit the Souls: Writings about Music*], edited by Hannu Tolvanen and Riitta-Liisa Joutsenlahti, 199–216. Helsinki: Finnish Literary Society.

Larsson, Asa. "Kulning – How to Call a Wild Swan with Traditional Swedish Singing." YouTube video, 2:40. N/D. https://youtu.be/Yy90wZbepiE.

May, Chris. "Le Mystère Des Voix Bulgares: How This All-Female Bulgarian Folk Choir Became a Timeless Cult Phenomenon." *The Vinyl Factory*. February 28, 2017. https://thevinylfactory.com/features/mystere-des-voix-bulgares-4ad-story/.

McCall, Jeremiah. *Gaming the Past: Using Video Games to Teach Secondary History*. London: Routledge, 2011.

Morgenstern, Erin. *The Night Circus*. Norwell MA: Anchor, 2012.
Pattison, Louis. "Musical World-Building: Albums Set in Lands of the Artists' Own Creation." *Bandcamp*. September 11, 2019. Accessed May 30, 2022. https://daily.bandcamp.com/lists/musical-world-building-bandcamp-albums.
Reacting to the Past. http://reacting.barnard.edu.
Romano, Aja. "Janelle Monáe's Body of Work Is a Masterpiece of Modern Science Fiction." *Vox*. May 16, 2018. https://www.vox.com/2018/5/16/17318242/janelle-monae-science-fiction-influences-afrofuturism.
Shaw, Fiona, and others. "Mother Courage Documentary (Featuring Duke Special)." YouTube video, 45:17, 2009. https://youtu.be/myhFbqnMDEc.
Sheldon, Lee. *The Multiplayer Classroom: Designing Coursework as a Game*. Boston: Cengage Learning, 2012.
Sibelius Folk Big Band. "Paimendisco (Levyn julkkari live)." Shepherd disco (trad. arr. Iida Savolainen, Irina Cederberg, Sirkka Kosonen, Petri Prauda & FBB) CD release live recording, YouTube video, 6:24. https://youtu.be/ORzty_b0WJY.
Smith, Christopher J. "Against the Grain and *Out Yonder*: Decolonizing the Music Conservatory via Vernacular Pedagogies." *Chigiana Journal of Musicological Studies* 51, (2021): 143–64.
———. Interview with Lucy Greenberg, *Evermore* magazine. Fall 2021.
———. "Reclaiming the Commons, One Tune at a Time." *New Hibernia Review / Iris Éireannach Nua* 10, no. 4 (Winter 2006): 9–20.
———. "Trusting the Tradition: The Meaning of the Irish Session Workshop." In *Cultural Diversity in Music Education: Directions and Challenges in the 21st Century*, edited by Patricia Shehan Campbell, John Drummond, Peter Dunbar-Hall, Keith Howard, Huib Schippers, and Trevor Wiggins, 69–79. Brisbane: Australian Academic Press, 2005.
———. "'What If It Had Been Different?': Role-Playing Games as Practice-Based Teaching and Research." Unpublished paper delivered at the History, Analysis, Pedagogy Conference, University of Nottingham, England. July 2016.
Smith, Christopher J., and Austin B. Caswell. "Into the Ivory Tower: Vernacular Musics and the American Academy." *Contemporary Music Review* 19, no. 1 (2000): 89–111.
Stimeling, Travis D., and Sophia M. Enriquez. "Building Relationships, Sustaining Communities: Decolonial Directions in Higher Ed Bluegrass Pedagogy." *Decolonizing Music Pedagogies* 39, no. 1 (2019): 57–72.
Taylor, Joseph. "Rufford Park Poachers." YouTube video, 1:33. 1908. https://youtu.be/4f6pXtZ2EEA.
Wharton, Anne. Interview with the author. August 2021.
Zelazny, Roger. *Lord of Light*. Garden City: Doubleday, 1967.

Index

active learning 18, 30, 171
affordances 112, 117
African popular music 124–8, 131, 137
Afrobeat 6–7, 126, 131–5
Afro-Brazilian religious music 8, 157–8, 165, 174–5
Agawu, Kofi 135
al-Andalusian music 24
Allar, Neal 17
allusion 124–6, 136
alternate history 204–8
American popular music 140–1, 145
Amiot, Jean-Joseph-Marie 4, 50, 54–7, 59
Anikulapo-Kuti, Fela 7, 124, 126, 131–5
anticolonization *see* decolonization
Appadurai, Arjun 129–30
Appalachian fiddling 5, 85, 87, 90–1, 94, 99
appropriation: avoiding 205, 214; as contested framework 6, 105, 107, 115–21, 124, 126, 169, 203; definition of 1; in popular music 141–3; and recontextualization 157, 169; in Western art music 4, 56, 62–3, 65–6, 70, 73, 76, 79–80, 97
assessment 188–9, 192–5, 197–9
assimilation 6, 58, 71, 105–6, 117–19, 121, 130, 133
audiotopia 114
authenticity: anxieties about 107, 158; as basis for evaluation 6, 106, 124–5, 142; dismissing concerns of 9; equated with precolonial 106; in folkloric performance 8, 168, 170–1, 173; as musical signifier 135; in old-time fiddling 91, 99; perceptions of 7, 140, 148, 151; as problematic 142; in Western art music 69
Averill, Gage 171

Baker, Theodore 64, 66–7, 71
Bakhtin, Mikhail 113, 120
Barber, Karin 130
Battle of Barbastro 22
Battle of Lepanto 26–7
Batuque 158–65
Bernstein, Leonard 179, 181, 185, 187–9, 192–3
bi-musicality 105, 109
Bithell, Caroline 145
Black Arts Movement 134
Black musical styles 114, 118, 141
Bobowski, Wojciech *see* Ufuķī, 'Alī
"Bonaparte's Retreat" 5, 85–9, 91, 94–8
Broyles-González, Yolanda 146, 148
Burman-Hall, Linda 96
Busoni, Ferrucio 4–5, 62, 70–80

Candide 181, 187–8, 190
Candomblé 8, 158–9, 164–74
canon (musical): centering of 2–3, 15, 40, 180, 197; efforts to expand 41; and intercultural interaction 129–30; juxtaposed with non-Western music 50, 58–9; looking beyond 4, 17, 30, 63, 81; of rock 'n' roll 140, 142; shedding new light on 42, 52–3; and systems of oppression 79–80, 198
capitalism 114, 129
capoeira 165, 167, 171
Carnatic music 6, 105–6, 108–14, 121
Carnival 8, 158, 166–7, 171–5

Catholic music: in China 4, 42, 50, 56–7; in Europe 25–6; in the United States 170
Chaillou-Amadieu, Christelle 24
Charlton, Katherine 141
Cheng, William 30
classical music *see* Western art music
close reading 18, **21**, **24**, **25**, **26**, **28**
Cochran, Timothy 80
Cohen, Ronald 145
colonialism 108, 110, 117–18, 125, 128, 135, 146–9, 202–3, 205, 214
complex thinking 3, 20
composer's ear, the 5, 85–7, 92, 99
Copland, Aaron 5, 85–7, 92–9
Costa, Amarildo 166, 171–3
creative music 109, 112
Crist, Elizabeth 93
cross-cultural: collaborations 115–16, 118, 121; comparisons 170–1; encounters 106, 157; fusions 149, 151; influence 115; learning 214; *see also* fusion, syncretism
crossover: in African popular music 124, 126; approaches to 106–7, 115, 119–20, 126, 189–90, 193–4; definition of 1, 192; in European music 3, 21; in Indian music 108–9; in musical theater 8–9, 179–82, 184–8, 194–5
Curtis-Burlin, Natalie 5, 62, 71–2, 74, 76, 80, 82

decolonization: and Afrobeat 131; and approaches to curriculum and pedagogy 16, 197–8, 205; as project in higher education 2, 9, 40; as project in the conservatory 199; and teaching music history 15–17, 30, 41, 79–80
de Mille, Agnes 92–4, 96
Derrida, Jacques 116, 120
dialogic encounters 129–30, 133
diaspora 6, 105–9, 114–21, 128, 149, 162
Díaz Meneses, Juan Diego 169
Dvořák, Antonín 4, 62–3, 69–73, 77, 80

Elegant Savages Orchestra 203–4, 216n26
Enriquez, Sophia 198, 205

enslavement 3, 21–4, 28, 146–7, 164
equity (in teaching) 127–8, 131, 136–7, 198
Eriksen, Tim 203, 205, 207, 212, 214, 216
Eurocentrism 2, 40, 49–50, 80, 121
European art music *see* Western art music
Ewell, Philip 10n1
exchange: in African popular music 124, 126; across borders 17; centered in al-Andalus 21–2; between China and the West 41–3, 49–50, 57; definition of 1; between Native American and Western cultures 69, 71–2, 78–9

Fick, Kimary 80
Figueroa, Michael 2, 41
Figueroa Hernández, Rafael 147
Fletcher, Alice 64, 69, 71
flipped classroom 18
Folk Big Band (FBB) 200–1, 206, 214
folkloric performance 8, 148, 158, 165–6, 168–9, 171, 175, 200–2, 204
folk music *see* vernacular music
fusion: Brazilian-jazz 164; of Chinese and Western music 50, 57, 59; Indo-jazz 6, 105–8, 115, 117–21; in son jarocho 7, 140–1, 146, 149–51

Gabrieli, Andrea 25–6
Gabrieli, Giovanni 3, 25
gamakka 105, 111–13
Garofalo, Reebee 141
Gershwin, George 179, 181, 185, 188–9, 192–3
Gibbs, Christopher **25**, **26**
Glissant, Édouard 17, 108, 115
globalism 50, 54, 58–9, 121, 136, 190–1
global music history 3–4, 40–2, 49, 57–8
Golden Apple, The 181, 183
gongche notation *see* staff notation
González, Francisco 147
Guettel, Adam 179

heteroglossia 113, 120
highbrow/lowbrow 9, 186
highlife 132–3
Hill, Juniper 145, 198–201, 206

hip hop 115, 117, 120, 150–1
historically informed performance practice 3, 24, **29**, 145, 212
historiography 18, 20, 22, 26–7, 30, 40, 79, 140
History of Western Music, A 10n1
hybridity 6, 7, 20, 105–7, 110, 114, 121, 124–5, 157, 174, 180–2
hyphenation 6, 107, 109, 114–15, 118–21

Iberian music 3, 20–1, 146
identity: cultural 17, 28–9, 81, 93, 118, 143–4, 146–8, 157, 203; diasporic 121; ethnic 4, 16, 23, 114, 117–19, 172; as fluid 30; gender 17, 23, 170; national 199, 212; and ownership 105; religious 17, 23, 27, 159; *see also* diaspora, hyphenation
improvisation: in Carnatic music 105, 111; cross-cultural 107, 109, 113–14; and European art music 16, 29; in Mexican folk tradition 147, 151; in a university folk band 199,–202, 206, 209, 213
Indianist movement 4, 62–3, 71, 80
indigeneity 5, 7, 58, 97, 126, 146–8, 198
indigenization 6–7, 125–8, 130–5, 201–2
Indo-jazz fusion 6, 107, 111, 115, 117
influence (narrative of) 25
intercontinental interaction 6–7, 129–31, 133–4, 136
intercultural: collaboration 117–18; encounters 1, 4, 19; interaction 6–7, 129–30, 133–4, 136, 147; learning 157–8, 166, 169–71, 175; transference 7; understanding/misunderstanding 54
interminority collaboration 117–18, 121

Janissary music *see mehter* music
Jarrell, Tommy 87, 95, 100

Kangxi, Emperor 4, 42–5, 47–9, 58
Kapchan, Deborah 116, 120, 157
Kartomi, Margaret 130, 133
Kidula, Jean Ngoya 124–5
Kohl, Randall 150–1

Koken, Walt 90–2
Kun opera 4, 42, 50–4, 56, 59
Kuti, Fela *see* Anikulapo-Kuti, Fela

"La Bamba" 7, 140–5, 148, 150–1
LaChiusa, Michael John 184
Laitinen, Heikki 200–1
Latouche, John 183
learning portfolio 18, 24
Leibniz, Gottfried Wilhelm 43, 48–50, 58
Light in the Piazza, The 179, 181, 187
liminality 1–2, 105, 214
listening: Carnatically 112; as classroom activity 18, **24**, 28–9, 56, 58–9, 85, 87–9, 120, 141–2, 144, 150, 188; and transcription 91; *see also* composer's ear, the; origin listening
Lomax, Alan 87–90, 96–8, 145
Lomax, Elizabeth 87, 89–90, 96–8
Loza, Steven 147
Lunsford, Bascom Lamar 89

MacDowell, Edward 4, 62–3, 65–8, 70, 72, 76, 80
Macedo, Jailton "Dendê" 8, 165–7, 169–71
Macedo, Leslie Malmed 166
Machado, Pai Antonio Carlos de Xangô 160, 162, 164
marginalization 4, 15–16, 24–5, 40–1, 69, 79–81, 118
mariachi 143, 147
Marie Christine 181, 184
Martín-Peñasco, Vera 23
meaning (musical) 8, 16, **21**, 64, 81, 120–1, 142, 145, 150, 157, 175, 197
medieval music 19–21, 24
mehter music 3, 27, **28**
mestizo 141, 146–9, 152
Meyer, Stephen 81
Milliner, Clare 90–2
minstrelsy 117–18
mode: in Carnatic music 109–13, 115–16; in Chinese music 54–5; and cultural reclamation 138; in Native American music 64, 75; in Ottoman music 29; in West African music 134, 136; in Western music 86, 110–11
Monáe, Janelle 205, 214

Moniz, Justin John 182
Morgenstern, Erin 213
Morin, Edgard 3, 20–1, 22
Moross, Jerome 183–4
musical theater 8–9
music industry 182, 186
myth of universality: in aesthetics 2–3, 58, 86, 97; in music as language 10; in truth 2, 46, 56

National Association of Schools of Music 197
Native American music: centering of 79–80; as commercial entertainment 69; historical recordings of 64–5; misrepresentation of 64, 67–8; and Western art music 4–5, 62–3, 69, 71, 73–4
Navarro, José 144
neoliberalism 9, 198, 202–3, 214
notation *see* staff notation

Of Agency and Abstraction 108
Oja, Carol 185–6
old-time fiddling 5, 87–8, 91, 98
Ologundê 8, 158, 165–9
On the Town 184–5
oral tradition: in Afro-Brazilian music 162, 174; in Appalachian fiddling 85, 95; and European art music 16–17, 20–1; in higher education 201, 203–4, 206, 212–13; in Native American music 64; in recording Qiyan music 24; *see also* staff notation
orientalism 57, 85, 107, 116–18
origin listening 6, 125, 127, 131, 132
Orquesta de Instrumentos Autóctonos y Nuevas Tecnologías, La (OIANT) 201, 206, 214
Osman of Timisoara 28–9
Other: as inferior 63; musical representation of 67, 75; versus self 50, 105, 116, 118–19; as threat 26
Ottoman: encounters with Europeans 16, 26–7, 31; identity 28–9; music 3, 29–30; perspective 27–9; *see also mehter* music
Oxford History of Western Music, The 10n1, 25, 26

participatory music-making 91, 98–9, 167–8, 171, 198
Passion 181, 184
pentatonic scale 53, 55, 75, 107, 135–6, 161, 167
Peony Pavilion 50–4, 56
Pereira, Thomas 43, 47–8
Pidgin English 135–6
Plotkin, Fred 182
popular music studies 143
postcolonialism 6, 107, 125, 127–8, 131
Powell, Elliott 113, 117–18
presentational music-making 8, 98–9, 167–9, 171
primary sources 3–4, 18, **23**, 27, 41–3, 79–80, 158, 184

qin music 42
Qiyan 3, 16, 21–4, 31

racism: in depictions of Native Americans 65, 77; and global race consciousness 118; and jazz 185; and phrenology 9, 186; protests against 175
Ramapo College 165, 169, 171–2
Rameau, Jean-Philippe 4, 42, 50, 53–8
reception 8, 181
recontextualization 8, 114, 157–8, 162–3, 165, 169, 171–5
revivalism 7, 98–9, 144–6, 148–51, 211
Robinson, Dylan 5, 97
rock 'n' roll 7, 140–5, 150
Rodeo 85, 92–4, 96
Roosevelt University 179
Rossi, Alejandro Iglesias 201–3, 206, 214

Seaton, Douglass 81
Seeger, Ruth Crawford 89–92, 96–7
Shelemay, Kay Kaufman 157
Sibelius Academy 199–201, 206, 214
Solís, Ted 173
Sondheim, Stephen 184, 187–8
Sonex 150–1
son jarocho 7, 141–2, 144–51
staff notation: combined with gongche notation 4, 56–7; as fixed instructions 98; limitations of 5, 85–7, 91–2, 121; used as teaching tool 9, 23–9, 120–1, 204, 211–12;

used to transcribe vernacular music 5, 29, 64, 72, 86, 89–92, 204
Starr, Larry 141–2
Stempel, Larry 185–6
Stepp, William 5, 85–9, 92–9
stereotypes 124–5, 127, 136–7
Stimeling, Travis 198, 205
Street Scene 181, 183, 187–8
Strohm, Reinhard 19
Swaminathan, Rajna 6, 108–10, 112–14, 118
syncretism 115, 125, 128, 159, 169, 174, 199, 205–6, 212, 214

Taruskin, Richard **25, 26**
Tesori, Jeanine 186–7
Texas Tech University 200, 203
Think-Pair-Share **20, 25, 28**
threshold concept theory 18, 20
tokenism 41, 80
Tommasini, Anthony 181
transcription *see* staff notation
transculturation *see* intercultural collaboration
transference 7, 140, 143–4, 151
Trimillos, Ricardo 173
troubadours 3, 16, 20–2, 24–5

Ufuḳī, 'Alī 3, 28–9
Universidad Tres de Febrero 200–1

Valens, Ritchie 7, 140–6, 150–1
values: in fusion 115–16, 120; negotiation of 10; participatory versus presentational 99; of unfamiliar music 54, 85–6, 99, 158; of vernacular practices 9, 197, 200, 202, 209–10
Veal, Michael 131
vernacular music: composers borrowing from 4–5, 85–6, 92–4, 97, 99; definition of 215; as distinct realm 96, 140; in higher education 1, 9, 214; and orchestration 201, 211–12; pedagogical idioms of 9, 197–8, 203; performance practices of 198, 209; pitfalls of treating as static source material 143; repertoires 210–12
vocal production 52–3, 105, 183, 186–7

Waksman, Steve 141
Walker, Margaret 40, 79
Waterman, Christopher 128, 141–2
Weill, Kurt 183–4, 186–8
Weinman, Jaime 182
Weiss, Sarah 106, 124
Western art music: in China 43; as culturally specific 85, 96–7; decentering 16, 18, 25, 40, 79–80, 97; definition of 10; denaturalizing 2–3, 99; as ethnic music 15–16; hegemony of 2–3, 15, 30, 40–1, 190, 197–8; from non-Western perspective 42, 58; normative stylistic elements of 67, 69–70, 73–5, 80, 86; shifting borders of 19–20; teaching courses in 2–5, 76, 143, 180, 190–1; values of 5, 99
West Side Story 181–2, 184–8, 195
Wharton, Ann 209
whiteness 2, 69, 80, 114, 118, 121, 205
work concept 94–6
world music: ensembles 158, 165–7, 171–4; teaching courses in 6–7, 40–1, 106–7, 124–7, 174

Yale University 124
Yongzheng, Emperor 4, 43, 45–7
Yorùbá 128–9, 132–6, 162, 164, 166–7, 170